in the shadows of the morning

BOOKS BY PHILIP CAPUTO

A Rumor of War

Horn of Africa

Delcorso's Gallery

Indian Country

Means of Escape

Equation for Evil

Exiles

The Voyage

Ghosts of Tsano

in the shadows of the morning

ESSAYS ON WILD LANDS, WILD WATERS, AND A FEW UNTAMED PEOPLE

PHILIP CAPUTO

THE LYONS PRESS
GUILFORD, CONNECTICUT
AN IMPRINT OF THE GLOBE PEQUOT PRESS

Printed in the United States of America
Book design by Casey Shain

1 3 5 7 9 10 8 6 4 2

1-58574-520-0

The Library of Congress Cataloging-in-Publication Data is available
on file.

contents

preface,   VII

NORTH AMERICA
the last of the big open 1995,   3
the farthest away river 1996,   23
up in michigan 1997,   55
alone 1998,   63

AFRICA
man-eaters of tsavo 2000,   81
dark skies of sudan 2001,   113
return to tsavo 2001,   141

ASIA
the enfield and the koran 1980,   157
the coils of memory 1999,   177

OCEAN AND ISLANDS
voyager 1997,   203
the ahab complex 1983,   217
blue water blues 1993,   233
yorke island 1999,   247
lost keys 1991,   253
dry tortugas 1996,   267

preface

I was born under a wandering star. I don't know how this came about. The first of my ancestors to emigrate to America arrived in 1884. A paternal great-grandfather laid track for the Great Northern railroad from Chicago to Seattle and for a while worked in the copper mines of Montana, after which he returned to Chicago and stayed put until his death in 1929. My mother's people also settled there in 1908 and never moved. So far as I know, they never had a desire to; nor did most of their children, grandchildren, and great-grandchildren. It was as if the perilous journeys undertaken by the immigrant generation had exhausted the family's reserves of wanderlust, which it probably had never possessed in abundance. Before the New World beckoned, the people I'm descended from had inhabited one small corner of southern Italy for centuries, so I have no idea where my own nomadic blood comes from.

It's stirred in me for as long as I can remember. My first eighteen summers were spent in the Wisconsin north woods, where my machinist father serviced canning factories, and where I acquired a love of the outdoors, an itch to see what lay over the next hill or around the next bend in a river, and learned how to fish and shoot, along with such obsolete skills as tracking game, building a campfire in a wet woods, navigating by the sun and the lay of the land. Some time later, as a newly minted college dropout, I hitchhiked, rode buses, and hopped freights through the West and down into Mexico—my Jack Kerouac phase. Still later, the U.S. Marine Corps took me to Hawaii, Japan, Singapore, and finally Vietnam. That was followed by a long career as a foreign correspondent in the Middle East, Europe, and the Soviet Union. Since the age of twenty-one, I've had fourteen different addresses, and have lived in, worked in, fought and covered wars in forty-eight countries on four continents, not to mention voyages in the South China Sea, the Caribbean, and the Atlantic.

I've written about these journeys for several publications. The stories that follow have appeared, in somewhat different form, in *Esquire, Islands, Men's Journal,* the *Miami Herald, National Geographic Adventure, National Geographic,* the *New York Times,* and *Sports Afield.*

Taken together, they form a record of adventure travel spanning some twenty five years. "Adventure travel" is a term I'm not entirely fond of, but I suppose we need it to distinguish modern modes of travel from those that entail some risk and hardship. By that definition, the act of getting from Point A to Point B on land or sea was an adventure for all travelers before the inventions of the steamship, the automobile, and the passenger plane, before there was a multibillion dollar tourist industry to make even remote corners of the world accessible and comfortable, before the United States was spanned by interstate highways with convenient rest stops, motorist call-boxes, and franchise eateries offering high-fat "Happy Meals."

Most of these stories are accounts of outdoor expeditions to wild places and on the open sea; some turn on hunting and fishing—pursuits I've followed since boyhood, without apologies. Readers will note a strong bias toward conservation and an equal disgust with the effects sprawl and overdevelopment have had on our landscapes—and on our collective soul. I'm not a pantheistic nature worshiper; nevertheless, my response to the natural world is essentially religious: I see the hand of God in mountains, forests, wild rivers, and think our society would be less troubled if there were more of those and less of shopping malls, sterile subdivisions, and all the detritus of a consumer-driven culture.

I've included three stories, from Afghanistan, Sudan, and Vietnam, that are about war or its effects. Those are not strictly tales of adventure because war, as Erich Maria Remarque told us a long time ago, never is an adventure to those who must fight in it.

— PHILIP CAPUTO
MAY 2002

NORTH AMERICA

the last of the big open

W e were twenty miles north of the Arctic Circle and
alone on the Jim River, three of us floating on one-
man rafts under a sun that never set. Tony Oswald
was in the lead, Marc in the middle, while I, feeling
the miles we had rowed as well as the effects of the late hour, brought
up the rear. Judging by the sky, it was late afternoon, but my watch
told me it was round about midnight. We'd been on the river for over
ten hours, making frequent stops to catch grayling from gravel bars littered with driftwood and printed with the tracks of moose, wolves, and
grizzlies. We hadn't seen any bears or wolves, but had passed a cow
moose and two calves, grazing on weeds in a slough. They raised their
heads to eye us, then trotted off with hardly a rustle into a stand of tall,
leaning spruce, where the cow stood vigilantly in front of her young.
Farther downstream, we'd come across a couple of otters, their bodies
making sleek, brown arches as they dove, and then a beaver slapped its
tail with a crack like a rifle shot. Except for the rare, faint, distant rumble of a truck on the Dalton Highway, the dusty supply road for the
Prudhoe Bay oil fields and the Trans-Alaskan pipeline, we hadn't heard
a man-made sound; nor had we seen a sign of our own species, not a
single bootprint.

That was welcome but not surprising. The Jim, a tributary of the
Koyukuk River, itself a tributary of the mythic Yukon, flows through a
wilderness bigger than California: Arctic Alaska, the last frontier of the
state that calls itself The Last Frontier, which in this case wasn't just a
slogan on a license plate. The nearest human settlements to us were

two tiny villages: Coldfoot, thirty-odd miles north on the Dalton, and Bettles, fifty miles to the west and accessible only by bush plane or by way of the Koyukuk. The isolation and wildness were a little daunting, but they were the reasons we'd come to Alaska's far north. There can be no true freedom without wilderness, no true wilderness without freedom, and neither comes for free. A toll is levied in sore muscles, sweat, and occasional spasms of fear; and sometimes, as we would learn before the float was through, the charges could be higher than you expected.

The trip was a college graduation present for Marc, the younger of my two sons, and for me the scratching of a fossil itch. In 1959, when Alaska was granted statehood, I was a restless high-school senior, steeped in the exploits of the French voyageurs in the north woods, a bit intoxicated on Jack London and Robert Service, and drawn to the beckoning classifieds that ran in the backs of the pulpy adventure magazines that constituted the bulk of my recreational reading. JOBS IN ALASKA. BUY LAND IN ALASKA. Fantasies of quitting school to become a fur trapper in the lands where, in Service's words, "the mountains are nameless and the rivers all run God knows where" distracted me from trig and English lit. I never went, and the itch went into a long hibernation. It was reawakened late last year, by the news that the Dalton Highway had been opened to public traffic.

The highway runs for over four hundred unpaved miles from its starting point at Livengood, north of Fairbanks, to the town of Deadhorse, on the Arctic Ocean. It was named for James W. Dalton, an oil explorer who played a major role in the discovery of the Prudhoe fields. He died at the age of sixty-four in 1977, only three weeks before the last weld on the eight-hundred-mile-long pipeline was completed. In those days, the road was restricted to pipeline service crews and truckers hauling supplies and equipment to Prudhoe Bay. In 1981, it was opened to the general public for part of its length, and, on December 2, 1994, the whole road was opened.

The Dalton is the only road in Alaska north of the Arctic Circle, a region of some 150,000 square miles. It bridges the Yukon River, climbs the White Mountains and the Brooks Range, and crosses the Arctic coastal plain. Along the way, it passes through or near four refuges and national parks whose total area almost equals the six New England states put together. The Arctic National Wildlife Refuge (20 million acres) is Maine, the Gates of the Arctic National Park (8.4 million acres) is

Connecticut and Massachusetts. The Yukon Flats Wildlife Refuge (8.63 million acres) is New Hampshire and part of Vermont, and the Kanuti Wildlife Refuge, a comparative postage stamp at 1.5 million acres, would accommodate more of Vermont and all of Rhode Island.

All of this has been thoroughly charted—there are no blank spots left. The maps now show to where Robert Service's rivers run, yet many of those rivers and creeks remain nameless, and still are highways for the epic migrations of salmon and Arctic char that grow to twenty pounds. Most of the mountains also remain nameless, their snow-mantled peaks ablaze in June's midnight sun or lit by the cold green fires of December's northern lights. Beneath them, caribou wander across fenceless ranges in numbers recalling the tides of bison that once inundated the Great Plains. Dall sheep speckle the tundra fells. Above all, there is the grizzly, the incarnation of all that was wild in North America before the arrivals of Cortés and the Massachusetts Bay colony. As many as thirty-five to forty thousand range through British Columbia and Alaska, compared with less than a thousand in the U.S. Rocky Mountains.

I was stirred by the idea of driving a road that is a 1990s equivalent of the Oregon Trail. Perhaps I would get an idea, however faint, of what America looked and felt like to the mountain men who had called the Rocky Mountain west "the Big Open." Having hiked, camped, canoed, fished, and hunted in many parts of the continental United States for more than half my life, I had come to the melancholy but inescapable conclusion that the "Big Open" is all but completely closed. The big cattle ranges are being carved into ranchettes for West Coast and East Coast refugees. Most "protected" wilderness areas, when they aren't being clear-cut, are becoming wilderness simulacrums—defanged, declawed, domesticated Disneylands teeming with video-recording tourists. Maybe, after the last "problem bear" in Montana is shot or tranquilized and relocated to British Columbia, Disney's imagineers will create virtual-reality grizzlies that will make suitable subjects for camcorders and have the added advantage of being perfectly safe for children and adults.

Even in relatively uncrowded national parks, there are enough bureaucratic regulations to make you consider joining a citizen's militia. You have to reserve campsites, as if they are hotel rooms. You have to draw permits. You are required to stay on marked trails, and, in some parks, you are not allowed to have ground fires.

John McPhee, in his 1976 classic about Alaska, *Coming into the Country*, observes that our society has "an elemental need for a frontier outlet, a pioneer place to go—important even to those who don't go there . . . Alaska is all we have left." He was right. Alaska is so vast that it's almost an insult to call it a state. England, Scotland, France, Germany, Italy, and Austria combined would fit within its 586,000 square miles. It's so sparsely settled that if its population density were applied to New York City, only 350 people would live in the five boroughs. And the biggest, most open part of Alaska is the Dalton region, where there aren't any marked trails. In fact, there are virtually no trails of any kind, and no permits are required. You can camp wherever you wish, walk wherever you choose, as far as your legs can carry you and a backpack across the tundra, over the mountains. Of course, there is a Yin to that Yang. If there are no rangers to hassle you with red tape, neither are there any to pull you out of trouble. No first-aid stations around the bend, no search-and-rescue teams. Suffer a broken leg or some other mishap in the middle of nowhere, and you will have to do what the prospectors and explorers did in the old days: send your friends for help and hope you don't die before it comes.

Late in June, Marc and I joined Tony Oswald and his friend Jeannie Chandler in Fairbanks. They had arrived from their homes in Colorado. For the next three days, we bought supplies and gear, and worked out a rough itinerary, pouring over topographic maps in our motel rooms. We would float and fish the Jim and Koyukuk Rivers for grayling and salmon, trek across the tundra to photograph caribou and musk ox, and hike the Brooks Range in the footsteps of Robert Marshall, the naturalist and explorer who had mapped a good part of those mountains in the late 1930s.

On June 25, we loaded our Chevrolet Tahoe and left Fairbanks. While a four-wheel-drive vehicle is not required for the Dalton, one is recommended. Driving that road, in the words of one oil-field trucker, "isn't a trip to Grandma's house, it's a real adventure." In the five hundred miles separating Fairbanks from the Arctic coast, there are only three gas stations and two general stores. You have to be self-sufficient and prepared for emergencies, which means you need a vehicle with a lot of cargo capacity. The back of the Tahoe was crammed with a tool kit, a tire-repair kit, first-aid kit, jumper cables, flares, tents, sleeping bags, four backpacks with our clothes, water bottles, food for ten days, fishing tackle, and Tony's extensive camera equipment. Atop the roof rack were the frames, paddles, and deflated pontoons of three rafts, along with two six-gallon jerry cans of gasoline. We carried a full-size spare tire in the undercarriage rack (if you have an older vehicle with mileage on the tires, it's a good idea to take two spares). A thick plastic rock guard had been fitted over the grill. The Dalton remains primarily a haul road, and the big trucks that barrel down it at fifty miles an hour throw up rocks and gravel that can shatter headlights or crack a windshield. We had two spare headlights in case the guard failed.

Heading north on the Elliott Highway on a somber, rainy afternoon, we were happy to get out of Fairbanks. Urban Alaska, what little there is of it, is remarkably drab and ugly—it's as if the overwhelming landscape suppresses the human impulse to build things that try to match nature in beauty or stupendousness. Eighty-four miles later, the Elliott ended. Ahead was a small green-and-white sign:

JAMES W. DALTON HIGHWAY
YUKON RIVER 56
ARCTIC CIRCLE 126
COLDFOOT 175

The Yukon River! The Arctic Circle! Coldfoot! Other names sang from farther up the road, some given long- ago by gold-fevered prospectors, some more recently by oil men, some by Eskimos and Athapaskan Indians in a time beyond recorded history. Bonanza Creek. The Kanuti River. Finger Rock. Cathedral Mountain. Sukapak Mountain. Disaster Creek. The Chandalar Shelf. Atigun Pass and Atigun Gorge. The Sagavanirkton River. The Sagwon Uplands. There we were, self-contained and headed up a raw and open road into the Far North's far north.

The rain had stopped when we crossed the Yukon on a steel-and-plank bridge, the only bridge to span the river in all the fourteen hundred miles it flows through Alaska. Half a mile wide and six fathoms deep, gleaming like liquid brass in the evening sunlight, it wound westward between high, wooded bluffs toward its meeting with the Bering Sea, where the great whales breached and blew.

We fueled up at a ramshackle gas station, where we got a look at two very different types of American traveler. One was a lonesome adventurer: a middle-age biker whose Harley was so mud-caked it looked like a clay model. He had ridden across most of the Lower Forty-Eight, up the

Canada-Alaskan highway, then up the Dalton to Deadhorse, and was now heading back to his home in Ohio—a round trip of some eighty-five hundred miles. The other type—several of them actually—climbed off a Princess Tours tour bus and walked into nearby café with the stiff gaits of people who spend too little time using their legs.

The sight of them in their sneakers and brightly colored synthetics got me down. If tour buses plied the Dalton, as they do almost daily, could it really be called a modern Oregon Trail? Worse yet, could concession stands, RV parks, flush toilets, and Best Westerns be far behind? It was hard to imagine them on the Dalton, but who could have imagined, in the 1890s, what Yosemite would look like in the 1990s?

Indeed, the opening of the Dalton has caused some conservationists to worry that it will draw even more tourists and leave wild places like the Gates of the Arctic as crowded and tame as some other national parks. One cause for worry lies in the conflicting mandates federal agencies have over the Dalton region. The Bureau of Land Management controls a five-mile-wide "recreation corridor" on either side of the highway and is already drawing up plans to develop visitor facilities and campgrounds. The National Park Service and U.S. Fish and Wildlife oversee the Gates of the Arctic and the Arctic National Wildlife Refuge, and are committed to preserving the "unimproved," pristine nature of those areas.

In Fairbanks, I'd talked to Jim Mills, superintendent of Gates of the Arctic, and Steve Ulvi, who manages the Inupiat Eskimos' subsistence hunting and fishing in the park. Ulvi makes a brief appearance in *Coming into the Country*. McPhee describes him as a "cinematically handsome" man of twenty-three, who was then pioneering near the Canadian border. He's forty-four now, but still cinematically handsome, with pale blue eyes, curly brown hair, and an extravagant mustache that gives him the antique appearance of a gold-rush prospector.

He prefers to describe himself and others like him as "representatives of the landscape, senators for the wilderness." He told me that park officials hope to maintain the Gates of the Arctic as a "black belt" park, meaning that it is not for the unfit, the unskilled, or the timid.

"The idea is to give hikers and campers a chance to feel like Bob Marshall did when he was exploring this country—a sense of discovery and adventure, and of solitude," Ulvi said. "Gates of the Arctic gets three to four thousand visitors a year. That's less than the number of people who ride the elevator in the Statue of Liberty in a day. We have people who go in there on real expeditions, sometimes for six weeks. We don't need to spend money on visitor facilities. We're at the point in management of this area where Yellowstone might have been in the 1900s. Hopefully, we've learned from places like Yellowstone how not to do things, but how to do things the right way. But now there's this raw road into this incredible wilderness. Open a road and you open a Pandora's box."

Mills, a balding man of solid, medium build, interjected:

"I don't think the road itself is a threat to the Gates of the Arctic. It's possible to develop reasonable access, but we hope the BLM manages its corridor as a buffer, and if we do this properly, we'll preserve the integrity of the Gates of the Arctic."

"We've got to," Ulvi added emphatically. "Because the Gates of the Arctic and the Dalton areas are as close as we've got to what America was like before European contact."

I reflected on those comments and concerns as we drove northward from the Yukon crossing, through mile after mile of taiga and tundra fells, ridges and hills that occasionally crowded close to the road but mostly opened up and stretched away forever. On the Dalton Highway, the world of the information highway seemed as remote as Mars, and all worries about the relentless pressures of modern civilization seemed unfounded. The only visible works of man were the road and the pipeline, zig zagging alongside on five-foot stilts. Building the two was an epic feat of engineering, but if the wilderness on either side were a football field, the corridor they cut through it would be no wider than a thread of spider's silk.

The road climbed gradually, the spruce trees grew shorter, to the height of the shrubs, and then we were rolling along a broad tundra plateau barren of trees. A stiff northerly wind was tattering the clouds, and patches of sunlight and shadow moved across the fells. A rugged jeep track that led westward beckoned us to leave the highway, and we did, bumping along for perhaps a mile to the base of a ridge. While Tony and Jeannie stayed behind to take photographs, Marc and I set off to climb the ridge and see what we could see.

From a distance, the tundra looks like an immense fairway that needs a little maintenance. In fact, it is rough, lumpy, boggy ground, composed of countless tussocks with tiny gullies in between. The tussocks roll under your feet, the gullies trip you, and you're lucky to make five miles in a day. I was making very slow progress, hobbled by a bad ankle, a souvenir of a bullet wound I'd suffered long before as a war correspondent in Lebanon. Marc soon outstripped me. Half an hour later, I caught up with him. He was sitting atop the ridge, reading a book by a Chinese poet of the T'ang dynasty. It was called *Cold Mountain,* an appropriate title—the wind was keening harder and a cloud dumped rain and sleet. We sat for a while, Marc reading while I glassed for caribou, whose tracks and droppings were all around. Before me were alpine meadows studded with dwarf spruce, valleys jeweled with glacial lakes, hills that might have been landmarks for the first aboriginals to cross the Bering Strait into North America twenty-five thousand years ago. Here was a world that reduced Marc and me to microbes, a world with the dew still on it, at once inspiring and humbling, exalting and intimidating.

By the next day, we were camped on the Jim, at the end of a rough track about a mile off the Dalton. Nearby were two big beaver ponds, where nesting yellowleg sandpipers went into noisy panics whenever we approached. The campsite was often used by bowhunters (hunting with firearms is prohibited within the pipeline corridor, for the obvious reason that a stray bullet could pierce the pipeline) and was hardly pristine. A fire ring, a couple of huge cable spools, a table jury-rigged out of scrap lumber. The camp lacked only the fifty-gallon oil drums that are the principal decorative item of Alaskan bush landscaping. But the frequenting by humans had not affected the wildlife in the area. There were wolf tracks and wolf scat, moose droppings like piles of small brown eggs, bear trails. I don't want to neglect the mosquitoes, which exist in Alaska in numbers as incomprehensible as the diameter of the known universe measured in miles.

At midday, we trucked the rafts to a crossing eleven miles north of our camp. Jeannie would drive the Tahoe back to camp and wait as Tony, Marc, and I floated back downriver.

Tony took Marc and me to a quiet slough and showed us how to handle the rafts, called Water-Otters and consisting of a seat mounted on a platform and two heavy rubber pontoons belted to aluminum frames. You faced the bow instead of the stern, and you rowed by pushing rather than pulling the oars except when the current threatened to sweep you into a rock or some other hazard. Then you turned the raft and rowed conventionally, diagonally across the stream.

"That's about it. You turn, face the danger, and row away from it," Tony said, wreathed in the smoke of a Swisher Sweet—the brand name of a thin, utterly foul cigar that was the most effective bug repellent he'd found.

After the lesson, we strapped our fly rods to the Otters, loaded rope, fly boxes, and essential survival gear into watertight compartments beside the seats, and launched in to a stretch of calm water above a mild rapids. Tony told Jeannie to expect us between eight and ten that night. The Jim is an easy river with only a few short white-water stretches, so we wouldn't be delayed by frequent portages around rapids. Besides, it was a fine, warm, cloudless afternoon. We weren't thinking about the fact that even easy rivers can be dangerous when you're north of the Arctic Circle and the water is somewhere between ice and forty degrees.

After traveling about a mile, we made the first of our fishing stops. Behind us, spruce ridges mounted in tiers toward a high mountain far to the northeast, its peak white against the unblemished sky. For a while, I was content to admire the scenery and to watch Marc, a novice fly fisherman, casting some very pretty loops. He made six presentations with a streamer and hooked three grayling. The grayling is a scrappy fish with a fanlike dorsal fin, a sleek, silvery body, and a low IQ. In fact, compared to the Mensa Society brown trout I have tried to outwit on eastern streams, it is a moron. The grayling struck at any fly we cast at them. When each of us had caught and released two, we rafted on.

The float went like that, hour after hour, until midnight, when we realized that the solitude and the perpetual Arctic daylight had bewitched us. We'd lost all track of time and were hours overdue, with still another three or four miles to go. That would take at least an hour more, so we decided to row hard for home.

As we pushed on, the Arctic dusk fell and the mosquitoes boiled out of the woods and muskeg bogs. I paused to apply a varnish of Alaskan cologne—one hundred percent deet—and to light up a Swisher Sweet. Ahead, Marc and Tony were setting up to negotiate a tricky passage. Just beyond them, the river drew into bottleneck between a high bank and a gravel bar, then picked up speed and curved in a frothing rush past an undercut bank. A lot of big spruce had fallen from the eroded bank, but their roots still clung to the soil, causing them to stick out in the current in long sweepers. A few yards downstream, more fallen spruce formed a nasty-looking jumble of snags, like a logjam.

Tony rowed bow-first into the bottleneck, then, as the accelerating current drew him toward the sweepers, turned the raft and paddled cross-current to stay clear of the trees. He sailed easily into quieter water below. Marc followed him. I was positioning my raft when I saw Marc's suddenly spin broadside into one of the fallen trees. His right oar jammed under it, and acting as a lever, flipped the Otter onto its side. In the next instant, unknown tons of water traveling at four or five miles an hour careened it into the snags downstream, where it stuck with one blue pontoon in the air, the other caught in the trees. Marc had been pitched overboard where the raft had first turned over. He was clinging to the sweeper, water rushing over him. I could see only his head, the top of his orange life vest, and part of his right leg, flung over a branch.

Tony paddled downstream to beach his raft and run to Marc's aid by land. That was the sensible thing to do, but when it's your son clinging to a log in an Arctic river, many miles from the nearest help, you don't think about what's sensible. I rowed straight into the fast water, back paddling to avoid striking the sweeper broadside and capsizing myself. Bumping into it bow-first, I sculled into a back eddy strong enough to brake the main flow. The raft slipped against the bank and was moored there by the opposing currents.

Straddling the sweeper, I inched out toward Marc, my plan simply to grab him and pull him to the bank. He was less than ten feet away.

The river was golden brown beneath me and then dark brown. It must have been seven or eight feet deep, and the current was stronger than it had looked at first. While I knew things were serious, I didn't think they were critical; then I realized that Marc's left leg was trapped underwater, probably in the crotch of a submerged branch. His waders had filled despite his cinched wading belt.

"Dad! I'm frozen! I can't hang on much longer!" he yelled above the river's rush.

Carefully, I stood and put all my weight on the tree trunk. It sank an inch or two, enough for Marc to free his leg. I inched farther out, almost prone as I reached to grab him. The standing waves sloshed over me, the cold numbed my fingers within seconds, but I somehow got a grip on Marc's arm with one hand. I couldn't budge his 180 pounds, not with the added weight in his waders, not against that current. For a second, I thought to tell him to let go and let the river carry him into the quieter water. Then I could pull him ashore without fighting so much current. But even with his life vest on, his flooded waders could draw him under; and if that happened, he could be swept into the snags and trapped. The chance of drowning was only the half of it; the other half was exposure. Anyone immersed up to his neck in water of forty degrees or less has only about ten or fifteen minutes to survive. I had to get him out quickly, but I was temporarily out of ideas.

"The rope!" Marc hollered. He was the one in trouble, but was thinking clearer than I.

I backed down the log and got the thirty-foot painter stowed in my raft. Tony stood on the bank and took one end, drawing it taut while I made a loop with the bitter end. I crawled out onto the sweeper but could only get the loop within inches of Marc's hands.

"I can't . . . ! Fingers . . . frozen! I'm going to let go!"

"No!" I said. "Grab it!"

Marc reached for the rope with his left hand and literally willed his fingers to open and grasp it. When he got hold with both hands, I scrambled to the bank. Tony took up slack and we both hauled him onto dry land, where he lay shaking, his strength spent.

We pulled off his waders—gallons of water spilled out—then helped him out of his drenched clothes and told him to walk around, to keep moving. Countless mosquitoes leapt on him ravenously. He was shivering violently, but couldn't get warm. He had been in close to the limit and was on the cusp of second-stage hypothermia, when the body begins to lose its ability to warm itself. It can be reheated only by an outside source—hot liquids, a fire, or another body. I was wet and chilled myself, but had more body heat than he. Stripping to the waist, I embraced him tightly and almost cried out from the sting of what felt like a thousand mosquitoes biting me all at once. Tony later told me that my back was almost black with them.

I held Marc for several minutes, and I like to think of it as a father holding a son in a life-giving embrace, but the truth was that it helped only a little. We tramped through the woods to a gravel bar about a hundred yards downstream, gathered a pile of driftwood, and Tony got a fire going with his lighter. Marc huddled beside the blaze. He was still shivering uncontrollably, and he was getting drowsy—another dangerous sign. We told him get up and gather more wood—anything to keep his blood moving, his mind alert.

For the next two hours, we three sat by the fire, the flames leaping and falling as the evening dusk blended seamlessly into the dusk of the Arctic dawn. As Marc began to recover, Tony and I went back to the logjam and retrieved the two rafts, but we couldn't find Marc's oars. Both had been sprung loose from the locks and sent downriver.

"They're probably halfway to the Yukon by now," Tony said as we returned to the gravel bar, where we found Marc ready to travel.

"Dad, Tony, I'm sorry," he said, standing up. "I was rowing away, but . . . "

"Listen, there's no sorry about it," Tony said. "There's no fault-finding out here."

"Well, thanks, you know, for saving my life."

Tony shrugged it off, and I said, "Glad you're still here, son," and then we set about solving the problem of how to get home with three rafts and only two sets of oars. Tony volunteered to tow Marc's raft, and that is how we went down the Jim—Marc's and Tony's rafts tethered, mine in the lead. When we were nearly back to camp, we swept past a great bald eagle standing on a jutting gravel bar. His head, white as sheep's wool, turned toward us, his dark wings spread to the breadth of a tall man's arm span, and he rose with his talons extended because he wasn't flying far, only to a high cottonwood at the end of the bar. There he perched, gazing down, but not at us because we were not his concern; he was looking for fish. Behind him the deep spruce forests stood silent in the shadows of the morning.

In the following days, Marc came to the recognition, so alien to a healthy young man, of his own vulnerability. As for me, I had wanted the true wild, and almost had gotten it in spades. I had wanted a taste of what North America was like for the mountain men and the pioneers, and nature had given a brief sampling. In the real wilderness, a small mistake or moment of blind, bad luck can have grave consequences, and there is neither anything nor anyone to rely on but yourself and your skills, your friends and their skills. Not that we came to look upon the wilderness as heartless or hostile. Nature and her creatures aren't cruel, nor are they compassionate. They are whole and complete unto themselves, and therefore indifferent to human fate and emotions, to human ideas of right and wrong. Curiously, Marc's close call made us feel more a part of the world we had entered, because it humbled us. We who live in civilization come to think of ourselves and those we love as special and deserving, but in the wilderness, where things die every day, we're merely more creatures, subject to nature's laws and deserving of nothing. I knew I never would forget the look on Marc's face as he clung to the log, nor my own thought that I was going to lose him; yet, if the worst had happened, the rivers, forests, and mountains would not have acknowledged my grief and loss any more than they would the she-wolf's loss of a cub to starvation, the female caribou's loss of her young to a wolf. Thus endeth the lesson.

We put the mishap behind us and went on.

MILE MARKER 175, Coldfoot—June 28. The blue road sign was painted with symbols familiar to any interstate traveler: a figure lying on a bed, a gas pump, a knife and fork, a telephone. The words beneath them would not be familiar: NEXT SERVICES—244 MILES. Coldfoot was founded in 1899 by gold prospectors and was originally called "Slate Creek." Its name was changed when a tenderfoot miner, after mushing up the Koyukuk River, took one look around, got cold feet, and headed back home. In the 1930s, Robert Marshall found it a crude mining camp consisting of "one gambling house, two roadhouses, two stores, and seven saloons." Today, after a brief incarnation in the 1970s as a camp for pipeline construction gangs, it consists of one roadhouse-cum-gas-station-cum-general-store, one motel-cum-bar-cum gift shop, the Arctic Acres Inn, and a rustic visitors center run by the Bureau of Land Management, the National Park Service, and the U.S. Fish and Wildlife Service. The big Dalton rigs stop in Coldfoot on their way to and from the oil fields, but the rugged old times they are a-changin'. Coldfoot now calls itself "The Coldfoot Resort." Tour buses and vans arrive every day, the passengers are run through the gift shop, and stay at the motel.

Prices match the surrounding landscape, we discovered. Gas was relatively reasonable at $1.75 a gallon, but a bottle of bug repellent cost $7 and a shower $3.50. The towel was extra. The roadhouse, however, offered an all-you-can-eat special for eleven dollars. Marc, dissatisfied with our Spartan camp fare, took full advantage and packed away the approximate caloric intake of a logging crew. Jeannie, Tony, and I fed our brains and souls in the bar, run by a stocky, blue-eyed Montanan named Jim. (Like a lot of full- and part-time Alaskans, he didn't volunteer his last name.) Jim said that cold feet remain a problem in Coldfoot. "A lot of Montanans work here. They stick it out. But we get people, some from as far as the East Coast, who don't last a week, hell, some of 'em don't last one shift before they quit. Don't know why. Too isolated, I guess. This place isn't even marked on a lot of maps."

M.M. 193, June 28: Sukapak and Snowden Mountains, peaks of the Brooks Range, shone with a magical light in the midnight sun. Their granite faces, barren and almost sheer, thrust up out of the forested lower slopes and took on subtle shades of rose, gold, and peach. At one in the morning, we were graced with a rare sight: four wolf cubs, two black and two white, scrambled out of a creekbed and crossed the Dalton. Two cubs were each carrying a rabbit carcass. They and their siblings ran up a wooded hill, paused to glance back at us, then vanished. We did not see their mother, but we spotted the tracks of a huge wolf in the sediment of Nutirwik Creek, where we camped for the night.

M.M. 235, June 29: We passed the northern limit of the tree line on the Dalton. The point was marked by a short white spruce and a sign that said: LAST SPRUCE TREE—DO NOT CUT. From there to the Arctic Ocean, 180 miles away, the tundra would be as treeless as a desert. As a matter of fact, the coastal tundra, receiving an average of eight inches of precipitation a year, would be a desert if not for the permafrost, which prevents moisture from soaking into the ground.

M.M. 240, the Chandalar Shelf, June 30: The grizzly's tracks led across the tundra and down the steep bank of a nameless mountain stream that tumbled toward the Chandalar River, two thousand feet below. The tracks were old, yet I felt a little apprehensive as Marc and I looked across the stream into a jungle of willow and alders dense enough to conceal a dozen grizzlies. I wasn't heartened by something I'd seen the night before, on a walk with Tony. A couple of square yards of tundra mat had been ripped away and gouged to a depth of two or three feet, an excavation that looked to have been dug by a psychotic backhoe operator but had been made by a bear. The grizzly had been after a marmot, a ground squirrel, or a vole, a rodent no bigger than a chipmunk, and you could almost feel its savage determination in the way it had torn the earth open. The brown bears of southern Alaska, fattening in rivers thick with salmon, had so much to eat that they grew selective and wasteful, just like humans. They often sucked the roe out of female fish and tossed the rest away. But on the Chandalar barren grounds, nature's shelves were not well stocked. Even the fiercest predator in North America had to settle for prey fit for a house cat, and he had to work hard to get it.

Yes, I had come to be where grizzlies were, roaming free in great numbers, but I did not want to run into one at close quarters. That led me to wonder if Marc and I should push into the thickets. The age of the bear tracks was no guarantee that their maker was not lurking in there; and an animal so famished that it had exerted tremendous efforts to capture a tiny vole might welcome an intrusion by two well-fed human beings. If I had to subsist on crackers, wouldn't I welcome a porterhouse delivered to my door? Of course, I was ignorant about grizzlies at the time, never having seen one outside of a zoo. All I knew about them was what I had read and heard; because much of that lore involved gory maulings and tales of their preternatural ferocity and power—even their scientific name, *Ursus horribilis*, inspired dread—I had a preternatural terror of them.

Tony, a veteran of literally hundreds of bear encounters during his years guiding out of King Salmon, had a deep respect for them, but they didn't terrify him. He had offered a tutorial on proper etiquette in bear country. It was mannerly, as well as prudent, to make noise if you thought a grizzly was near. Talk, sing, ring bells. Marc and I had no bells, nor firearms, so we started chattering and bantering and thrashed through the alders like a whole troop of urban Boy Scouts on their first outing off pavement.

We passed through without any ursine confrontations and tramped on to the finger of a ridge, where we glassed the valley for caribou. The big migrations take place in the fall and spring, herds of a hundred thousand or more surging over distances of a thousand miles. But in the summer, in flight from the tormenting mosquitoes, smaller herds of, say, ten or twenty thousand move from the valleys and coastal tundra into the high ranges.

Late on the twenty-ninth, after passing that last spruce tree, we had backpacked into the Chandalar, hoping to spot one of those summer caribou treks. (That beautiful name, Chandalar, is a corruption of *Gens de Large*—nomadic people—the name French employees of the

Hudson's Bay Company gave to the Gwich'in Indians who roamed the valley and who still live there.) After hauling ourselves and forty-pound backpacks over the tussocks for three full hours we had seen a pair of shed antlers but no caribou. And we had covered a mere three miles. I felt as if I were walking on a waterbed with a sack of rocks on my back. A thunderstorm, building up over the Brooks Range, gave us an excuse to stop and pitch our tents on a lonely, barren, windswept pitch above the valley.

Now Marc and I swept binoculars across the valley and the river, its braids like the strands of gray, frayed rope. The valley was empty of game, and so were the mountains on the far side, their slopes green at first, then black with scree, then white. The silence was dense and primeval, a silence that never had been sundered by the clatter of industrial and postindustrial civilization. Compared with it, the voices of statesmen and politicians arguing about even the gravest issues of our time would have sounded as trivial as the nattering on a TV talk show.

Another thunderstorm was approaching, and we hoofed the mile back to camp. It rained hard for a while. When the storm passed, Marc opened our tent fly and said, "Dad, look at this." A rainbow, its colors so vibrant that it appeared solid, arched over the river. It must have been a thousand feet across and a thousand feet high, and we were looking down on it. Yeah, yeah, I thought. No caribou, but this is enough, more than enough.

M.M. 275, Galbraith Lake, July 2: We camped beside a creek a few miles off the Dalton for two days and nights. Galbraith Lake, its thousand acres glimmering in the tundra, was overlooked by the snow-capped peaks and glaciers of the Brooks Range. But gazing upon such beauty amid so many savage insects was like being trapped in hell while in sight of heaven. I had been in buggy places, from the Ontario woods to the Everglades, from Vietnam to the Yucatan, and had never seen mosquitoes to compare with those around Galbraith. Not in numbers, not in viciousness. They would have caused the most fanatical eco-maniac to have visions of B-52s carpet-bombing the tundra with DDT.

We caught grayling, fried them with potatoes, and ate wearing head nets so we wouldn't swallow too many bugs. If speedy bowel movements were an Olympic event, we would have been gold medalists. At night—a term of convenience in the Arctic summer—we lay in our tents, listening to a whine that sounded like a badly tuned, one-note violin orchestra. In a quavering, high-pitched, horror-movie voice, Marc pretended to be a mosquito. "Let us in," he lisped. "We won't hurt you. We only want to be with you." I could think of only one use for them—they will keep the Arctic wilderness from being overrun with tourists.

M.M. 417, Deadhorse, July 3: This was it, the end of the road (or the beginning, if you were heading south). We voted Deadhorse as the strangest and ugliest town any of us had seen in our lives. Every structure, whether warehouse, office, or airplane hangar, looked the same, built of extruded steel or aluminum and set on pilings (to avoid melting the permafrost and causing the buildings to collapse). There were no churches, schools, bars, banks, or shops—except for one general store where a box of Triscuits went for five dollars. Deadhorse exists solely to house and feed the fifteen hundred men and women who work in the oil fields.

There are no horses in the Arctic, so how did the town get its name? Some years ago, a rich New Yorker set up a six-million-dollar trust fund for his son, but stipulated that he could not collect until he was thirty-five years old. The young man went to Alaska to work at odd jobs and wait for his thirty-fifth birthday. One day, he decided to start a hauling business and talked his father into cosigning a loan for vehicles and equipment. The company almost went bankrupt, and the Father became financially responsible for several dump trucks, graders, and the like. He said, "I hate to put money into feeding a dead horse." The company then became known as "Deadhorse Haulers." In the 1960s, as the first North Slope gushers came in, Burgess Construction won a contract to build the first airstrip at Prudhoe Bay. Burgess hired Deadhorse Haulers to do the gravel work. Soon, everyone began calling the airstrip "Deadhorse" and the name stuck.

On the way up from Galbraith Lake, we had not seen any caribou, so Tony chartered a bush plane in Deadhorse from a company called "Forty-Mile Air." It was run by a young, dark-haired bush pilot, David Duke. "No guarantees on seeing caribou," commented Duke's partner, an insouciant flyboy named Rick. "Those animals were born under a wandering star."

While Tony zoomed off into the wild blue, Marc, Jeannie, and I were given an unofficial tour of the oil fields by twenty-year-old Teddy Westlake, who knew his ethnic makeup down to the fraction: thirteen-sixteenths Eskimo, the rest white. I knew my friends in the EcoCorps would have drummed me out if they'd read my thoughts. I liked the oil fields. I liked seeing caribou trails and even bear tracks within sight of the well-heads, liked seeing eiders, tundra swans, red-throated and Pacific loons nesting in thaw lakes in the shadows of drilling rigs. But most of all, I liked being in a place where real people worked at real jobs, a place blessedly free of "knowledge workers" who make lots of money simply by pushing numbers around on their computer terminals.

The tour finished, Teddy drove us to the northern limit of North America. We got out of the truck and dipped our toes in the Arctic Ocean.

M.M. 188, Wiseman, July 4–8: Wiseman, three miles off the Dalton down a gravel track, is a helter-skelter collection of mud-chinked log cabins, sled dogs barking in kennels, narrow, rutted dirt lanes, a general store with a wood-burning stove. It was founded back in 1907 as a supply depot for gold miners. Robert Marshall used it as a base for his explorations, and described it as a village "two hundred miles away from the twentieth century." The opening of the Dalton has brought it closer, and there are signs of the twenty-first century: in a few cabin yards, amid the huskies' cages and oil drums and battered pickup trucks, satellite dishes point skyward, seeking signals of Oprah and Monday night football.

Eleven miles from Wiseman, deep in the mountains at the end of a jeep trail, was the Silverado Mine. It would be our jump-off point for a four-day hike into the Brooks Range and the Gates of the Arctic. Despite its name, the Silverado was a gold mine, and it was a big out-fit: thirty miners and Cat-skinners whose huge bulldozers had removed half a mountainside. Here was my chance to work up enough outrage for reinstatement in the EcoCorps. Alas, I didn't. The manager, a soft-spoken, bearded man who called himself Bill and left it at that, hos-pitably showed us where his men had cleared a space for campers to stay overnight. His security chief, Merle, an Arizona deputy sheriff when he's not looking for gold, gave us mosquito coils. He excited my own greed when he told us that the miners had dug up a forty-one-ounce nugget this season. Somehow, it seemed fitting to be among such men in the middle of nowhere, on Independence Day.

We backpacked into the bush, following a dogsled trail westward toward the Glacier River, ten miles away. About two miles in, we crossed from private land into the Gates of the Arctic. All around us, mountains soared, patched with dark green spruce and the lighter greens of alder and willow swales. After covering five miles, we took a lunch break beside a lake where a widgeon hen swam with her ducklings in tow.

"Howdy!"

The voice startled us. Up the trail came a man of twenty-eight or thirty, with a blond goatee. He wore a floppy hat, and an old Stevens side-by-side shotgun was in a scabbard strapped to his bulging backpack. A gold pan shone from underneath the pack's top flap. Beside him trotted a mongrel carrying a saddle bag of dog food.

We invited him to join us for lunch. He declined the food but sat down. His name was Doug, a body-and-fender man from Homer, Alaska. He was camped near Wiseman, on the Koyukuk, where he was waiting for his partner to arrive from California.

"We got a little gold claim we work up at Wild Lake," he explained, gesturing vaguely at a hundred thousand acres of wilderness. "Summer's my slow season, so I take some time off to work the claim. My partner's late, and I got restless, thought I'd wander for a bit."

He noticed me eye the shotgun.

"Only twenty-gauge, but with rifled slugs, it'll penetrate a bear's skull." He patted his cartridge belt. "Birdshot in case I run out of food. I wouldn't shoot one of those widgeons, unless I got real hungry. Mallards and pintails, that's what I like."

We chatted for a while, then Doug shouldered his pack, saying, "Be seeing you around." Off he went with his dog, his gun, and gold pan, as free as anyone can expect to be.

It was 10:30 P.M. when we crested a six-hundred-foot ridge, from which we looked down on the Glacier River, shimmering in the soft Arctic glow. We pitched camp on a bluff across the river from an abandoned trapper's or miner's cabin, and built a crackling fire. With the sun below the ridges, it got chilly, but the cold kept the bugs down. Downstream, the land opened up, and we could see for miles, the reach of our eyes finally blocked by a high mountain. There were wolf tracks in the riverbank below, and the rocks in the riverbed were hued like coral and laid like the tiles in a terrazzo floor.

We caught grayling and explored the Glacier River valley the following day. If we hadn't seen Doug, we would have thought ourselves the only people within fifty miles. He visited us again, telling Marc that he had seen a grizzly. Marc asked him what he liked most about Alaska. "The greatest thing," he replied, "is that you have to dig down only a foot to keep your beer cold."

As for me, it was the country that went on and on, the absence of marked trails and fences, and the presence of bears and wolves. It was the bald eagle on the Jim River, the golden eagles soaring above the high, windy Atigun Pass, the Dall sheep on the Atigun's meadows. It was the lone caribou bull whose rack rose like a king's crown as he trotted across the tundra while we were heading back south from Deadhorse. It was the beautiful yellow blossom that's called the tundra rose and the fireweed that blazed on the mountainsides with a violet flame. It was nameless mountains and lakes.

And it was watching Marc hike out of the wilderness on his own. He had grown impatient with our plodding, middle-age pace and declared he would push on ahead of us, out of the Gates of the Arctic. Still a bit shaken by the accident, I was reluctant. I thought about the grizzly Doug had seen, the fresh tracks we had spotted by a nearby creek. And the ten miles of Alaskan bush that lay ahead of him. But he was twenty-two. Robert Marshall had been in his twenties when he mapped the Brooks Range. Time to let go. Past time.

"Well, take off, then," I said, and watched him stride across a broad tundra valley, his figure growing smaller and smaller until it was gone.

the farthest away river
1 9 9 6

I t was the name that beckoned—Kongakut—"The Farthest Away River" in the language of the Inupiat Eskimos in Alaska's far north. Someone told me they call it that because it's the most distant river from Kaktovik, a native village some sixty or seventy miles west of its mouth. Whatever the reason for it, the name fits; the Kongakut is the farthest away river from anywhere in the United States. In the extreme northeastern corner of the Arctic National Wildlife Refuge, it begins on the north slope of the northern Continental Divide in the Brooks Range, flows for a little over a hundred miles into the Beaufort Sea, and at one point comes to within a day's hike of the border with the Yukon Territory. The country it passes through is arguably the wildest in North America, an uninhabited land exempt from our Yankee-Doodle drive to tame the untamed, where nature still roars and rages and most of the rivers and mountains don't have any names, native or otherwise. All that beckoned even more than the lyrical "Farthest Away River."

I'll try to keep the romanticism within bounds, the call of the wild being a summons more attractive to the man snug in his living room than to the subsistence hunter who has to wrestle nature to get through the week with a full belly; nevertheless, the Kongakut did call because all I could think about for the past year was getting back to Alaska. Once again, I was depressed by the neutering of the wilderness that remains in the Lower Forty-Eight. I'd read in a recent issue of *Sierra* magazine that there is no place in the continental U.S. farther than twenty miles from a road of some kind. The nearest one to the

Kongakut is 180 miles away—the Dalton Haul Road that I'd traveled the previous summer.

There were other becauses:

I woke up on June 10, 1996, to find myself fifty-five years old. Still in good shape, but those two digits looked weird whenever I had to fill out a form asking my age. They reminded me that the window of opportunity for high adventure was closing. I had an urge to go big-game hunting again. Except for wild boar in Australia, I'd shot only waterfowl and upland birds since I quit deer hunting almost thirty years before, driven out of the woods by trigger-happy bozos, one of whom had put a round over my head in 1967, another of whom, the following season, fired through my tent just as I was getting out of my sleeping bag. Maybe I wanted to find out if I still could endure the dangers and hardships of going into the Big Wild, after quarry larger than grouse or ducks, and if I could still shoot straight. A willingness to face danger and hardship and an ability to shoot straight are not relevant virtues in our let's-stay-home-and-surf-the-net, safety-obsessed, consumer culture, but one advantage to getting older is the freedom to be reactionary.

Alaska means "The Great Land," and it is. Its wolf population, estimated at between seven and ten thousand, is several times larger than that of the *entire* continental U.S. I wanted to get to know it as well as a *cheechako* (a tenderfoot) could. Hunting in it, hunting in the right way, that is, the hard way, seemed a path to that knowledge; the hunter achieves a depth of intimacy with his environment denied the hiker, the rafter, or the trail-biking athlete for whom wild country is an outdoor fitness center. All the good hunters I know are excellent naturalists because their success depends on acute powers of observation and hearing, on a knowledge of game and habitat. Wilderness tourists generally see only the bold print of the natural world; the hunter reads the fine print, and if he's really skilled, that part of nature's book written in invisible ink. At the deepest level, he becomes an actor in the primeval drama between predator and prey.

My companions would be Dave Brown, Alan Richey, and Frank Stanskanis, all of whom work for Alyeska, the company that operates and maintains the Trans-Alaskan oil pipeline.

A two-hundred-pound six-footer, Brown at forty-four has gray hair and a gray mustache and bears a slight resemblance to actor

Donald Sutherland. The son of a U.S. Army rifle champion, he's a crack shot himself and has lived in Alaska for almost thirty years. Thirteen Dall rams are mounted in his Fairbanks house. He's hunted them every season for twenty-six years and was a hunting guide in a previous incarnation. Today he oversees the security force that patrols the pipeline.

Forty-nine year-old Richey came to Alaska in 1976 from his native Alabama, where he began shooting and fishing at an age when city boys are trying on their first baseball mitts. He worked on a pipeline construction crew and is now an engineer with Alyeska, a job that's taken him into the Brooks Range when it's sixty below. He's fished all over Alaska and in Costa Rica and the Florida Keys. An accomplished archer as well as rifleman, his bow hunting achievements include a caribou that just missed setting a Boone-and-Crockett record, and a grizzly bear that he shot at a range of twenty yards.

Stanskanis, with his sandy brown hair and trim physique, looks ten years younger than his sixty-two years. He should be an inspiration to other senior citizens who think that passing sixty is a one-way ticket to an A.A.R.P. life of golf courses and rocking chairs. Carrying a pack and rifle, he can outwalk men half his age over the ruggedest terrain, which isn't surprising; until a few years ago, he'd been a line-walker for the Trans-Alaskan, inspecting the four hundred of its eight hundred miles that are above ground. Through muskeg bogs over tundra and mountain passes, he would be out for six weeks, covering twelve to twenty miles a day. He began sheep hunting with Dave about a decade ago. Sheep hunting takes you into some very hazardous, vertiginous terrain, but Frank took it up because, he says, "I figured I'd lived long enough that it wouldn't be so bad if I got killed."

We would do our own outfitting, skinning, packing, and camp chores. Whatever the difficulties of the do-it-yourself approach, it's less expensive and more gratifying than buying a hunt. Ours also would be an old-fashioned hunt, with none of the modern doo-dads, like Ground Positioning Systems (maps and compasses would do for navigation, thanks) or ATVs (all travel would be by raft or on foot). Almost everything the hunter carries into the bush, from rifle to boots, is artificial, but there is a degree of artificiality that alienates him from the surroundings and makes the hunt unworthy of the dignity of the quarry.

All of us sought to catch a trophy-size Arctic char on fly or spinning tackle. A sea-run relative of the eastern brook trout, char leave the

Arctic Ocean in August and September to spawn in North Slope rivers.

Alan, Dave, and Frank each hoped to shoot a Dall ram, a grizzly, and a wolf.

I had tags to kill two caribou. (You won't find the euphemism "harvest" anywhere in this story. Big-game animals are not cash crops, and we hunters should avoid the politically correct obfuscations that muddle speech in our universities and in the media.) There were two reasons I limited myself to caribou.

The first was practical: Alaskan game laws prohibit nonresidents from hunting brown bears or Dall sheep without a professional guide. Dave Brown, still licensed to guide, had generously offered me his services for a nominal fee. I declined because he would have been barred by law from hunting.

The second reason was mystical. I wasn't ready to shoot a grizzly. It wasn't only the long hiatus from big-game hunting that made me reluctant; it was my belief that a grizzly has a powerful spirit. I didn't feel that my own spirit was commensurate, didn't feel that I had yet earned the right to shoot so magnificent a beast. Maybe next year, maybe the year after, maybe never, but definitely not now.

The plan was for a fifteen-day hunt. We would land by bush plane near the headwaters of the Kongakut, then raft downstream, fishing along the way, stopping every few miles to hunt side creeks and drainages. To an extent, we'd be living off the land, supplementing our freeze-dried rations with whatever we shot and caught. This wasn't to be a stunt, an attempt to play hunter-gatherer. Bush plane fares in Alaska are expensive (ours would be over five thousand dollars, and that was a bargain). The more stuff you carry, the more flights required to get you in and out. With the raft, paddles, and its accoutrements weighing almost two hundred pounds and a four-man base camp tent adding another fifty, we had to keep our food and personal gear as light as possible—an average of sixty-five pounds per man including rifles and ammunition.

There are ski bums and surf bums, so I guess Stu Ballard, a bush pilot for Alaska Flyers, is an aviation bum. He has no wife, children, or fixed address, and stays with friends or pitches his sleeping bag in the hangar in between hops. A green beret usually covers his thinning hair, and he wears a goatee and a cracked leather jacket that might have belonged to a World War Two ace.

"I've never landed there, so I'm going to make three or four passes and if I don't like what I see, I'll take you to Kaktovik and Walt will fly you in," Ballard said to us as we stood on the airstrip at Deadhorse. Walt was Walt Audi, owner of Alaska Flyers, and "there" was a gravel bar on the Kongakut, about two miles upstream from a feeder stream with the unlovely name of Drain Creek. "Is that okay with you guys?"

Bad weather had delayed our departure by three days (it was the third coldest August on record in the Brooks Range; blizzards had dumped half a foot of snow on the mountains), but Ballard's caution was okay with us. Not that caution and flying skill were guarantees of a happy landing. A few days before, two very experienced bush pilots died in a crash in the western Brooks Range.

Ballard's Super Cub could not carry all of us, the raft, and our gear in one flight; we would have to shuttle in, two men at a time. Frank and I went first. We took off into a crystalline blue sky, the first clear sky we'd seen in days, and flew along the northern rim of America. On one side, between the shore and the ice pack where polar bears ranged, was a dark blue corridor of the Beaufort Sea. In a few weeks, that lane of open water would be frozen solid and you could walk to the North Pole if you were so inclined. On the other side, the Arctic coastal plain, flat, brown, fissured by cracks in the permafrost into polygonal shapes resembling rice paddies, stretched east and west as far as we could see, and southward fifty miles to the jagged wall of the mountains. The plain is the spring calving grounds for the Porcupine caribou herd, two hundred thousand animals, and ground zero of the fight between, on the one side, oil companies that want to drill in the Arctic Wildlife National Refuge, and on the other, environmentalists and the Gwich'in Indians whose lives and culture depend on the caribou, much as the lives and culture of the Lakota and Cheyenne had on the buffalo. (Personally, I'd like to see the Indians win this time around. Yeah, yeah, an oil field would take up only a tiny fraction of the refuge, but to my mind that's like installing roulette tables in a cathedral and then saying, well, they only cover a few square yards of floor space.)

I looked down, hoping to see caribou. The herd's migration, an awesome, ever-moving tide of flesh and antlers, has earned the coastal plain the nickname "America's Serengeti" and is a sight never forgotten by the few who've seen it. But the early winter storm appeared to have sent the caribou south already. Empty of game, the plain was a depressing monotony of tundra grasses broken by small thaw lakes and the silver, serpentine braids of rivers. The Canning, named by British explorer Sir John Franklin for Prime Minister George Canning, passed beneath us, then the Hulahula, christened by Hawaiian whalers who'd hunted bowheads on Yankee ships in the last century; then came a succession of rivers with Eskimo names that hobbled the most nimble tongue: the Okpilak and the Okerokovik, the Niguanak and Aichilik and Ekaluakat. Finally, with the British Mountains of the Yukon Territory in sight, Ballard turned south and we winged over the Kongakut.

Within half an hour, we were skimming the shining peaks of the Romanzof Mountains. Ballard, accustomed to the low ceilings of the North Slope, was ecstatic; he hadn't flown this high in weeks. Cresting at nine thousand feet, the Romanzofs are the tallest mountains in the Brooks Range. That isn't much by the standards of the Alps or Rockies; yet their rise from the plain is so steep and sudden that they possess a forbidding drama, their sharp peaks, razor-edged ridges, and spired battlements giving an impression of a guarded sanctuary in which you may not find a hospitable welcome.

There was snow everywhere, from the summits down to the Kongakut valley, and great gray boulders and limestone crags and long black rivers of shale and scree showed through the snow. Meandering sheep trails striated slopes so steep I could not imagine any creature surefooted enough to walk on them. The river, now a bright pewter in the sun, now a deep jade, twined and braided past stands of willow and browning aspen. It might have been August on the calendar, but down there it was late November.

Ballard made a pass over the landing strip, which didn't look any different than any other gravel bar to my untrained eye. We made a second pass, and saw patches of maroon and blue in the snow of the valley: the tents of a hunting camp. Those hunters and their guide, along with a handful of Eskimo and Gwich'in subsistence hunters, were the only human beings in the refuge's thirty-two thousand square miles. You have to imagine Maine with a population of about twenty.

A third pass, Ballard peering out to check for ruts and large boulders on the strip. I began to ponder, somewhat tardily, the concern my wife, in-laws, and parents felt for me, going into so remote a place at my age. No doctors or hospital or telephone within two hundred miles. In bush Alaska, you come as close as a modern American can to experiencing what our country was like in the days of Lewis and Clark. It's a wilderness that doesn't forgive mistakes or rashness, and randomly metes out bad luck even to the prudent and experienced. If a freak downdraft doesn't cause you to die in a bush plane crash, you might stumble into a sow grizzly with cubs (a hiker from Washington, D.C., had been mauled to death in the western Brooks Range a week before we flew in). If a bear doesn't get you, your raft might overturn in a river so cold you have, oh, about five minutes before you go into fatal hypothermia, as my son Marc almost had last year. Or you might die in a fall from a cliff (the body of a British hiker who'd tumbled into a gorge this summer was found about six weeks after he disappeared). It's not surprising that bush Alaskans don't worry a lot about their cholesterol levels.

After a fourth pass, Ballard decided to go for it. The Super Cub touched down, bouncing crazily over the rocks. This is what Frank called "blue-collar flying." We rolled to a stop. Frank and I off-loaded our rifles, packs, and other gear. Ballard taxied to take off and got his nose wheel stuck in sand. We helped push him out—and then the plane lofted away to pick up Alan, Dave, and the raft.

All around was a world of white mountains and white tundra meadows, and when the echoing buzz of the plane faded away, a world utterly silent except for the whisper of the cold, green, transparent river. John Voelker, the novelist and outdoor writer (*Anatomy of a Murder, Trout Madness*), once said that he fished for trout because he liked to be where trout are. I thought about that, and realized that I wasn't after caribou or char. The hunt was important, imposing a kind of logic and discipline on what otherwise would have been aimless wandering. If I saw a suitable bull, I certainly would shoot it; if I caught a two-and-a-half-foot char, I would keep it; but the true quarry wasn't on land or in the waters. These days of budget air travel have made it easier than ever to put several thousand miles between you and home, but cell phones and CNN, among other things, have made it harder than ever to flee the familiar, the pressures and trivial media chatter of modern civilization. I had come to the Farthest Away River, not only to *be* far away, but to *feel* that I was. And I did.

The day was calm and pleasantly warm, about fifty degrees. We idled away the next three hours. Frank fished for a while, then took a nap. I talked and drank tea around the fire with the guide, Dave Marsh, and his two clients. A wiry, bearded man of medium height, Marsh had been in the mountains for several weeks, without much word from the outside world. Said he'd heard something about an airliner blowing up near New York, and did they find out what caused it? Nearby was evidence of a successful hunt—a boar grizzly's hide, fleshed and salted, a caribou rack, a Dall ram's skull and horns, and game bags packed with meat. The blizzard had made things miserable for a while, Marsh said, and one of his packers had been charged by an angry sow with cubs. The grizzly swiped the man across his backpack, knocking him flat, but she must not have been in a murderous mood; having made her point, she ran off to rejoin her young.

Ballard landed with Alan and Dave. Marsh gave us a hand packing the raft, then photographed us as we shoved off. He was the last human being we would see until we flew out.

The river carried us down, through the mountains. We pitched our first camp on a gravel bar at the mouth of Drain Creek, which wound away to the west, galleries of yellow aspen along its banks. There were wolf tracks in the fine black sand, and in the last glimmer of the long Arctic twilight, a young bull caribou plodded along the Kongakut, only thirty yards from our tent and crackling driftwood fire. Caribou aren't known for their intelligence, but this one's obliviousness struck me as monumentally stupid, if not evidence of a death wish. Shooting him would have been no honor; he was too small in any case. But I took his appearance as a good omen, and after a meal of freeze-dried beef and noodles, had a jolt of Johnny Walker and crawled into my sleeping bag. The four of us lay awake for over an hour, maybe mildly insomniac by the anticipation and unrealistic expectations that precede every hunt or fishing trip.

Waking to a frosty but cloudless morning, my Alaskan friends marveled at the weather. The North Slope of the Brooks Range wasn't supposed to be so benign in late August and early September. The excellent visibility allowed them to scan a distant mountainside for Dall sheep, first cousins to Canadian bighorns. With the naked eye, they spotted a dozen or so, all ewes and lambs. Even with binoculars, all I could see were patches of snow or white rocks.

Alan, whom I've fished with in Mexico and the Florida Keys, told me the art of spotting sheep was a little like the art of spotting bonefish wakes on a tidal flat.

"When you've done it a thousand times, you know what to look for," he drawled. "They're a dirty white, not like snow or rocks, and you look for a little movement. Rocks don't move sidehill or uphill."

Finally, I focused on them, clinging to what looked like a sheer rock face in apparent defiance of gravity. My next problem was how to discern their age and sex. I couldn't tell which were adults, which had ram's horns and which didn't, so I had to take my companions' word that the flocks were ewes and lambs. Hunters are allowed to shoot only mature rams—males with a three-quarter to a full curl. Dall rams rut in the late fall, but they are not nurturing fathers and loving husbands; for the rest of the year, they live apart in small bachelor groups. We went off to find them, or caribou, or bear.

Stuffing spotting scopes, game bags, survival gear, and food into our backpacks, Alan and I crossed the Kongakut in hip boots to hunt a drainage on the east side. Frank and Dave hiked up Drain Creek on the west.

That stream and its surrounding ridges (which had equally unpoetic names, like Bathtub Ridge—the surveyors of that country must have been plumbers in another life) were rich in game, particularly sheep. The reasons why offer a lesson in why the hunter has to be able to read nature's fine print. In the Brooks Range, as in most other wild areas, nature doesn't believe in equality, distributing plants and animals unevenly. One stretch of terrain is full of game, another is not; but because nature is also jealous of her secrets, she often makes the differences between the two landscapes too subtle for most people to notice.

From morning till early afternoon, Alan and I hunted five miles up one side of the eastern drainage, then the other side back to base camp. We saw a few old caribou tracks, a golden eagle's nest, and two or three female Dalls; Frank and Dave, striking ten miles up Drain Creek, saw two dozen sheep (though none were legal rams), a moose, ptarmigan, mergansers, and teal, in addition to fresh sign of caribou and grizzly. The mouths of the two watercourses were separated by less than a mile, the banks of both were covered with willow and aspen; both were surrounded by identical natural communities—wetland, alpine tundra, treeless mountainside. What accounted for the abundance of the one, the barrenness of the other?

Anyone but a blind man would have noticed that Drain Creek had more water in it; slightly less obvious, but still apparent even to the casual observer, was the density and age of the vegetation—Frank reported seeing aspen with trunks eight inches in diameter (in the austere Arctic, trees that size are the equivalent of sequoia). But there were other, more hidden answers to the puzzle, inscribed in the shale on Drain Creek's bars—fossilized corals and marine organisms that lived in the primeval sea basin from which the Romanzofs arose sixty million years ago. That's recent by the geological calendar, so the shale is still rich in nutrients that not only help vegetation flourish in the creek valley and on the lower elevations, but also provide minerals that the sheep need in their diet. Periodically, they come down from the safety of their high ranges (whose limestone formations are comparatively sterile) to lick up the phosphorus and nitrates leached out of the rocks.

The rest of the answer lay in the architecture of the land. The creek Alan and I followed was narrow, its canyon almost sheer-sided—a still, shadowy corridor that rose steeply toward its source. The Drain Creek valley was several times as wide, and ascended gradually. Its width made it a natural wind channel, while its gentler sides allowed more sunlight to fall on the south-facing slopes above. Dall sheep like wind channels and also south-facing slopes. In the winter, the gales that make the Brooks Range only slightly more congenial to human life than the moon scour the snow from the high meadows, exposing tundra grasses the sheep graze on. In the warmer months they move onto the ridges with southerly slopes because those are the first to green up in spring and remain the most luxuriant through the summer. All of this illustrates another lesson, an old one learned by Native Americans through millennia of experience, by ecologists through science: if you significantly alter one thing in nature, you alter everything else, because all things are connected, in time as well as space. Interred within the very rocks are creatures that died when dinosaurs reigned, yet their microscopic skeletons help sustain animals living today.

Two golden eagles, wings black against the blue sky, gyred on thermals rising from a limestone pinnacle, swooped across a tundra meadow, and then soared away and vanished over a distant ridge.

Taking a break from fishing, I sat on a gravel bar and watched the eagles, just because their grace and effortless speed made me feel good. The Kongakut surged slowly against a cliff on its far side. The river looked like liquefied jade, so pure that only the color and the movement of the eddies told you it was water and not air. The clarity created an illusion of shallowness—shoals and bars that appeared no more than a foot or two down were in fact four or five feet deep. The greenish rock bottom was speckled with gray oblong spawning beds, or redds, scraped out by the tails of mating char, hundreds in this pool alone, the females long and silvery, the males with black, red-spotted flanks, bellies the color of fire.

It was our third day out, and we were a few miles down from Drain Creek, on our way to another campsite. Earlier, we had caught and released over a dozen fish in less than twenty minutes; at this hole we'd hooked twice that many, using blue-and-white streamers and Egg-Sucking Leeches on the fly rod, orange and red Mepps on the spinning tackle. I'd caught a twenty-two-inch male on fly and was fairly content with that, but now I was watching Dave tussling with a big fish. He pumped it in and beached it—another male, with a kype jutting pugnaciously.

"Twenty-three!" he exulted. laying the tape on the fish, a grin breaking under his mustache.

The eagles had returned, but I'd done enough bird-watching. Competitive juices flowing, I began casting a red Mepps. After releasing three or four females, I felt a solid hit. The rod bowed, then came that ever-wonderful sound of a big fish pulling drag. The char ran hard downstream, but I quickly got below him, to stop him from using the current to his advantage, and beached him in two or three minutes. A full-girthed male that looked seven or eight pounds. I thought he would make thirty inches, but the tape said twenty-six. I released him without disappointment; it was enough to have fought a wild fish that size in a wild river, with eagles in the sky.

Another pool a couple of miles downstream proved even more productive. In less than an hour, we caught so many that it became boring—a char for almost every cast.

Looking northward, we saw dark clouds filling the notch of the Kongakut valley. The mountains were through giving us a break on the weather, so we decided to move on.

Unless your plan is to turn yourself into bear bait, it's imprudent to walk through grizzly country with dead fish on you, which was why we hadn't kept any char for dinner. We weren't going to spend the night in base camp. As soon as it was set up and the raft secured, we would trek up another unnamed drainage and spike out, deep in mountains where friends of Alan's had shot and seen everything there was to be shot and seen a couple of years ago: That wilderness teeming with game that has been a sportsman's fantasy for centuries, and the Indian shaman's vision for much longer than that.

There is a saying that everything in Alaska is twice as far as it appears, and twice as hard to get to. With some thirty pounds on our backs, we tramped over the jumbled rocks of dry creek bottom, through muskeg, over tussock tundra, the tussocks rolling underfoot like bowling balls. We must have crossed and recrossed the creek a hundred times, and the icy water eventually breached the triple layer of waterproofing on my boots. The moose trails that wound through the willow and alder brakes were a comparative joy to walk on; the monsters had tramped the tundra to the hardness of pavement. But there was a certain tension in the thickets, and we had rounds chambered and scope covers off in case of a point-blank grizzly charge.

Frank and Dave, those marathon hikers, had gone on ahead. Their spike was to be pitched about ten miles up, Alan's and mine half that distance, under a mountain on which one of his friends had bagged a ram with a thirty-nine-inch curl. I was happy to have Alan as companion, because he was hobbled by bad knees and I by a bad ankle and right foot. Traumatic osteoarthritis in the ankle, traumatic nueroma in the foot, the trauma having come from two AK-47 bullets, fired at me by Muslim militiamen back when I was a war correspondent in Beirut. I've often wondered if the experience of being hit by a high-powered rifle had had something to do with my reluctance to shoot big game. A certain empathy.

We came across a long stretch of stream that inexplicably flowed underground. It must have dried up suddenly; dozens of juvenile char, caught unaware, lay rotting on the rocks.

The tracks of a very large wolf were printed *over* Dave's and Frank's tracks in the snow, and every spooky Russian folktale I'd heard came back to me.

At dusk, we pitched the small mountain tent near a stand of dead willow. The mountain rose to the northwest, its summit slightly bent, like a half-straightened fishhook, and crowned with limestone slabs. The peaks to the east glowed in the light of a sun we could no longer see. The days were still long, sunset arriving about ten P.M., but we were losing light at the rate of eight minutes a day. For the next hour, we watched steam rise from our drenched boots and socks, arranged around the fire, and then ate some more freeze-dried rations before turning in. With the bolts open, to quickly chamber a round if necessary, we slept with our rifles beside us, the muzzle of Alan's .300 pointed to the back of the tent, the muzzle of my .30-06 toward the front. In Alaska, grizzlies always stalk your imagination, but never so much as at night.

Rain and sleet crackled against the tent when we woke up. A breakfast of instant oatmeal and coffee, and then a short walk in our rain gear to a low bluff downstream. From that perch, we watched the valley for caribou and bear, glassed the mountains for sheep. The easterly wind turned north, and banks of fog and cloud settled into the draws and canyons above. If there were any Dalls up there, we could not see them now; and not a living thing appeared in the valley, though it was criss-crossed with game trails. The Arctic is a spare environment, its climate severe, but with two thousand caribou in the Porcupine herd, I expected to see a lot of *Rangifer tarandus;* and with an estimated 960 grizzlies in the refuge, at least one *Ursus arctos horribilis.* But even in the West early in the last century, white explorers and Indians alike often faced starvation. In his biography of Meriwether Lewis, *Undaunted Courage,* Stephen Ambrose notes that the Lewis and Clark expedition, in country abounding in elk, antelope, buffalo, was sometimes reduced to eating dogs and horses, as were a few of the tribes they encountered. Hunger was such a constant threat to Native Americans that it haunted their souls as well as the bellies. The Ojibwa of the northern Middle West and central Canada believed in the *windigo,* an evil spirit that resorted to the unthinkable practice of cannibalism. In Alaska today, the Koyukon have a similar myth—Woodsman, a human being exiled to the forest because game shortages have driven him to survive on human flesh.

The idea that the amount of game is directly proportional to the degree of wildness is partly illusion. Of course, you won't find grizzlies in Manhattan, nor bison in Iowa cornfield, but true wilderness is vast and unpredictable. I wasn't seeing any caribou because the Porcupine herd ranges over an area as large as all six New England states put together—plenty of space in which to disappear. They can be whimsical nomads, born under a wandering star, and often change their migratory routes without giving prior notice. True wilderness also is harsh on game populations. Sheep in the Brooks Range have lost half to three-fourths of their population in the past several years because severe winters (severe even by Arctic standards) have buried their alpine pastures under several feet of snow. The sheep have either starved or have been driven to concentrate in valleys where they can find graze—and where they are easy prey for wolves. The moose season was closed in the northern part of the refuge this year because the calf survival rate was close to zero. In the Kongakut herd alone, only three of the two dozen moose calves born last year lived through the winter. The calves couldn't forage in the deep snows, and those that didn't die of hunger were killed by grizzlies, which often stake out a calving area and devour the newborns.

After four fruitless and chilling hours atop the bluff, Alan and I decided to return to camp, put on an extra layer of clothes, and move to another spot farther up the valley. I was scouting the creek for a ford when Alan whispered:

"Get down! Stay quiet! Big bull caribou!"

I caught a glimpse of it through the willow and alder thicket behind us. It was meandering along the side of a ridge about four hundred yards away. In the open, with no trees or shrubs to make a contrast, the bull did look big. Its velvety rack branching handsomely, its cape a grayish brown, its flanks dark brown, it moved at a stately pace, pausing to browse on tundra grass. Alan raised his binoculars and said in an excited whisper:

"He's got a double shovel! There's only one in a thousand with a double shovel!"

A double shovel is two antler spades that jut from the base of the rack, parallel over the caribou's forehead.

My heartbeat immediately shot into buck-fever range, and I was telling myself to calm down as we stalked through the thicket, bent low, trying hard not to crack branches underfoot. I was thinking "Trophy!" and about camp meat and that it was up to me to bag insurance in case we got weathered in—a frequent emergency in Alaska. In his guiding days, a storm had trapped Dave Brown in the mountains for seven days. His partner had broken his leg on the last day of the hunt and their food was almost gone; if they hadn't shot a sheep the day before, they would have been half starved by the time the weather broke and the plane picked them up.

I took three or four deep breaths to steady myself as we came out of the thicket and crouched down. Between us and the bull was a wide-open muskeg bog, perhaps two hundred yards across, and the caribou was standing some fifty or sixty feet above it, his whole side toward us.

"Better shoot him now," Alan muttered.

I had a four-power fixed scope on my Weatherby, and there wasn't anything but a flimsy willow shrub to rest the rifle on. An offhand (standing) shot of over two hundred yards was longer than I cared to make, especially in the rain. On the other hand, I didn't dare venture farther into the open muskeg even a dumb caribou would spook if he saw me. I'm not too bad an offhand shot—ten years ago in Australia, I'd dropped a wild boar from the standing position, with one shot and with iron sights. And on the rifle range at home, I'd put twenty killing rounds in a row through a silhouette target at one hundred yards. But that was at a cardboard deer, on a warm, sunny day . . .

I shouldered the rifle, slipped the sling under my arm for stability—and found myself looking into a fog. The scope had misted over in the rain. I wiped it off with a bandanna, raised the .30-06 again. The bull was on the move again, almost prancing, his head held high, and I led him slightly, fired, and saw him stumble. "Good shot!" Alan said, looking through his binoculars. The caribou didn't think so—he was still moving, although a little more slowly. The rifle was sighted to hit dead-on at two hundred yards, but there must have been more bullet drop than I'd counted on. I figured I'd hit low, on the upper part of the foreleg. Still, the 180-grain bullet should have knocked him down. Maybe I'd led him a little too much and had only winged his leg. (I found out later that that's what I'd done.) Overcompensating, I put the next shot high, and watching the round throw dust in the ridge, was amazed that the animal didn't sprint off—or at least try to.

Now he was atop a knoll, and I saw he was going to turn into a thickly wooded draw. The last thing I wanted was to have wounded him and lose him in the woods. I rested on a willow branch, but it was, well, willowy, and gave way just as I centered the crosshairs on his lungs and fired again. The bull's legs crumpled. On his knees, he raised his head, and seemed to look momentarily toward the strange noise that he may or may not have connected with the terrible thing that had happened to him. Then his head dropped and he rolled over onto his side and lay still. Alan was sure he was dead, but I wasn't; the shot must have been thrown off when the willow bowed under the weight of the rifle.

The *cheechako* was right—after slogging across the muskeg and up the knoll, we found that the bull had hobbled into the draw, where he now knelt on all fours, blood matting his fur from a wound behind his lungs. He was looking at me from thirty yards away, and I saw in those dark eyes glowing from under the antlers all that I had felt when I'd been shot—not pain, because I can attest that you don't feel a bullet wound's pain right away but a stunned bewilderment. I also saw that the rack was not as big as it had appeared from a distance, but there was no choice now. I sat down and made sure the rifle was as solid as if it were bench-rested. Watching the caribou's legs give a few final kicks from the shoulder-breaking shot, I told myself, "Remember this and how it make s you feel and maybe next time you won't come hunting until you've made *five hundred* bull's-eyes at the range." I'm not sentimental about the deaths of animals, and anti-hunting zealots who aren't strict vegetarians strike me as sanctimonious hypocrites. Our lives are sustained by the deaths of other creatures, whether they're steers or free-range chickens or wild caribou; but when you hunt for any reason other than to stave off starvation, you have a moral responsibility to kill as quickly and cleanly as possible.

"That wasn't shooting, that was butchery," I murmured as we began to skin and gut the carcass.

"Hey, we all like 'em to be pretty, one shot and down, but they can't all be pretty. You got the job done," Alan said, forgiving me.

I wanted to say that's what it had felt like—a job, and a messy one at that—but there is nothing more tiresome than the whine of self-recrimination.

Stripped of felt, bloodstained, the rack lay near the fire we'd managed to get started in the steady downpour, and chunks of caribou tenderloin were roasting on willow sticks when Frank and Dave tramped in, soaked with rain and sweat after a five-mile walk from their spike camp.

"You guys are just in time for dinner," I said.

"Yours?" asked Dave, gesturing at the rack.

I nodded.

"One shot, right?"

"Not quite."

Dave dropped his pack and squatted by the fire and sampled the meat.

"What the hell's going on here?" he said. "The Connecticut gentleman, the East Coast dude catches the biggest fish and shoots the only game?"

"Anytime I can provide for you sourdoughs, give me a call," I answered.

He and Frank reported that they had seen a number of ewes and lambs, but not a ram, a moose with a rack of fifty-five to sixty inches, and about ten caribou, filing along a far ridge and led by an enormous bull with antlers like a small tree.

"That's the kind you'll want next, you'll have to be selective," Dave said, commenting indirectly on the size of my caribou's.

Through the afternoon and into early evening, we boned the quarters and stuffed meat into game bags. I was hoping for a leisurely night, but Dave, who was more or less in charge, noted that the creek had risen several inches and that the clouds were racing overhead. We couldn't feel the wind, broken by a wall of mountains to the north, but we could be sure it was howling down the Kongakut. A blizzard was coming. We'd better hoof back to base camp and make sure all was secure—if the big river rose, our raft could be carried away and then we'd have to walk the fifty-odd remaining miles to the pickup point. That's a five-day march in the Brooks Range.

With the meat adding twenty pounds to Frank's, Alan's, and Dave's packs (as the resident East Coast dude, or perhaps in deference to my bum ankle, I was given the lightest load), the return to base camp took over three hours. Alan's bad knees grew wobbly under the sixty pounds on his back. I relieved him for an hour, and that was penance enough for shooting badly. And so was tramping through bear country stinking of caribou meat and blood.

It was snowing by the time we got back, a little after nightfall, our feet drenched and half frozen. The tent was still standing, but billowing and snapping like an unsheeted sail in the thirty-mile-an-hour wind. Too tired to build a fire, we stripped off our wet clothes and leapt shivering into our bags.

The gale blew all the following day, and more snow fell, and dense gray clouds shrouded the mountains. The water in our water bottles froze solid. We built a roaring fire behind a tall willow bush and rigged tarps over the bush to further break the wind and hung our wet socks and trousers over the branches on the lee side to dry them by the fire. Despite the weather—the Brooks Range was through showing us its smiling side—there was a kind of cozy domesticity about camp and an atmosphere of cheerful comradeship. We reorganized gear, trimmed and roasted caribou meat, dried our boots. One of the benefits of hunting the hard way is that it teaches you how most of humanity once lived—you hunted, you ate what you killed, you did your best to stay warm and dry.

By late afternoon, we were on the river again, and set up another camp some three or four miles downstream. Hunting long and hard the next day, each team of two covering at least fifteen miles, we saw the usual ewes and lambs, golden eagles, and plenty of moose, caribou, and grizzly sign, but never the animals that made them. The day wasn't without its rewards. Once, I found a perfectly preserved mayfly in a field of aufeis—overflow ice that remains frozen all year—and the ice itself was beautiful, seven or eight feet thick, with aquamarine chambers beneath it.

Later, far up a canyon as innocent of human footprints as Mars, I sat on a bed of glacial till and experienced the absolute "otherness" of the natural world, a world independent of human endeavor, careless about human fate, whether one person's or the entire race, a world complete unto itself. The silence was different than the silences of wild places in the Lower Forty-Eight; there, even when there isn't a man-made sound to be heard, the atmosphere seems to carry echoes of the logger's chain saw or of mine machinery or of tourists' laughter and shouts. The stillness in the Brooks Range was virgin, a quiet never broken by humanity's industrial and commercial clatter. Compared to it, the noise I'd left behind—campaign speeches, sound bites, talk-radio yelps—seemed as significant as the chirping of crickets. I listened for an hour, and once thought I heard voices, faint with distance. It must have been a trick of the wind, but I like to think the mountains were talking, though in a language I couldn't understand.

The next morning dawned foggy and cold, and there were fresh wolf tracks in the sand only yards from the tent. Half a mile away, three caribou appeared like apparitions out of the mists. Tossing willow leaves in the air to test the wind, Dave and I stalked to within 250 yards of the animals—a bull, a cow, and a calf. We crept a little closer. The bull raised his head majestically, and grew wary; the cow and calf paced nervously. We'd been quiet and were well downwind, so they could not have seen or scented us; then we realized that they'd cut the trail of the wolf. The bull had a fine cape that fell like a silver apron over its front and made a beautiful contrast with its chocolate-brown flanks and haunches; but its rack was no larger than the one I already had, so I didn't shoot, just watched the three animals walk off, and was happy to do so. What a sight that silver-chested bull made, prancing with his crown of antlers beneath the mountains.

At midday, it was downstream again to a new camp, a new drainage, the river falling now, its rapids becoming more frequent and more demanding. Beaching the raft near a summit called Mount Greenough, only twelve miles from the Canadian border, we caught several fat char in a half-mile stretch of smooth, swift water. The fish were seasoned with salt, pepper, and lemon-pepper, then wrapped in tinfoil with chunks of butter and baked in coals. Though it was sleeting and we ate hunched over the fire in foul-weather gear, picking the meat off the bones with our hands, that meal tasted better than anything I've had in those Manhattan restaurants where the waiters are called "servers" and the numbers on the menu look like the down payment for a used car.

The weather partly cleared later on. Alan, glassing a ridge some three miles off, announced, "I see my ram!"

I was again amazed by his ability to pick it out among the snow patches and rocks, but eventually found it with my binoculars; it was grazing on a ledge in the concave face of the ridge, two and a half thousand feet above.

Checking it out through the sixty-power spotting scope, Dave said that it had a full curl, and Alan declared that he was going after it. I couldn't see how he would manage the climb, but decided to go along to photograph the ram and to help pack out the meat if Alan bagged it.

Off we went, following a bluff alongside the Kongakut to mask our approach. Dalls, Alan said with only slight exaggeration, had eyesight equivalent to his spotting scope. The horizontal part of the stalk, the easy part, was hard enough—for almost two miles, we picked our way over and around boulders strewn above a roaring rapids. A cross-fox half arctic fox, half red fox scampered across our path.

Coming to the base of the ridge, Alan pointed toward two slabs of rock, rising from near the crest like the humps of a camel. If possible, he would make his shot from there.

The ridge was covered with immense rock slides too treacherous to climb on. Though many of the boulders were the size of small cars, they were precariously balanced and could give way under a man's weight, and then that man would be dead, if not immediately from the fall, then eventually from exposure as he lay with his legs or back or arms broken. We scaled the tundra fells and willow thickets between the rock slides, the slope far steeper than it had looked from below, so steep that we had to turn the bills of our caps up to keep them from bumping into the mountainside.

Sometimes the willow brakes were too dense to get through, forcing us onto the slides. Never in my life have I been so careful, watching and testing every step, feeling a pain in my chest like a heart attack when a boulder shifted or I heard scree sliding away from under me with a sound like breaking crystal.

The weather changed again without warning. The wind picked up—twenty miles an hour, thirty, forty. Great sheets of snow swooped down like curtains from the onrolling clouds to the north. It was 7:45 P.M. by the time we got above the willow line, roughly halfway to the top and a thousand feet above the Kongakut. As we sat with our fingers digging into the mountainside (because the wind threatened to blow us off), I remembered that my mother-in-law had warned me not to do anything stupid or take unnecessary chances. *This* was stupid. By the time we got to where we were going, it would be too dark for a shot with rifle or camera. I told Alan that we should pack it in. He said he was going on. I considered advising him not to, but there was a bright, wild, predatory determination in his eyes, and I knew he wouldn't listen.

Some three hours later, in pitch blackness, I stumbled back into camp, very happy not to have broken a leg or bumped into a bear. Dave and Frank were snug in their sleeping bags.

"Christ, we were wondering when you guys would give it up," Frank called out.

"Make that 'guy.' Alan's still up there. He wanted to go on," I said, now embarrassed that I hadn't insisted he return with me. "Maybe I ought to go back and find him. . . "

"The hell you will," said Dave. "Then we'll have two guys stranded up there in this weather. If he's not back by morning, we'll backtrack him and find him."

We lay awake for a long time, listening to the wind that blew so hard it made snowflakes crack like hail against the tent. We didn't say it, but each of us wondered how Alan could survive such a night up there. Then, around midnight, we saw the beam of a flashlight outside and heard him say:

"High adventure on the Kongakut!"

He'd made the climb, arriving at the two humped rocks at last light—just in time to see that the ram had moved to a pinnacle almost a mile away. He'd returned by the same route as I, navigating by starlight and moonlight. While working his way back along the river bluff, he heard something snarl in a willow thicket above him. Was it the fox we'd seen earlier? Bear? Wolf? He couldn't identify the sound, what with the wind and the noise of the rapids. When the creature snarled again he whirled around, leveling his rifle an turning his flashlight on. But he couldn't see a thing.

"So I started talking to it," he said. 'Now listen, whatever you are, I'm just trying to get back to camp and into my sleeping bag, all right? I've gotta three-hundred Weatherby here, but if you don't fuck with me, I won't fuck with you.'

Sometimes nature had a sense of black humor. When Alan and I woke, late the next morning, we spotted the same ram standing on the same ledge. Had we waited, we would have had a whole day to stalk him. Now, so worn out it tired us just to gather firewood, we couldn't muster the strength.

With only three hunting days left, Dave and Frank had left camp at first light. They made their most epic trek, walking out of the Romanzofs and into the British Mountains to within a long rifle shot of Canada. Somewhere up there, at a point Dave later described as "several miles east of Jesus," they saw ten sheep—all ewes and lambs, but with a beautiful ram nearby, his horns curling into near-perfect circles. The two men began their stalk, scaling scree meadows past waterfalls and glaciers. When they finally reached the top, some forty-five hundred feet up, they watched the ram amble over another ridge and out of sight.

They had to settle for the scenic rewards, which were not inconsiderable. Mountains climbed and fell and climbed again, tier upon tier, for a hundred miles in all directions, the ranges stitched by rivers and jeweled with glacial lakes—a world as pristine as when those crags and peaks were born in the thunder of the earth's colliding plates.

The two then climbed down into the drainage they had followed from camp. In midafternoon, rounding a bend in the creekbed, they spotted a fine grizzly of some seven feet and 450 pounds, with a honey-brown coat. Frank had never killed a bear. Taking the rifle off sling, he eased the safety, and they saw a cub come out of an aspen stand. You do not shoot a sow with young because you have then killed more than one bear. It was unusual to see a female with only one cub; possibly the brother or sister had been killed by a boar. Like lions, male grizzlies sometimes commit infanticide to induce females to go into heat.

If that's what had happened, this sow probably would be super defensive, so Dave and Frank looked for a way around her. But she scented them first, bolted up to a knoll above the aspen, and rose onto her hind legs to get a fix on them. (Grizzlies have acute senses of smell and hearing, but poor eyesight, and stand upright to see better.) For a few seconds, men and bear faced each other; then the sow tossed her wide head side to side and popped her jaws. Dave and Frank could hear her teeth clacking, even from over a hundred yards away. It's one of the most dreadful sounds in nature. It means you're going to be charged, an experience that can be approximated if you stand on a football field while two enraged NFL linebackers, each with a fistful of jackknives and roofing nails for eyeteeth, come at you at full speed.

Dave pointed to a spot some thirty or forty yards away and said: "She gets to there, I'm afraid that cub will have to fend for itself."

With a whoof, the sow dropped to all fours, bursting through the underbrush at racehorse speed, ears flattened, saliva flying from her jaws, her teeth still popping, her claws clattering on the rocks of the creekbed. The two men raised their rifles, but the sow suddenly turned, just short of Dave's imaginary line in the sand, and lunged off toward her cub. It was a false charge, a bluff. One could say that Frank and Dave sighed with relief, but it was more than a sigh. The bear's agility stunned them.

"She didn't slow down before she turned, like a man would," Frank said later. "I never saw anything reverse field like that."

Now only two full hunting days remained. My three companions were getting anxious; they'd been skunked so far. There was much strategizing around the fire that night, discussions about the dearth of sheep in the Brooks Range and how much blame to assign to bad winters, how much to wolves. Nothing could be done about the weather, but if a wolf pack appeared, my companions intended to do some serious culling. I said I wouldn't join in because, coming from the Lower Forty-Eight, where wolves have been trapped, poisoned, and shot to the edge of extinction, I viewed the wolf as an almost mythic animal. They had a more pragmatic outlook about that much-maligned creature. They weren't paranoid about wolves, like, say, farmers and ranchers, and they appreciated having them around; on the other hand, they didn't look at wolves or anything in the natural world through Disneyworld glasses. Living in a land where the wild dominates, they saw the wild for what it is—a place of astonishing beauty and freedom, but also of an indifference that amounts to an unbearable ruthlessness.

Some years ago, when he was a guide, Dave was glassing for sheep when he saw a pair of wolves attack a bull moose many times heavier than their combined weight. For almost an hour, they worked the moose like skilled *banderillos* preparing a Spanish bull for the matador's kill.

"The first wolf would charge the moose from the front, and the moose would go at him, hocking its antlers," Dave said, "but the wolf would dodge away in time. Meantime, the second one would back off, then charge the moose from behind. The moose would turn to face that one, but then the other would charge from the back, and it would have to spin around again. Finally, the moose was exhausted. His head was hanging down, his legs were spread wide. One of the wolves paced back and forth in front of the moose, made quick charges, and then ran away. The moose was distracted by him. The other one circled around behind and waited. Then something told that wolf it was time to go in for the kill. Don't know what, but something did, and it charged, so fast I almost couldn't see it, right between the moose's hind legs and bit into its belly and ripped it open."

The moose's guts spilled out like groceries out of a bag. Both wolves tore at the intestines, snapping them up in sections, while the moose stumbled and weaved.

"He was being eaten alive but he was still on his feet," Dave went on. "Then one of them jumped onto his hindquarters and tore out a big chunk of meat. The other one jumped on from the other side and ate some of that leg, and the damned moose was still on his feet, his insides trailing on the ground, two wolves hanging on and tearing at his hindquarters. . ."

At last, the huge beast fell, though Dave could see by the motions of its head that it was still alive as the wolves devoured it, sometimes from the inside out, sometimes from the outside in.

"There's nothing up here that dies easy," said Alan, supplying the moral to the story.

We paddled ten or twelve miles the next morning, after a frigid night. The sky was clear, the wind down, but the river got serious, falling more sharply toward the coastal plain, flinging itself around cliffs in frothing bends, tumbling down rocky staircases with a steady roar. There were Class Three rapids in places, with standing waves a yard high and enormous boulders with back eddies and whirlpools spinning behind them. Experienced white-water rafters would have found this four-mile stretch a piece of cake, but for us, it was exhilarating and occasionally a little scary. Complicated eddies combined with our let's say modest rafting skills to sling us into rocks or careen us against cliff sides; once, in a booming rapid, we wound up high-centered atop a boulder roughly the size of a pickup truck. We shifted our weight and rocked the raft, ever so careful not to capsize in that beautiful, clear, absolutely deadly water, and then piked with our paddles, and at last succeeded in refloating ourselves.

The Kongakut swept us around a conical mountain and into a wide, wooded valley below Whale Mountain, so- called, I assumed, because it was shaped like a whale or because its massive breadth made it a whale of a mountain. To the east, a broad side drainage split through the Romanzofs for miles, showing us the snow-crested, serrated wall that marked the Yukon border.

Dave and Frank hunted this drainage in the morning, while Alan and I worked the meadows on the west side of Whale Mountain. We came across fresh bear sign—tracks and holes dug by a grizzly hunting for ground squirrels. Sometimes called "parky squirrels" because Eskimos make parkas from their fur, they are a mainstay of the interior grizzly's diet (moose and caribou are rare treats, the ursine equivalent of a night out at a five-star restaurant). Otherwise they subsist on berries and the roots and leaves of boykinia, or bear flower, which is why their meat (unlike that of the fish-eating bears of coastal Alaska) is excellent, tasting a little like sweet pork.

We trailed the bear all morning without success. He must have doubled back on us because our partners, we found out later, spooked a grizzly only a fifteen-minute walk from camp. They didn't get a shot at it, but, three miles farther up the drainage, they encountered another bear, feeding on a caribou. Here was Frank's chance. He raised his .300, fired high on the first shot. A second dropped the bear; it leapt up and started running, and the third shot killed it. At almost the same moment, a wolf burst out of the trees and raced up a ridge, out of effective range. The wolf let out a howl, and another answered, and then a third. The caribou must have been killed by a wolf pack, which the bear had driven off. While the two men skinned and dressed out the grizzly (it taped at six feet, eight inches, and weighed about four hundred pounds), the wolves circled the ridges above, calling to one another. What were they saying?

Miles away, Alan and I were perched on a spur of Whale Mountain, looking for a sheep. I was a little woozy, from fatigue and a touch of vertigo, for we occupied a narrow shelf, above a long, almost vertical shale slide. After a couple of hours of glassing, we saw only a shaggy musk ox, climbed down, and hunted our way back to camp, arriving there about an hour before dusk. Having eaten nothing but a few granola bars and boxes of raisins all day (we'd run out of oatmeal the day before), our first act was to fire up the camp stove and boil water for a luscious meal of freeze-dried chicken gumbo. I hitched my belt another notch. I was shedding a pound a day by consuming twenty-five hundred calories while burning three times that much. It made for an efficient weight loss program, though I doubted I could market it to the general public.

After dinner, Alan went toward the river to draw more water for coffee. He was back fifteen seconds later, with that focused, predatory brightness in his eye.

"I see him!" he said in a tense undertone, jacking a round into his Weatherby. "See my bear and he's coming this way."

I pulled my binoculars from my jacket pocket. The bear was a little more than a quarter of a mile downstream, ambling along the side of the mountain on the opposite side of the river—a big, classic grizzly with dark brown fur silvered at his hump, a long nose, and short, powerful legs. Each bristling hair seemed alive as he walked, his nose down a little, his small black eyes in a head as wide as an average man's chest looking straight ahead, his gait exuding sovereignty.

Between us and the river was a broad gravel bar with no cover except one big boulder the color of weathered copper. We low-crawled to it, Alan resting his rifle on a clump of brush alongside. The bear was downwind of the caribou meat we'd cached well away from camp, on the near side of the river. We figured he would be drawn to the scent and come down to the bank on his side, giving Alan an easy shot of less than a hundred yards. Instead, he climbed up to some scree, as easily as I might climb a short flight of stairs. The light was fading and the bear did not make a distinct target against the black shale. He was almost directly across from us now, about 225 yards away and a hundred feet above the river. He hadn't scented us any more than he had the cache; he possessed that total absence of wariness that marks the predator at the top of the food chain.

Alan didn't want to risk a long shot in the dim light. In a crouch, he stalked quickly to where the raft was moored and used the raft for a bench rest. I followed him with my camera and the binoculars.

My light meter told me I would need a flash, but I didn't dare use one before Alan fired.

"Put the glasses on him and mark my shot," he whispered, tracking the bear as it sidled down onto the tundra just below the shale.

Lying flat, I felt my heart thumping against the gravel. The bear was just a little to our upstream side by this time, his whole broad, brown side facing us, and his pace quickening a little. In a couple of seconds, he would be in a willow thicket and out of sight, and in my mind I was shouting, "Shoot! For Christ's sake shoot!" when the .300 cracked. All four of the grizzly's legs left the ground and it cartwheeled in midair and the next thing I saw were its haunches as it ran into the willows. Alan looked at me.

"You hit him solid, but he took off. He's in the brush," I said.

If going in there after a wounded bear with night coming on quickly was unthinkable, not going was unconscionable. We walked upstream, glassing the mountainside, and saw his head showing from behind a rock. Just then a big gray wolf, seeming to materialize out of nowhere, came loping down the mountain. It seemed to be making a beeline for the bear, then squatted to pee. Alan's snap shot hit close enough to convince the she-wolf to leave. She ran back up and vanished.

We then launched the raft, paddled across the river, tied up, and climbed well above where the grizzly had fallen. If he was still alive, he would either flee or charge. If he fled, it would be downhill; if he charged, the steep slope would slow him enough to give us time for a killing shot.

Rifles in our shoulders, safeties off, we crept toward the willows, thick and shadowy. In another five or ten minutes, we would need flashlights. Well, I thought, with some resignation, if the son-of-a-bitch comes and kills us, I sure wouldn't blame him.

"There he is!" Alan said, pointing downhill.

The grizzly lay on his side, his back toward us, and though he was motionless, those rippling hairs suggested life. We went down cautiously, stopped, went down a little farther, stopped again. When we were perhaps ten yards away, I centered the crosshairs of my scope on the grizzly's upper back while Alan circled around behind it and poked it with the muzzle of his rifle, once. twice, a third time. The bear never moved.

The bullet—a 180-grain Federal with the appropriate brand name of "bear-claw"—had gone through his lungs and out the other side; the short run he'd made had been more reflex than anything else.

We dragged him from behind the rock and onto a flat spot to begin skinning, and I was awed by how heavy he was and by the black claws as long as my fingers and by the fangs and jaws that could have broken my neck as easily as I could crush a bug. The emotions I'd felt up until then, a fusion of exhilaration and fear, swiftly changed to relief and . . . well, I don't know what to call it. Pity seems too cheap, and so does guilt. A kind of reverence, I guess, an awareness that the death of that great animal had been no small event. At such moments, the hunter understands in his bones and guts why Native Americans apologized to the spirit of an animal they'd killed.

Night fell before we could start skinning. That would have to wait until morning. We laid our packs and stinking undershirts on the carcass, figuring our stench would keep scavengers away. It would have kept almost anything with a nose away, except a skunk.

That night, we built a big fire against the cold and roasted caribou and pieces of succulent bear tenderloin from Frank's kill. That seemed fitting: after they have killed a grizzly, Koyukon hunters eat the bear's best parts to placate its spirit. Later on, we each poured our customary nightcaps. As we drank, a partial moon rose, and the snowy mountains stood out in stark relief in its light; they looked in fact as pale and unearthly as the lunar mountains themselves. Dave pricked his ears for a moment and gestured for us to be quiet. Far off a wolf was howling, possibly the female Alan and I had seen. The northern lights came out. We'd seen them almost every night, but they put on their most dazzling display that night, appearing first as ever-shifting, pale green curtains, then as rising columns that whirled singly, like ghostly tornadoes, or twined around each other, forming gigantic double helixes. A moment later, in silent explosions of pink and rose, the lights shot horizontally across the skies, dancing rings over the rims of the mountains with movements so vigorous and rhythmic I swore they would make music next. Two bears killed on the same day, game meat roasting on a campfire, whiskey drunk from a tin cup with good friends, wolves and the moon on wild mountains and the aurora going crazy overhead—oh, that was one night for the record books.

Alan's bear taped out at six feet ten. It probably had weighed 425 pounds. While skinning it the next morning, the biggest bull moose either of us ever had seen lumbered to within a long stone's throw before he whiffed the stench of bear and man and trotted off. His rack would have gone over five feet.

The wind turned north in the early afternoon. Ahead of us lay a twenty-mile float to the pickup point at Caribou Pass. The bush plane was coming for us the next day, weather permitting. For the moment, it looked to be in as permissive a mood as an Iranian ayatollah. Snow-laden clouds tumbled in, fog lay in the valleys. I was sure we'd be weathered in for at least two days. We were nearly out of freeze-dried rations, and I was glad for the game bags of bear and caribou stowed in the bow of the raft.

We paddled with the wind in our faces. Some gusts were strong enough to almost stall the raft despite our efforts and the four-knot current. It got colder and colder. Wearing wool long underwear and lined fleece trousers, a thick wool shirt, lined wool sweater, and a pile jacket, I shivered nonetheless. And so did the others. "I have envied the early explorers not for their discoveries but for their sufferings," says a character in André Malraux's *Man's Fate*. Not me; no more penances.

After covering some six miles, we had to beach the raft and build a fire behind a clump of alders. Those flimsy bushes made an enormous difference, cutting wind and windchill in half. But the vegetation downriver began to grow sparser, the mountains lower and more rounded; we were getting closer to the coastal plain. The barren land-scape took on an alien, menacing quality. It looked Paleolithic.

Twelve miles. Another stop. Another fire.

"Only eight to go," said Dave cheerfully. "Maybe this will let up soon."

Back on the river, with no feeling in our fingertips and little in our feet, the snow started to fall harder. Actually, it wasn't falling—it was whipping along almost parallel to the water.

"Yes, this *is* better," said Frank dryly. "Really splendid conditions."

More than cold troubled us.

"Man, we don't find that thing, we're screwed," said Alan, voicing our concern. He meant the landing strip at the pass. Ballard, our pilot, had told us we couldn't miss it, and I don't suppose we could have on a clear day. But in the blizzard, with clouds and fog obscuring landmarks and darkness only a few hours away, all we would have to do was take the wrong braid in the river and we'd shoot right past the strip.

Considering that possibility, what happened next was just this side of totally insane. Hawk-eyed Alan spotted a grizzly, trotting down to the river. Dave, the only one not to have shot anything, went after it, with Frank backing him up. From the riverbank, Alan and I watched the whole show. We saw the two men skirting an alder-choked ravine, and we saw the bear (which Dave and Frank could not see), about two hundred yards away on the other side. The hunters thrashed through the underbrush, but the bear heard them. It reared on its high legs, then dropped and bolted off, making for the hills at top speed. We watched Dave raise his rifle, heard the shot. Considering the range, the weather, and a fast-moving target, the miss wasn't surprising. The bear ran on, vanished for a moment in a gully, then reappeared, lunging up a hill in the snow, dark brown against white.

"You know, I'm glad I missed. If I'd killed him, we'd be here all night dressing him out," Dave said when he got back with Frank.

Maybe there was another reason to be glad. The great bear, gal-loping across the snow-covered tundra, made a sight that might have been seen by the first nomad hunters who crossed the Bering Straits into North America thousands of years ago.

At twilight, we caught the briefest glimpse of a blue fuel barrel peeking through some underbrush. Above it, a shred of pink surveyor's tape fluttered from a tall willow branch—the bush pilot's wind sock. That tattered little ribbon was what we weren't supposed to miss. It was miraculous we hadn't.

It was midnight by the time we had the tent pitched, the raft deflated, and our gear ready for loading. Our (possibly) last campfire, more caribou and bear meat for dinner, and then the last of our whiskey. Never had a warm sleeping bag felt so good.

The storm began to break up the next morning. September 8, and the clearing weather brought one of the most memorable events I think I'll ever see. The cold winds had convinced the snow geese and specklebelly geese, fattened on the cotton grass of the coastal plain, that it was time to leave the Arctic. All morning and into the afternoon, the birds staged for their three-thousand-mile journey to California's San Joaquin valley and the bosques of New Mexico. On the ground, the snow geese were grouped so thickly they resembled drifts. In the sky, with high, shrill cries, skein after skein after skein flew by, hour after hour without end. I learned later that many of the refuge's game biologists have never seen the migration at its beginning; we four felt graced and privileged to witness it.

In a chapter in his book on the wars in North America, military historian John Keegan mentions that some anthropologists have noted that the life of the nomadic hunter, for all its privations and hardships, is the happiest. Watching the geese, I fully understood what the anthropologists meant, not with my mind but with my heart and in my belly, which may be the premier seat of understanding. The night before, I was ready for a warm bed and the pleasures of the hearth, so it now surprised me to feel a hope that we would get weathered in for a few days. The far-off buzz of the approaching bush plane, which we heard around midafternoon, was a not entirely welcome sound.

We were going to be shuttled out again, and in my enthusiasm, I volunteered to be the last one to leave.

Dave said:

"You've seen how fast the weather changes up here. He could bring us back and then get socked in before he can pick you up. You could be out here for days, on your own. It's your call, Phil."

I pondered for a few seconds and answered:

"Nope. This is no place for an amateur."

From Ballard's plane, I looked down five thousand feet to the

Farthest Away River, twisting out of the Brooks Range and onto the coastal plain that reached to the Arctic Ocean, where ice floes sailed on the currents. Out of the corner of my eye, I saw what looked to be a bright, low-flying cloud; turning, I saw that it was a wedge of snow geese, necks like white arrows, pointing southward.

up in michigan

1 9 9 7

I t is 1,067 miles from my door in Norwalk, Connecticut, to Mike Ballard's in Grand Marais, Michigan—a ridiculously long way to go to shoot ruffed grouse and woodcock when I could hunt them next door in Massachusetts or Vermont. But it's not the shooting that lures me to Michigan's Upper Peninsula every fall; it's a lot of other things, like having room to roam in wild country. The New England states are small and crowded; the U.P., slashing east to west for 325 miles between Lakes Superior and Michigan, is a fair-size state unto itself, with millions of acres in national and state forest, and millions more owned by pulp and paper companies that allow public access to their land.

There aren't a lot of people (locals call themselves Yewpers) in all that territory. That makes it congenial for wildlife. Robert Voelker, author of *Anatomy of a Murder* and a U.P. native, described it as home to three of the noblest creatures on earth: the white-tailed deer, the eastern brook trout, and the ruffed grouse. He could have added brown and rainbow trout, steelhead, black bear, coyote, bobcat, moose, beaver, otter, bald eagle, several species of hawk, several of duck, Canada geese, woodcock, and sandhill crane. A few wolf packs have established themselves on the Peninsula and on Isle Royal, way out in Lake Superior. If you're very lucky, you'll hear them some night. You'll know they're wolves because their howl will sound deeper and some-how wilder than the warbling yap of coyotes, will in fact pierce your upper brain, wherein you have stored lots of comforting information that wolves are not dangerous to human beings, and enter your lower brain, wherein you retain primeval memories of a time when wolves *were* dangerous to human beings.

Still, it requires an elastic notion of truth to call the Upper Peninsula a real wilderness. It was before the lumbering boom at the end of the last century and the beginning of this one annihilated its virgin white pine forests. Today, with logging roads, jeep trails, and paved highways crisscrossing the bush like the mazed creases in an animal hide, you could describe it as a used wilderness with lots of miles on it.

Its landscapes do not stun or mesmerize, like the Rockies, ruling it out as a second-home destination for the sort of media moguls and software kings who are transforming parts of Montana into a high-end exurbia. The Lake Superior shore is largely unspoiled and not without its cold grandeur; the Huron Mountains in the north and the Porcupines in the west provide attractive vistas, but most of the land is a rather level, unstylish expanse of hardwoods, birch and aspen, with hummocks of spruce and hemlock that make green islands in autumn's seas of gold and fire. Tamarack bogs lie here and there in quiet indolence. There are countless lakes created by the recession of the Wisconsin glacier thousands of years ago, but they're puny compared to western lakes. The Snake and the Colorado would chuckle at the U.P.'s narrow streams and rivers, browned by the tannin of cedar swamps. Yet there is a beauty, of a haunted, melancholy kind. The hush of north woods sunset, spired pines against a primrose sky, a young owl glides on silent wings from across a river. Scenes like that seep into you and make you feel at peace, and that's another reason for my going.

And this too: a chance to shake hands with the part of me that's still a boy. I shot my first grouse on the Upper Peninsula in 1961, caught my first trout there, got my first deer—all passages of one sort or another. When I came home from another kind of passage in Vietnam in 1967, the first thing I did was to call my old hunting and fishing buddy, Bill Remacks, and take to the big north woods to start the long process of spiritual restoration. Sure, I was borrowing a page from Hemingway's *The Big Two-Hearted River,* but one of the functions of literature, whether you're talking Hemingway or the Book of Isaiah, is to show us how to get through life without going crazy.

I have stayed long periods on the Upper Peninsula, up to six weeks, but I've never lived there, full or part time. I spent my boyhood summers in Wisconsin, but I grew up mostly on the outskirts of Chicago, in western Cook County. As a teenager in the mid- to late 1950s, I could hunt pheasant and rabbit with bow and arrow inside the city limits of my hometown, Westchester, Illinois. If I wished to use a gun, I only had to drive twenty or thirty minutes into rural areas of neighboring DuPage County. I shot my first pheasant in a cornfield out there when I was sixteen.

I went back recently to find that field, and of course it was gone, interred beneath a mega mall surrounded by corporate parks where glass towers rise above artificial ponds and the preternatural green of chemically nourished lawns. I watched today's sixteen- year- old boys, wearing baggy pants and baseball caps turned backward or sideways, wait in line for the multiplex matinee to start, or idle around in sunless corridors, ogling the made-in-Taiwan (China, Indonesia, Honduras) sweatshop offerings of Benetton, The Gap, Nike. I wanted to tell them, "I shot a pheasant here almost forty years ago, right here, and I wish you could shoot one now, and know the hunter's joys of walking in pure air and making a good wing shot, and of eating what you've shot instead of Big Macs, imitation tacos, chickens chopped into nuggets unrecognizable as anything once living." But they would not have known what I was talking about, would have seen me as a comical emissary from another time, a goofy old windbreaker as unhip and alien to their world as *Reader's Digest*.

Anyhow, I'm grateful that there aren't any malls in the U.P., except in the larger towns like Escanaba, Marquette, and Sault Ste. Marie. Otherwise, bruised and battered though it's been by the logger's ax and chain saw, it's been spared our national love of asphalt. I can go to places I fished or hunted thirty years ago and still find my way around. The compact with the land and the past has not been broken, the landmarks of my youth are still there, and they connect me to who I was then. Those river bends and trail crossings, those woodcock marshes, grouse coverts and fishing holes help me make a more or less coherent narrative of my life. And that's another reason for my going.

And finally there are people I hunt with. Maybe the people are the main reason. Of them all, Mike Ballard most clearly fits the image, and lives the life, of the U.P. backwoodsman. The only time I've seen him in a suit was in his wedding picture with his second wife, Kathy; he doesn't look comfortable, as though the jacket's lined with steel wool. I have known him for fifteen years, hunted with him for ten, and can report that in a culture that worships celebrity, which is to say a culture that worships people who earn their bread making images and playing make-believe, he is that rare and refreshing phenomenon: the real thing. I guess it would be interesting to have a drink with Tom Cruise, but if I were in a tight spot, I'd rather have Ballard at my side. Especially if that tight spot is out somewhere where you can't call 911 or search and rescue. He's as good in the woods or on a stream as anybody I know. As if he had been born to it, though he wasn't. He was raised in Detroit, the capital of Rustbelt industrialism, in a tough neighborhood where he had to learn a different set of survival skills. Some were taught by his father, a former prizefighter, and Mike later did a little sparring in Kronk's gym, famed for its gym wars and for producing ex–welterweight champ Thomas "Hit Man" Hearns.

Ballard's in his midforties now, his ginger red hair is receding, and though he would be considered only average size in today's NFL, his six-foot-two-inch, 230-pound frame projects an impression of bearlike leverage. Like a lot of Yewpers, he's had to do whatever he could to bring in a dollar or a dime: gypsy logger, surveyor, saloon keeper, construction worker. Today, he has his own contracting firm, building and renovating houses, while Kathy works part time as a counselor in an alcohol rehabilitation clinic (the dark side of life in the U.P. is that its isolation and interminable winters breed alcohol abuse, which leads to other forms of abuse). Together, the couple own and operate a small resort, the Hilltop Motel and Cabins in Grand Marais.

Once a lumberjack's boomtown, Grand Marais is now a charmingly dilapidated little community of some four hundred people, situated on a bay of Lake Superior. An IGA, a general store, a couple of bars and restaurants, not the sort of place rushing into the twenty-first century. Owing to the town's small size and remoteness, Mike and Kathy and his two children from his first marriage have to rely on their own resources. The nearest medical care is in Marquette, ninety miles away by two-lane blacktop; once a month the couple stock up on staples at Marquette food cooperative. Their lives are not without touches of modernity—they listen to NPR on their boombox, watch cable TV, and are on the net; otherwise, they live pretty much the way Americans did a century ago, the way a lot of Americans today think they would like to live (but probably wouldn't know how). They cut their own firewood, because fireplaces and wood-burning stoves are not used for their aesthetic effect in a climate where the winters are almost Alaskan in length and severity. Kathy cans and puts up preserves, makes jam from blueberries picked with other women in town, some of whom carry .357 revolvers in case they encounter bears in the berry patches. Mike does his own carpentry as well as electrical and plumbing repairs, and his skills with a rod, gun, and bow ensure that there's always fish and game in the freezer. Once, I kidded him that his lifestyle might cause people to wonder if he was a Michigan militiaman, a right-wing survivalist. A lifelong liberal on most issues, Ballard chewed on that one for a moment, then said, "Hell, no. I'm a *left-wing* survivalist."

But how did a Motor City boy wind up in the north woods? He went to Northern Michigan University in Marquette, got a degree in botany, and then, in his words, "found out there were three botanists in the world and two were unemployed." He worked on construction crews in Oklahoma and Florida, but found that he missed the land where the cold rivers ran and the grouse drummed in the springtime. Back in Michigan, he picked up a chain saw and became a pulp cutter, then a forester surveying timber, and then, in the early 1980s, went into the saloon business, buying one of Grand Marais's two bars, the Dunes Saloon. A shot-and-a-beer joint patronized by downstate hunters, Finnish loggers, and Canuck commercial fishermen, with the occasional Chippewa thrown in—a mix not conducive to always cordial social relations—Mike's tutorials at Kronk's often came in handy. In his spare time, he guided bear hunters, more to get out from behind the bar than to earn extra money, and today his thick neck is adorned by a rawhide thong from which a bear tooth hangs, an ornament of wonderful political incorrectness.

I carry around in my head snapshots of days we've hunted together. On an October afternoon so splendid I hope it will never end, the birches and maples glowing like neon in the sunlight, we are tramping across a moorlike expanse that was once the floor of a white pine climax forest. The great trees, tall as radio towers, were slaughtered in the boom years, and their stumps rise out of browned bracken fern like the tombstones they are. Stands of popple and balsam fir, ideal grouse cover, have grown in their place, and there are vast swales of thorn apples where woodcock hide from terrestrial and airborne predators, like the red-tailed hawk we watch circling far overhead. Far off, sandhill cranes let out their Jurassic squawks, while out in front of us, Mike's springers enter a thorn apple thicket. One is a black-and-white named Charley, a calm, methodical dog; the other is the liver-and-white Buster, young, inexperienced, a bit rangy for a flusher, but so enthusiastic you forgive him for putting up birds you couldn't reach with a missile. We hear Charley snuffling like a rooting hog inside the bristling thicket—a sign that he's making game. We get set. A woodcock, a fat flight bird, explodes from out of the thorns with a piping whistle and its rufous wings spread wide. I shoot and miss. Mike drops it. A few minutes later, the roles are reversed when Mike misses another bird as it flies straight away. It's thirty-odd yards out, too far, I think, for my 28-gauge Beretta, and I'm surprised by the puff of feathers in midair, the falling bird. We move on, put up more birds, hit some, miss at least as many as we hit—the essence of woodcock shooting is humiliation—and then Mike reminds me of the day, several seasons ago, when an inch-long thorn buried itself in the back of his calf. He couldn't reach it, so he asked me to pull it out; but it was in so deep, I couldn't get a grip on it with my fingers. To relieve the pressure on his leg muscle, Mike got onto his hands and knees while I knelt behind him and tried to extract the thorn with my teeth.

"Jesus Christ, I hope nobody sees us," he said. "I'll never be able to show my face in town again."

Another day, as gloomy and wet as the one above was bright and cheerful. With three woodcock apiece in our game bags, we hoof toward the truck, and come upon a lone white pine, an old giant that escaped the timberman's greed. Beneath it is a bluish gray stone with the name "Oscar" chiseled into it. Oscar was Mike's old springer, and Charley's father—very possibly one of the best and most delightful flushing dogs ever to fly a bird. He died before his time of cancer, a death that struck Mike almost as hard as the death of a child. Any pet owner knows the feeling, but it's several times as intense with a hunting dog because they aren't pets; they're comrades with whom you've shared joys and disappointments, miles of rough walking, all kinds of weather. On a sodden day like this one, Mike buried Oscar in this spot, near the thorn apple meadows where they had hunted so often. He looks at the grave and reminisces about a day when his friend ran off on him.

"It was just before opening day. Now Oscar wandered a lot around town, chasing girls mostly. Something we've all done. He'd be gone overnight usually, but this time he was gone two days, three, four, and I was sure he'd been hit by a car or maybe kidnapped or got himself lost in the woods and killed by coyotes. I'm not religious, but I had a talk with God, made a bargain. Told him that if he gave Oscar back to me, I wouldn't drink or lose by temper ever again, that I would do all in my power to be a better person. Well, that afternoon, I'm not kidding, that *very* afternoon, the phone rings. It's this guy I know in town. Said Oscar was in his garage. The guy had been out of town for a few days, and he had a bitch in heat, and Oscar must've got her scent and followed his nose and tried to get into the house through a grate in the garage. He got trapped there, until the guy found him. I was so happy! Oscar, you're back! Fed him, watered him, and we hunted and got some birds. So I had my dog again, but now I had a real problem. Went to the Methodist minister in town and told him the whole story, about the deal I'd made with the Big Guy, and then asked him, 'Is there any way I can get out of it?' He didn't cut me any slack, told me that God doesn't like people who break contracts."

Mike has never said what happened next, but no one has observed any radical changes in his habits or personality.

Another afternoon, another season—I've had a perfect morning, one of those mornings with which wingshooters are occasionally blessed. I couldn't miss. Two grouse, five woodcock. All I need now to limit out on grouse is one more. With Mike and a Lansing financial planner named Gary Slaughter, I have had a birdless afternoon, however. Not because I've begun to miss, but because I haven't seen a grouse to shoot at; it's as if some giant vacuum cleaner has sucked them all up.

As we sit, debating about where to go next, the conversation turns to experiences we've had getting lost in the woods. Gary mentions that he is going to buy a GPS. Mike is a man after my own heart, something of a Luddite when it comes to outdoor equipment. He believes that technology puts a barrier between man and nature, that it makes you lazy and stupid if you rely on it too much. A standard compass is as sophisticated an instrument as he uses, and he tells Gary, "If you show up here with one of those goddamned things, I'll never hunt with you again!"

Later on, some seven or eight miles from town, we are pushing through a patch of woods as thick as mangrove swamp. I hear Mike making strange vocalizations—it sounds as if he's reciting a poem. I cannot now recall the words, but it might have gone something like this: Come to the black stump/Bend of the trail/Look to the forked birch for the rest of the tale.

I asked what he was doing.

"That's my song line," he said. "I've got a deer stand out here and the way I find it at night is with a song line."

He explained hat he'd decided that even compasses were too high tech for him. Reading that the Australian aborigines find their way across the featureless Outback with songs describing their routes, he thought he'd try creating a directional composition of his own. Sure enough, he sings us right to the deer stand. There are no whitetail, but a grouse is in a tangle of popple at the edge of a meadow. Buster puts it up, and though we don't see it, we hear the always startling whir of grouse wings. Going for the reflush, Mike circles around the popple thicket, while I push into it. In a few minutes, I hear that whir again and Mike hollers, "Bird!" It appears like an apparition, all browns and whites and blacks, weaving in and out of the trees. In a nanosecond, he's winging straight past me, a right-to-left crossing shot about fifteen yards out. I swing, shoot, and he's down as if he's hit an invisible wall.

That night, in front of Mike's house, with a moon plating Lake Superior, woodcock are on the grill. Mike bastes them in butter. I am leaving for home the next morning. The grouse are wrapped in newspaper and freezer bags and stowed in my cooler. Beside it is a box containing two jugs of maple syrup Mike has tapped from his own trees, jars of pickles Kathy has put up, jam made from blueberries picked that August. Mike, his face half lit by the grill's coals, spears a woodcock, and with a nod, pronounces it done. I take a bird, bite into its meaty little breast, wash it down with cabernet. "Hey," Mike says. "Hey." And I know what he means—hey, this is wonderful, not just the rich, wild taste of the bird, but all of it, the woods and the shooting and the moon on the lake.

I would be too easy to romanticize the rustic simplicity of his and Kathy's life. I couldn't say that they are happier than the people I see, rushing to catch Metro-North's 7:42 to Grand Central Station every morning. I do know Mike and Kathy are a lot happier than they would be if *they* were running to meet the 7:42.

alone

1 9 9 8

F inding connections between apparently disconnected facts or events can be a sign of genius or madness. Isaac Newton linked the rise and fall of tides to the differences between the gravitational attractions of the earth and the moon. At the loony end of the scale is the right-wing militiaman who weaves the federal government, the United Nations, and the helicopter he heard fly over his house the night before into a conspiracy to land saboteurs in preparation for a U.N. takeover of the country.

I'm no Isaac Newton; therefore, I wonder, as I sip whiskey beside a campfire deep within New Mexico's Aldo Leopold Wilderness, if I'm a little nutty. For the past several days, something has been causing my brain to find conjunctions between and among things that any normal person would say have nothing to do with one another. Maybe it's too much solitude: for nearly three weeks prior to starting this solo backpacking trip I was living alone on a remote Arizona ranch, which is where the symptoms first showed up.

One night when a violent storm knocked out the power, I was crumpling newspapers to get a fire going in my adobe cabin. Two horrific crime stories on the front page of an *Arizona Republic* got my attention, and I found myself reading them by candlelight and then clipping them instead of consigning them to the fireplace. As I continued to pull papers from the pile beside the canvas firewood carrier, a few other stories about subjects seemingly unrelated to the homicides also caught my eye. I read them and cut them out too, and then, without quite knowing why, joined them to the crime stories with a paper clip.

Now, leaning against a log close to the campfire, I'm pondering what relationship the stories could possibly bear to each other. Whatever it is, I sense that it also has something to do with why I am here, a man in his midfifties, walking about alone in what is one of the vastest, and possibly one of the last, authentic wildernesses left in the contiguous United States.

The region is called "the Gila," a term of convenience that applies to the fifty-two-hundred-square-mile Gila National Forest in southwestern New Mexico, as well to the three wildernesses that form its primitive core: the Gila, the Aldo Leopold, and the Blue Range. Logging, mining, livestock grazing, roads, and motor vehicles are prohibited in the wilderness areas. Within them are mountain ranges nearly two miles high—the Mogollon and the Diablo, the Mimbres and the Black. Ancient forests of ponderosa pine, Douglas fir, and Engelmann spruce bristle up the mountain slopes, while agave and prickly pear cling to the canyon bottoms. Rare Gila trout hold in the pools of the perennial streams and rivers, waiting for what food the swift currents bring them; elk graze on high alpine meadows, desert bighorn sheep stand poised on vertiginous ledges, black bear prowl remote gorges. All in all, it's territory that at least resembles the America that stretched from sea to sea before the "stern impassioned stress" of Pilgrim feet began to beat the path that appears to have led our civilization to the shopping mall.

Human feet left their marks on the trail I followed this afternoon; so have the hooves of shod horses, but the prints were old and outnumbered by those of wild game—the heart-shaped tracks of mule deer, the pads of coyotes. It is early spring and, because of the freakish weather stirred up by El Niño, still-cold nighttime temperatures of ten degrees at the higher elevations. The Gila region is most heavily visited in summer and early fall, though it draws only a small fraction of the mobs that descend on Yellowstone and Yosemite. Now, with the weather nippy and unpredictable, it is virtually unpopulated, solitude all but guaranteed.

Before I hiked in, I told John Kramer, the chief wilderness ranger (I'd love to have a title like that), that I wanted to minimize or, if possible, eliminate, any chance of running into my fellow bipeds for the next five days. He suggested a route in the Aldo Leopold, which is named for the great conservationist who wrote *Sand County Almanac*.

The Gila Wilderness, twice the size of the Aldo Leopold and bordering it on the west, draws more people because it contains prehistoric Indian cliff dwellings, and its gateway is reachable by a paved road. The Aldo Leopold has no tourist attraction, and New Mexico State Highway 61, a narrow, rutted, washboarded dirt track, is the only way to get to it by car.

Shortly before noon, I started up Route 61. It was posted with a sign almost designed to daunt interstate namby-pambies: CAUTION. ROAD AHEAD RESTRICTED TO 4-WHEEL-DRIVE, HIGH-AXLE VEHICLES. NO FOOD LODGING OR GASOLINE NEXT 120 MILES. The road turned out to be less formidable than advertised, but the side track to the trailhead for the Continental Divide Trail was a real axle breaker if taken at speeds faster than five miles an hour. I tucked my dust-cloaked, mud-splashed Pathfinder behind the ruins of a corral, shouldered my pack, and hiked off. In the distance, scraping a heaven scrubbed clean of clouds, was my destination: the 10,100-foot crest of the Black Range, mantled in snow and covered with the dark spruce and firs that, I surmised, give the range its name.

On this, my first night in the boondocks, I am somewhat pleased with myself. With only six years to go before I am officially considered a "senior citizen" (loathsome label that; when coupled with "citizen," the word "senior" doesn't connote a veteran worthy of respect but a doddering geezer who gets discounts at movie theaters), I have hauled a sixty-pound backpack through some five miles of wilderness, all of it uphill: a gradual ascent for the most part, but in a few spots fairly steep and with the trail a treachery of shale and rock rubble. I have pitched my tent, gathered firewood, strung my food bag high up in trees to avoid presenting bears with an occasion to sin, cooked my dinner of freeze-dried beef stew, and managed to get a good fire going in a woods still wet from the storm that passed through here a couple of days ago. I feel fit, vigorous, competent, even—dare I say it?—virile.

But I haven't come all this way to prove what a manly fellow I am. Been there, done that, bought that T-shirt ten times over as a marine platoon commander in Vietnam, a war correspondent in the Ethiopian desert and in the Hindu Kush in Afghanistan. I don't regard the great outdoors as a fitness center or an arena for athletic contests, as seems to be the case with some yuppie enthusiasts I have met in my travels. You know—the extreme sports studs with sweaty nylon shirts plastered to their Michelangelo pecs as they race three-thousand-dollar mountain bikes straight up the north face of Denali. Having hunted, fished, backpacked, and run rivers everywhere from Alaska's Brooks Range to the Florida Everglades, I've learned that merely getting from Point A to Point B in wild country provides sufficient challenge and exercise for anyone.

I have come all this way to take a kind of American walkabout. My reasons are contained in a remark Theodore Roosevelt Jr. made to one of his brothers. T. R. Jr. was expressing his loathing for the sort of holiday we would call a "family vacation" today. "When I go," he said, "I go hard and I go alone." Marvelous. That should be every backpacker's motto.

I am going hard because I think it's important to challenge yourself; the older you get, the more important it is, lest thou find thyself one day, gray-haired and fat, driving a Winnebago with a bumper sticker that says, WE'RE SPENDING OUR GRANDCHILDREN'S INHERITANCE! I am going alone because I wish to follow my own agenda, not a guide's; and because I don't want to deal with the needs, wishes, and complaints of a companion or companions. I am seeking more than escape from the toe jam of contemporary American civilization. I seek to touch the mystery, and it's hard to touch the mystery when there are other people around. The mystery of the wild, which is the mystery of creation. Wilderness somehow engenders in me the feeling and state of mind that I am supposed to have in church but seldom, if ever, do. Joy. Fulfillment. Happiness. Ah, what is happiness? you ask. I can't top the definition I recently came across from Willa Cather: "to be dissolved into something complete and great." The natural world is whole and sufficient unto itself; it doesn't need us or want us. Doesn't care about us or know about us. It is stunningly indifferent, and yet, to immerse yourself in its completeness, if you can manage that surrender, is to grasp happiness. And the Constitution says I have a right to that, or, rather, to its pursuit.

Unfortunately, those ugly stories keep intruding. They hobble my pursuit, reminding me that if I am in a vast and beautiful cathedral, it is one surrounded by a much larger aesthetic and moral slum.

On February 24, 1998, in Phoenix, a thirty-one-year-old unemployed laborer, John Sansing, high on crack with his wife, Kara, telephoned the Living Springs Assembly of God Church, asking for help in feeding his family. The church sent Elizabeth Calabrese, a fourty-one -

year-old mother of two, to deliver a box of groceries. This is what the police report said happened next: when the Good Samaritan appeared at Sansing's door, he pulled her into the living room, threw her to the floor, beat her over the head with a club, and then, with his wife's help, tied her to a chair. The couple did this in full view of their children, ages nine through twelve, who couldn't understand why their parents were hurting the lady who'd brought them food. Their father explained it was for the money and showed then the cash he'd netted from Mrs. Calabrese's purse: $1.25.

Sansing then blindfolded and gagged her, dragged her into the master bedroom, and raped her while Kara watched. When he was through, he got a kitchen knife and stabbed Mrs. Calabrese to death. It had been quite a day for John and Kara; they left the body in the bedroom and went into the living room and promptly fell asleep.

On March 22, 1998, the *Arizona Republic* reported mixed responses to the news that Maricopa County, which encompasses Phoenix and its suburbs, was the fastest-growing county in the nation. It even outpaced Clark County, Nevada, where a burgeoning Las Vegas has been spreading like a gigantic oil spot. Between 1990 and 1997, according to the U.S. Census Bureau, Maricopa County welcomed an astonishing 574,097 newcomers.

Developers and cheerleaders of laissez-faire growth were elated: "I think it's very exciting," gushed Jan Brewer, chairwoman of the County Board of Supervisors. But some Phoenix-area residents thought their desert Eden was repeating all the mistakes of postwar Los Angeles: urban sprawl, overcrowded schools, polluted air, traffic jams, and spreading crime.

About the same time that the Census Bureau report was issued, this headline appeared in the Phoenix newspapers: MOM TORCHES KIDS. Kelly Blake, a thirty-four-year-old unwed mother of three, telling her children that they were going to play a game, lured them to a shed beside their Phoenix house. They were John Fausto, fourteen, his brother, Ramon, twelve, and their nine-year-old sister, Vanessa. Once they were inside, their mother poured gasoline on the shed door and set it on fire. The two boys managed to escape, but not Vanessa. While John was trying to extinguish the flames that engulfed his brother, Kelly Blake doused herself in gasoline and set herself ablaze. Firefighters arrived on the scene and saved her life and the lives of the two boys, but Vanessa burned to death.

Meanwhile, back on the growth front, one of Tucson's newspapers, the *Arizona Daily Star,* reported in its March 29 edition that there are now 247 golf courses in the state, 129 in Phoenix (average annual rainfall, eight inches) and another 35 in Tucson, average annual rainfall, twelve inches. The metastasizing of greens and fairways is devastating the Sonoran Desert's ecology and draining Arizona's aquifers. It takes 185 million gallons of water per year—as much as is used by about thirty-six hundred people living in single-family homes—to keep the average eighteen-hole course looking lush and pretty. Conservationists were gearing up to battle developers and politicians eager to draw more tourists and retirees to the state by building still more links, the *Star* said. But one statistic cited by the newspaper suggested that the conservationists have about as much chance of halting the advance as the Polish horse cavalry had of stopping German tanks in 1939: golf in Arizona brings in approximately a *billion* dollars a year.

And finally this item: scattered across a ridge northwest of Albuquerque, New Mexico's capital and another Sunbelt city bursting its seams, are some fifteen thousand petroglyphs that ancestors of today's Pueblo Indians carved into boulders spewed from five now-extinct volcanoes. The figures of horned serpents, masked men, flute players, birds, spirals, and stars are revered by Zunis, Hopis, Sandias, and Cochitis, who believe that the volcanoes link living people to the spirit world and the afterlife.

A six-lane commuter highway abruptly stops at the foot of the ridge, which was designated a national monument in 1990. Beyond it, out in the pristine Chihuahuan Desert, subdivisions for sixty thousand people are going to be built soon, and the developers and their political allies want to extend the highway through the monument to connect the new communities with the rest of the city. They defend this intrusion into public lands by saying that the extension would slice off only a sliver of the petroglyphs: a little over 8 acres out of a total of 7,244 acres. To the highway's Indian opponents that is like saying that a proposed widening of Fifth Avenue in New York City will only lop off the front of St. Patrick's Cathedral.

"In Albuquerque, major roads stop at golf courses," a Cochiti Indian leader, William Weahkee, told a reporter. "Are those sacred sites to you guys?"

He must have known the answer. A proposed alternative to the route had already been dropped, after citizens realized it would amputate a few holes from a golf course in the suburb of Paradise Hills.

So now I am a good long way from the places where little white Spaldings soar over the bones of Anasazi shamans, farther still from neighborhoods where sociopaths prompted by drug-jangled neurons rape and murder church women. But I am still no closer than I was days ago to connecting the dots between golf and homicide and Indian petroglyphs.

Two or three coyotes yap eerily on some distant ridge or in some far barranca. A few yards in front of me, down an arroyo that would be dry in a normal year, a stream burbles pleasantly. A waxing half-moon directly overhead turns night into twilight, and the pine trees cast distinct shadows over the carpets woven by their shed needles. Leo glimmers in the east, Taurus's horns make a V in the west, and bright Sirius appears as a blue-white lantern strung between the two giant ponderosas just south of my camp.

I stoke the fire, flick on my penlight, and begin rereading *Sand Country Almanac*, both because I like it and because it seems a good way to express my gratitude. June 3, 1999, will mark the seventy-fifth anniversary of the creation of the Gila's wilderness areas. If God was their father and nature the mother, Aldo Leopold was the midwife. He was working for the U.S. Forest Service in the early part of this century, and thanks to his impassioned advocacy, the wild heart of the Gila National Forest was spared from the ax, the chain saw, and the bulldozer.

The first paragraphs of his book, published fifty years ago this year, have always struck me for their clarity:

"There are some who can live without wild things, and some who cannot. These essays are the delights and dilemmas of one who cannot . . . Like winds and sunsets, wild things were taken for granted until progress began to do away with them. Now we face the question whether a still higher standard of living is worth its cost in things natural, wild, and free. For us of the minority the opportunity to see geese is more important than television. and the chance to find a pasqueflower is a right as inalienable as free speech."

Amen. The campfire burns down to embers. I fill a pot from the stream and pour it on the round red eye, which winks out in a plume of smoke. For a while, I watch the constellations wheel slowly westward. Taurus has fallen behind the ridge beyond the stream, and the quadrant occupied by the moon has been appropriated by the Dipper, its pointer stars aimed at Polaris, which is blotted out by the trees.

Dawn: a glorious light floods through the woods and turns the tops of the tallest trees into golden torches. While I'm waiting for my coffee water to boil, three mule deer come trotting down the ridge to the west—all does. I freeze, waiting for a buck to appear, but if one is around, he keeps out of sight, as bucks are wont to do. The deer continue on down in single file, their big donkeylike ears erect and alert for sounds of danger. When she is seventy-five yards away and about to cross the stream, the lead doe senses that something is wrong and pauses. She turns toward me, her whole body a study in tension. The other two follow suit. We stare at each other for a long, quiet thirty seconds. This is the sight hunters dream of—no brush or branches in the way, the quarry broadside and close enough for a sure shot. I am as enthusiastic a hunter as anyone, and I would rather eat game killed in the wild than a steak from a feedlot cow or a chicken butchered in some agribusiness abattoir. Yet thinking about what a dandy target the doe makes doesn't feel right on this innocent morning. I flick my hand and that's all the movement it takes. The deer bound away. There is no transition. One instant they are still as statues, the next they are lunging off through the trees, and in two or three ten-foot leaps, have vanished.

The only thing wrong with backpacking solo is that you have to do everything yourself. The chores involved in pitching and striking camp take twice as long, but the brain-cleansing effects of solitude make it worth the effort. It is past ten-thirty before I am on the trail again. The going is pretty easy, but that sixty pounds on my back makes my progress less than Mercurial: a little less than two miles an hour. Why sixty pounds? Because of the weather, I'm carrying more warm clothes than I'd originally planned on, and because Kramer told me the springs up ahead have run dry, I've tanked up on water—a two-quart saddle canteen, and two one-quart water bottles. True, the burden is eased by my new, nifty internal-frame backpack with load lifters and other design marvels; still, sixty pounds represents a little over one-third of my body weight. I am amazed that in my youth, before the advent of load lifters, lightweight tents, and freeze-dried food, I used to hike in the Michigan and Wisconsin north woods carrying eighty pounds in a big canvas Duluth bag with leather shoulder straps and a tumpline—a rig virtually identical to the kind used by the French voyageurs in the eighteenth century. But that's one of the many melancholy differences between being twenty-one and fifty-six.

For a while, the track winds through the transitional zone between juniper upland and pine forest; but as it climbs, the conifers take over completely; a few firs and Engelmann spruce begin to join the crowded company of ponderosas. After an hour, I take a short break (faintly hearing in memory's ear a drill sergeant barking, *Take five, troopers. Lamp is lit. Smoke 'em if you got 'em*). Don't got 'em. Quit 'em, though I have brought five cigars: one for each night. I am looking westward, out across Rocky Canyon at a landscape of such breadth and beauty that it seems to stretch the ligaments of my soul. The tiered foothills and mountains go from dark green to blue to purple at the horizon, where the Mogollons rise and their highest summit, Mogollon Baldy, is so slabbed with snow it might be in the Canadian Rockies. In the middle distance, a pair of hawks, too far away to identify, orbit over a side canyon. They ride the thermal until something is revealed to their keen eyes, and they glide down and away, in a line so perfect it's as if they are sliding down an inclined cable. In thirty seconds, they disappear over a ridge that looks to be a mile from where they'd been circling. It would take me half an hour to cover that mile on the ground. Backpacking in rough country revalues the currency of distance; the mile cheapened by the car and rendered almost worthless by the jet plane once again costs something, and so means something.

I set off again. I do not intend to wander aimlessly on this walkabout: my plan is to reach Reed's Peak (now some six miles away and another two and a half thousand feet up), follow the Black Range crest southward past Mimbres Lake to McKnight's Peak, and then descend to the South Fork of the Mimbres River, following that to the main stem of the Mimbres, which will eventually lead me back to the trailhead. Thirty-five to forty miles altogether. Kramer warned me that I might not make it, however: there is deep snow on the crest, and there could be drifts up to my waist on the north faces of the slopes below it.

And they almost are, as I discover around noon, when I reach eighty-five hundred feet. I am following fresh elk tracks, in the hopes of photographing the animal, but for the moment, my attention is focused on the impressions the elk's hooves have made in the drifts. I try to walk where the prints are only a few inches deep and to avoid those places where the snow is soft and elk's legs have drilled what look like postholes. The technique is sometimes successful, more often not. As the day warms, the frozen crust thaws fast, and several times I plunge to my thighs. With the help of my walking stick, I work my way out, wishing that I had four-wheel drive like my Pathfinder—or like the elk for that matter. The most treacherous spots are those in the deepest shade of the trees; there the crust is firm and supports my weight and deceives me into thinking I can stride along—until it betrays me and I suddenly find myself two feet shorter. It takes an hour to get around the north face of this particular hill, and I'm chilled from the thighs down, drenched in sweat from the waist up. I've also worked up a raging thirst and empty one water bottle and half the other, but save the saddle canteen for cooking; melting snow for water is tedious business. The map says that Aspen Spring is about a mile and a half farther on. Maybe, with all the precipitation, it has water in it.

The hike there is easy and exhilarating for the first half; but the trail then wraps around the north face of another slope and I am hobbled by snow again. Aspen Spring is dry. I am too, and drain my second water bottle. It is now two in the afternoon, and realizing that I will have to find a decent campsite in an hour or so, preferably near water, I strike off toward a side canyon to look for a stream. All around, not surprisingly, are groves of old-growth aspen, eighty feet tall with straight, clean, gray-white trunks.

The canyon bottom is waterless and deep in snow, and then I come upon one of those mysteries the wilderness sometimes offers. It is a monolith, an oblong slab of sandstone perhaps forty feet high and fifteen feet wide, with a tunnel drilled through its middle by, I presume, the waters that once ran through the canyon. There isn't any other rock around, beyond the small ones in the creekbed. It rises there all by itself among the trees, improbable, fantastic, inexplicable (though I suppose a geologist could explain it), and it possesses in its strangeness and its solitude a kind of power. I can imagine shamans from the Mimbres Indian culture that flourished here a thousand years ago chanting and drumming beneath it. I feel like doing a bit of chanting and drumming myself, in the hopes that the Great Lone Rock will point me to water and comfortable campsite.

Taking my binoculars and the saddle canteen, but leaving my locker-size pack at trailside, I head off to reconnoiter the route. I encounter very deep drifts at about nine thousand feet. Reed's Peak and the western face of the Black Range loom ahead. A brisk wind has risen from the south, and the sound it makes as it moves through the pines is sometimes like a waterfall, sometimes like the rush of an approaching train. Scanning the crest with the binoculars, all I can see is snow, cascading down the slopes. It looks very cold and forbidding up there, and I remember that only last week Kramer and his rangers rescued seven young adventurers who had been trapped in the Gila by a sudden storm. They had run out of food and two were into advanced stages of hypothermia and had to be taken out on pack horses. "That's our best-case scenario in search-and-rescue work, a large group of fit young men," Kramer had told me, leaving unsaid what was a worst-case scenario: a middle-aged man on his own. I decide to leave my trek along the crest for the future, maybe the fall, when the aspen turn gold. Blame it on El Niño. Why not? El Niño is getting the rap for everything from the Monica Lewinsky scandal to the Asian currency crisis, but all that snow can be legitimately laid on its shoulders.

Now I am camped in as flat and sheltered a spot as I can find on a ridge overlooking the named and unnamed canyons that lace their way downward into the Mimbres River valley. Small white flowers with yellow stamens cluster under the young firs that shield my tent from the wind. I don't know if they are northern bedstraw or wild candytuft; nor am I sure if the small, gray-winged, white-breasted birds flocking around are solitary vireos or gray vireos or some kind of gnatcatchers. As a naturalist, I make a good plumber.

Another night passes. I spend the next day rather idly, reading from *Sand County Almanac,* and rediscovering the wisdom in it . . . *Conservation is a state of harmony between men and land . . . Recreation is valuable in proportion to the intensity of the experiences, and to the degree to which it contrasts with and differs from workaday life . . . Mechanized outings are at best a milk-and-water affair . . .* I take a couple of short day hikes, sit on promontories, scanning the vast country for elk or the rare desert bighorn. I'd seen those elusive creatures on my first trip to the Gila in 1992, when my wife and I were horse-packing through the Whitewater Canyon country, many miles to the west of where I now am. We had seen hardly any game in five days, and suddenly there they were, a ram and his ewes, perched way up on a cliff.

Evening falls again. I gather pine needles, pinecones, and dry grass, cut shavings from a dead stick of gambel's oak, then make a tepee of twigs over the tinder and strike a match. Advocates of minimal-impact camping frown on fire-making. I carry a backpacker's stove, but mostly for emergencies or for use in places where ground fires are prohibited. I think it's important to know how to make a cooking fire out of what's around rather than relying on a gas bottle. And a backpacker's stove can't keep you warm or provide cheer in the darkness.

At around eight-thirty P.M., while I am thinking about absolutely nothing and savoring my nightly whiskey ration, I hear the most bizarre noise I have ever heard in the wilderness. It is coming from the east, near where the land falls steeply into a small canyon: a piercing screech with a pulse as regular as a metronome. It reminds me of a smoke alarm or an electronic alarm clock, considerably amplified. Indeed, I'm sure it is not a living thing, but some sort of device. With my flashlight, I walk toward it, and it never varies in tone, pitch, or rhythm. Could it be some newfangled high-tech signaling device used by lost hikers? "Is someone there?" I call out. "Somebody in trouble out there?" The noise stops. "Hello? Anyone there?" Silence. Ten or twenty seconds later, it starts again. Now I can hear that it's coming from up in a tree somewhere. A bird? I cannot think of a bird capable of making such an absolutely unearthly cry. Other possibilities come to me. Some sort of tracking collar? But tracking collars don't emit noises. A weather balloon that's fallen to earth and is sending a distress signal? But weather balloons are pretty big. In the bright moonlight, I would see one if it had fallen this close. How about space aliens? This is New Mexico, land of Roswell. Once more I shout, once more it falls silent. All right, to borrow a line from the horror flicks—*it's alive!* I'm sure of that now. It also flies, because in a few seconds, it starts coming from the south, and from high above. Shrill, insistent, not frightening so much as it's irritating. At one point, I yell, "Shut the hell up!" And it does, but soon resumes and doesn't stop. After a while, I get used to it, so used to it that I actually crawl into my tent and fall asleep to that SCREEP-SCREEP-SCREEP.

In the morning, while I'm melting down for my breakfast and morning coffee, I scour the woods all around, looking for bird droppings. I scan the branches overhead, but can't find a clue about the night's strange visitor. Well, I think, I wanted touch the mystery, and I've certainly been touched by one. Two days later, the biologist for the

Gila Wilderness will clear it up for me. I will learn that I've had an encounter with a famous endangered species. The screech was the alarm cry of the female spotted owl, and I was what she was alarmed about.

If climbing through the snow to the crest would be too much adventure, backtracking to my truck would be too little. I break out my topo map, orient it, and see that the anonymous canyon below me strikes southeastward and joins another, which in turn tumbles down to meet the Mimbres River. On paper, a trek of about two and a half miles, but figure a good three and a half to four on the ground. And a fairly rugged walk for the first two, judging from the crowded contour lines. Even in a wilderness, following blazed trails dilutes the adventure. The idea of going off trail, into unnamed canyons, appeals to me. Also, there is sure to be fresh running water in the bottoms—my coffee and breakfast were seasoned with dirt, bark, and bits of leaves embedded in the snow I'd melted. Silencing the memory of the Robert Service poem that Aldo Leopold quotes in his book—

Where nameless men by nameless rivers wander
And in strange valleys die strange deaths alone.

—I hoist my pack and start on down.

Soon, I hear the rush of water: a clear, swift stream, no more than a foot across, descends in a series of rocky steps. I fill my water bottles, drop in some iodine tablets, and while I'm waiting for them to take effect, I shoot an azimuth down the length of canyon to make sure I've read the map right. The canyon is almost a slot canyon, with nearly sheer walls of sedimentary rock—sandstone, mudstone, conglomerate, ash tuff fused by volcanic eruptions and the collapse of calderas thirty million years ago. I am walking on earth perhaps trod by dinosaurs. I haven't seen a human being for three full days, but I've seen signs of them. Down in No-Name Canyon I don't see any. The only trail is a game trail, blazed by elk and bear. The going is tricky, for the canyon falls in rocky ladders, creating tiny cataracts. There are windfalls and deadfalls everywhere, but I can see where the elk and bear have gone around these obstacles. I follow their lead—what the hell, they live here. Several times, I have to do some nontechnical rock climbing to find a way around narrow gorges. I am very careful. The surtax for lack of caution or a lapse in attention could be a broken ankle or leg; and I know Ranger Kramer and his rescue team would have a devil of a time finding me here.

An hour and a half later, I reach the junction of No-Name Canyon #1 with No-Name #2, which is twice as wide. The stream tumbling through it is like a brook trout stream, with many deep, delightful pools and small, sparkling waterfalls that are a joy to hear and see. For a while, I hike above the dancing water. A mountain on the other side climbs to snow-covered meadows, and the sky is so blue it seems to be the *idea* of blueness. The game trail is as well trod and defined as any made by man. I come across a recent bear dig, ten feet long by four wide by nearly two deep, and I see the paw prints of the beast that made that excavation as it dug for ground squirrels or mice. To be on the safe side, I call out, "Bear, hey bear," and make a lot of noise as I walk along. Grizzlies are gone from the Gila; the last one was shot in the 1920s by Ben Lilly, the famous mountain man and hunter. But I am not complacent about black bears; it's a matter of record, I've been told, that they have killed more people than the infamous *Ursus horribilis.*

Another two hours brings me to the Mimbres. There is a lot of satisfaction in navigating cross-country with map and compass. I prefer to do it that way than to turn everything over to a GPS. For one thing, you never know when the little box of microcircuits will go on the fritz; for another, not knowing where you are right down to the yard creates a certain pleasurable *frisson.*

The Mimbres winds away southwestward, glittering like a brightly jeweled cord. I make good time for the next three miles. Compared to the side canyons, the river valley is a park. White and violet wildflowers are beginning to bloom in the meadows. Far above rise cliffs fissured by eons of rain, sculpted by millennia of wind into towers and minarets and spires. They look like temples built by some race of devout titans. Hawks wheel over them. I delight in the beauty of a wide bend in the river as it curls against a low bluff, forming a gray-green pool created by the friction of water against water.

Farther downstream, I have to make eight river crossings within a mile—and that slows me down. Tired, I decide to pitch a camp in a trail-tromper's Eden: a knoll above the river, soft, flat ground, and plenty of standing and fallen deadwood. Looking toward the ridge on the other side, I see a three-quarter-moon, risen just above the rim and bracketed by two tall firs.

I perform the usual chores, wolf down dinner, and take up *Sand County Almanac* while there is light enough to read. The line, "Now we face the question of whether a still higher standard of living is worth its cost in things natural, wild, and free" leaps out from the page and discloses the common thread in the stories I clipped from the newspapers.

It is growth. The one thing our society does hold sacred is growth. Not intellectual or spiritual growth but economic growth; and not stable, sustainable economic growth but let-her-rip, boomtown, pave-it-don't-save-it growth. Our grail is an ever-higher standard of living that must be sought and grasped at almost any costs: polluted air, a high crime rate, degraded quality of life. But there is this difference between today and Aldo Leopold's day: then getting and spending was a big part of what we Americans were all about; now it seems to be all that we are about. Our national religion is a kind of Evangelical Consumerism. We even consume things that aren't really things—we swallow the salt water of information by the gallon even when our throats are parched form the springs of wisdom; we consume violence in computer games and on tabloid TV while we gorge on a home-delivered pizza.

Of course we pay a price for a culture such as ours, a culture that demands its instant gratifications. It isn't paid only in the coinage of rivers drained dry to irrigate golf courses or of sacred petroglyphs bulldozed to make travel more convenient for commuters. Our bodies pay a price: study after study has shown that we are today more obese than at any time in our history; we are the fattest people on earth. We pay in lowered quality of our moral lives. Heinous crimes like John Sansing's and Kelly Blake's are not anomalies, but signs of our spiritual emptiness; signs that what we have built in America over the past half century is not civilization. It may be development, but it's not civilization. It seems that the more we despoil the land and divorce ourselves from the rhythms, cycles, and beauty of the natural world, the less civilized we become.

Well, I am still no Isaac Newton, so am I crazy for making these connections? Hope not. In the past, this country needed a frontier as an outlet for people seeking to build new and better lives for themselves. I wonder, here beside the Mimbres River, if we need more wild places like this one as sanctuaries in which we can restore and renovate our inner lives. I think we would all benefit if more of us spent more time watching geese instead of television; if more of us devoted more time to absorbing the information wild creatures leave in the earth instead of filling our brains with the data-babble on the Internet. There is wisdom in the woods, "books in the rivers and sermons in the stones" that can teach us lessons about patience and humility, about the interconnectedness of all living things, about discerning what is important and lasting and what is trivial and transient. Thoreau said that in wildness lies the salvation of mankind. Another of our great naturalists, John Muir, said virtually the same thing in one of his essays on the California Sierras. Each alpine wildflower, he wrote, was "a window unto the Creator." Maybe you don't believe in a Creator; so put it like this: through that window we can see the grandeur in all creation, from atoms to galaxies; we can catch at least a transforming glimpse of something bigger than ourselves, something ineffable to remind us that consumption isn't the point of being human.

Tomorrow, I will hike the remaining four miles to the trailhead, get in my truck, and return to what is commonly called the real world. But I'm not so sure it is.

AFRICA

man-eaters of tsavo

2 0 0 0

There are few words as disturbing as "man-eater." Instantly, it dissolves hundreds of thousands of years of human progress and carries us back to our beginnings, when we were puny hominids, slouching across the African savanna where man was born, huddling in fireless caves, waiting for death to rush us from out of the long grass. The thought of being devoured offends our sense of human dignity, subverts our cherished belief that we are higher beings, "the paragon of animals," to borrow a line from *Hamlet*. The man-eater's actions say to us, "I don't care if you're the president of the United States, the queen of England, the inventor of the Internet, a bankable movie star, or an ordinary Joe or Jill, you're no paragon in my book, but the same as a zebra or gazelle—a source of protein. In fact, I'd rather hunt you, because you're so slow and feeble."

We didn't know if the big male lion in front of us had ever tasted human flesh. He did inhabit a region of Kenya that had given birth to the two most infamous man-eating lions in history, and that still harbors lions with a proclivity to hunt man: only two years before, a cattle herder had been killed and devoured by a lion not far from where this male now lay, looking at us with eyes that glowed like brass in firelight. He must have gone four- hundred pounds, and he was ugly in the way certain prizefighters are ugly—not a photogenic, Oscar de la Hoya sort of lion, but a Jake La Motta lion, with only a scruff of a mane and a face and hide scarred from the thorny country he lived in, or from battles with rival lions, or from the kicks of the zebra and buffalo he killed for food. He was only twenty-five feet away, but we were safe, provided we stayed in our Land Rover. Panting in the late afternoon heat, his gaze impassive, he rested in the shade of a tall bush, beside the carcass of a young Cape buffalo killed the night before. Around him, five lionesses lazed in the short yellow grass, well- fed and yawning. Two cubs licked and nibbled the buffalo's hindquarters, the ragged strips of meat in the hollowed-out cavity showing bright red under the black skin. Nothing else remained of the animal, except for the horned head, the front hooves, and a few scattered bones.

I ran out of film and dropped through the roof hatch to fetch another roll from my camera bag. Photographer Rob Howard, trying for another angle, boosted himself through the hatch and stood. Immediately, the drowsy, indifferent expression went out of the male's eyes as they focused on Rob with absolute concentration. Rob's camera continued to whir and click, and I wondered if he noticed that he'd disturbed the lion. Now, with its stare still fixed on him, it grunted out of one side of its mouth, then the other, gathering its forepaws into itself and raising its haunches. The long, black-tufted tail switched in the grass.

"Say, Rob, might be a good idea to sit down again," our guide, Iain Allan, advised in an undertone. "Move slowly, though."

He had barely finished this instruction when the lion made a noise like a man clearing his throat, only a good deal louder, and lunged across half the distance between us and him, swatting the air with one paw before he stopped. Rob tumbled through the roof hatch, almost landing on top of me in a clatter of camera equipment, a flailing of arms and legs.

"Jesus Christ!" he said, obviously impressed. The big male had settled down again, though his tail continued to sweep back and forth.

"The short, happy life of Rob Howard," I wisecracked. "It's embarrassing to see a man lose his nerve like that."

A bit of bravado on my part. We were going to spend only half of this safari in a vehicle. In the second half, we would try to track and photograph lions on foot. How would my own nerve hold up then? Perhaps Rob was wondering the same thing about himself. He asked Iain and his partner, Clive Ward, if the lion could have jumped on the roof.

"Could have, but he wouldn't have," Iain replied, a vague smile cracking across his rough, ruddy face. "That was just a demonstration, to let you know the rules. Of course, you had no way of knowing that."

There was a lot we didn't know about lions, practically everything, and we had come to Kenya to begin filling in the gaps in our knowledge. After hiring Iain, whose safari company, Tropical Ice Ltd., is one of the most experienced in the country, we journeyed by Land Rover from Nairobi to the eastern section of Tsavo National Park, the largest in Kenya, with an area of 8,036 square miles (that's the size of Massachusetts). Here you can at least get a taste of the wide-open wilds that Isak Dinesen described in *Out of Africa,* that her lover, Denys Finch-Hatton, hunted for elephant, and that aviator and adventurer Beryl Markham explored by air. It is the Africa that's all but vanished from the rest of Kenya's national parks and game reserves, which have become vast outdoor zoos, except that the animals are free while the visitors are caged in mini vans.

Iain loves Tsavo—the dense palm and saltbush forests of the river valleys, the sere red-and-khaki plains that seem to go on forever.

"Africa without any fat on it." he termed it, taking a line from Dinesen's book. "It's raw and primitive and it doesn't tolerate fools or forgive mistakes."

But Tsavo also has a dark history that's centuries old. Its name means "Place of Slaughter" in a local tribal language—a reference to massacres committed by Masai warriors in the distant past. Ivory traders told spooky tales about men who vanished from their midst when their caravans stopped at the Tsavo River for water and rest. The traders blamed the mysterious disappearances on evil spirits.

The region's forbidding reputation spread worldwide in 1898, when two lions literally stopped the British Empire in its tracks by killing and eating over one- hundred workers building a railroad bridge over the Tsavo River, in what was then called Kenya Colony. Their reign of terror lasted nine months, until they were hunted down and shot by the British army engineer in charge of the project, John H. Patterson. Working as a team, the pair sneaked into the construction camps as night, snatched men from their tents, and consumed them, often within the hearing of the victims' fellow workers. Patterson, who'd had considerable experience hunting tigers in India, used every trick in the big-game hunter's playbook, and devised ingenious traps and ruses to bring the killers to bay. They outwitted him time and again, proving so crafty that the workmen—mostly contract laborers imported from India—came to believe the ancient legends about body-snatching demons, and then added an anti-imperial spin to the myth: the lions were the incarnate spirits of African chieftains angered by the building of a railroad through their ancestral lands. "Beware, brother! The devil is coming!" the men would call to each other on nights when the lions' roars fell silent, for silence meant they had begun to stalk.

In 1907, Patterson, by then a colonel, published a best-selling book about the ordeal, *The Man-Eaters of Tsavo*, widely regarded as the greatest saga in the annals of big-game hunting. Still in print, it has inspired two feature films, *B'wana Devil* in 1952, Hollywood's first 3-D movie, and *The Ghost and the Darkness* in 1996, with Val Kilmer portraying Patterson.

Seventeen years after its publication, while lecturing in the U.S., Patterson donated the lions' skins and skulls to the Field Museum of Natural History in Chicago. A taxidermist turned the hides into life-size mounts, and they were put on exhibit and have been there ever since, a source of grim fascination to countless visitors. I saw them in 1958, when I was in high school, and though I can't remember any other exhibit I looked at that day, I've never forgotten those two lions, posed on a replica of sandstone, one crouched, the other standing, right paw slightly raised, both looking intently in the same direction. They had no manes, and the absence of the adornment that give postcard lions a majestic appearance made those two look sinister; it was as if nature had dispensed with distracting ornamentation to show the beasts in their essence—stripped-down assemblies of muscle, teeth, and claws whose sole purpose was to kill. But it was their eyes that impressed me most. They were glass facsimiles, yet they possessed a fixed, attentive, concentrated expression that must have been in the living eyes, when they spotted human prey decades before, on the plains of Africa.

Patterson's account of their deadly raids reads like a Gothic novel.

"The ground all about was covered with blood, morsels of flesh, and the larger bones, but the head was left intact, save for a couple of holes made by the lion's tusks. It was the most gruesome sight I had ever seen," Patterson wrote, describing his discovery of the remains of his Sikh servant, Ungan Singh, seized by one of the lions the previous night.

Singh was one of the lions' early victims and his ghastly death sent Patterson in pursuit of the lions. He didn't know what he was in for, but found out soon enough. The construction camps were scattered up and down the railroad right-of-way. The lions would strike at a particular camp one night, Patterson would stake it out the next night, waiting with his .303 rifle, but they always seemed to know where he was and would attack elsewhere.

The workmen meanwhile surrounded their camps with high *bomas*, or protective fences, made from thorny *Commiphora* shrubs. For a while, the attacks stopped. One night, a few workers figured it was safe to sleep outside their tent but inside the *boma*—a bad decision. One of the lions leapt over the fence (a lion can make a vertical jump of twelve feet) and grabbed a man. His friends threw stones and firebrands, but the lion calmly dragged his victim through the thorns. Outside, it was joined by its partner, and the two savored their meal within earshot of the dead man's friends. Some were armed and fired at the lions through the fence, but the bullets missed, and the cats, not in the least disturbed by the gunshots, leisurely finished dinner.

Perhaps Patterson's worst memory was of the night when he was in a tree stand and both lions carried their most recent kill close to him. It was too dark to aim and fire. He sat up there, listening to the crunching of bones and to what he described as a contented "purring"—sounds that he could not get out of his head for days.

The cats did not confine themselves to humans. In December, 1898, they killed a donkey. Scared off by Patterson, they abandoned the carcass. Patterson, inspired by his tiger-hunting days in India, built a *machan*, or platform, with four poles and a wooden plank, from which he could shoot in relative safety. He used the partially eaten donkey as bait, lashing it with wire to a nearby tree stump. That night, Patterson stood vigil. Soon, he heard a twig snap and a lion sighing with hunger. It ignored the donkey, however, and began to stalk Patterson, circling around and around his rickety perch. All it had to do was knock out a pole or jump, and Patterson would have been a dead man. The lion growled, then moved in for the kill. Patterson fired. The lion snarled—it had been hit, but it ran into the bushes. Patterson blazed away into the brush; the snarls grew weaker and finally ceased. The first man-eater was dead.

The next day, its body was recovered. The unmaned male, measuring nine feet, eight inches from its nose to the tip of its tail and fourty-seven and a half inches at the shoulder, was so heavy it took eight men to carry it back to camp.

To dispatch the second lion, Patterson tried one of his tricks. After the cat killed a goat near the railroad inspector's shanty, Patterson tied three live goats to a length of railroad track, then entered the shanty and waited. The lion came just before dawn, killed one of the goats, and began to carry it away, *with* the other two goats and the 250-pound rail. Patterson fired, missing the lion but killing one of the goats.

The rail left a trail easy to follow; the lion escaped nonetheless. The dogged Patterson stalked it for almost two weeks, and finally managed to wound it. He and his gun-bearer followed the blood spoor for a quarter mile, and at last spotted their quarry, glaring back at them with bared teeth. Patterson took careful aim and fired. The lion charged. A second shot bowled it over, but it got up and charged again. Patterson fired a third time without effect, reached for his second rifle, and saw that his gun-bearer had fled into a tree. Patterson had no choice but to join him; if one of the bullets had not broken the lion's hind leg, he never would have made it. Once in the tree, Patterson grabbed the rifle and shot the lion again. It fell heavily. Patterson foolishly climbed down—and was stunned to see the lion jump up and charge him again. He put a round in its chest, another in its head, and the lion went down for good, snapping at a branch even as it died.

The second man-eater taped out at nine feet, six inches in length and forty-five inches at the shoulder, and its death ended the reign of terror.

Throughout history, the beast with a zest for human flesh has been regarded as an aberration, even as an outlaw, as if there is an ordinance against making meals of people. Patterson's book often refers to the lions in terms commonly applied to criminals or psychopaths. Even the more objective scientific literature tends to explain man-eating as the exception that proves the rule—humans are not normally on the predator's grocery list. Lions are generally believed to turn to man-eating only when injuries or old age prevent them from pursuing their usual prey.

It's true that old, sick, or wounded lions have been responsible for most attacks on people. However, modern field researchers have come up with—well, it would be an exaggeration to say "evidence," so I'll say "hints" instead—tantalizing hints that there may be some lions with a more or less genetic predisposition to prey on humans, even when strong and healthy enough to bring down a zebra or buffalo. The explanation for this behavior would then subtly but significantly shift from the pathological to the Darwinian: conditions in a lion's environment, as much as changes in its physiology, can drive it to hunt people—and there's nothing aberrant or criminal about it.

Still, such a beast poses a mystery, and the key to that mystery may be found in the lions of Tsavo, which truly are a different breed of cat from the glorious, regal lions of, say, the Serengeti plains. Most Tsavo males are maneless, and larger than average male lions, which measure thirty-six inches at the shoulder and weigh between 385 and 410 pounds; Tsavo lions are up to a foot taller and can tip the scales at about 460 to 520, giving you a cat the size of a grizzly bear. They are also distinguished by their behavior. On the plains, adult males mate and protect the pride, leaving the hunting chores to females. In Tsavo, where scarcity of game makes prides smaller, males share in the hunting and may do most of it.

"There's no doubt in my mind that Tsavo lions are different," Iain told us on the drive from Nairobi. "They're total opportunists, just killing machines that will attack and eat even little African hares. They're also more cunning than pride lions, often killing from ambush instead of stalk and spring. There's something sinister about them."

Iain is not a big-cat biologist, but twenty-one years of leading walking and driving safaris in Kenya and Tanzania have given him the kind of direct experience that compensates for any lack of scientific training. He's never had an experience more direct, and terrifying, than the one he had on a Tsavo safari last July.

It was late in the afternoon, past the time when he usually checks in with his Nairobi office by satellite phone (nowadays, even safari guides cannot escape the tyranny of instant communications). He ambled down to the wide, sandy banks of the Galana River, where reception was better than it was in his tree-shrouded tent camp. As he chatted with his secretary, he observed a waterbuck poke its way through a saltbush thicket some distance upriver, then lower its head to drink. Suddenly, the animal raised its head and froze; an instant later, a lioness sprang from the saltbush still farther upriver, and the waterbuck bolted down the shore in Iain's direction, the lioness in pursuit. When she was about fifty yards from Iain, her intended meal disappeared into the brush, and she veered off without breaking stride and headed straight for him, bursts of sand flying behind her as she ran. Iain tossed the phone away, and in a microsecond that seemed like minutes, realized that he needn't worry about her teeth and claws; he was going to be killed by the impact of three hundred pounds of sinew and muscle smashing into him at twenty-five miles an hour. He remembers that and how, when she was only ten feet from where he stood, she veered again and kicked sand all over him.

Iain suspects that the lioness charged him because she was confused, annoyed, or curious. "That's the closest I've ever come to getting killed," he added.

Are the lions of Tsavo predisposed to prey on people? Why are they maneless? Why are they larger than average? Can they tell us anything new about the king of beasts? Those and other questions are being looked into by a team of researchers from Chicago's Field Museum headed by Dr. Bruce Patterson (no relation to the colonel). They are also the questions that prompted us to go to Tsavo.

On our first day, after settling into Iain's tent camp on the Voi River, we drove down a red, laterite road to the Aruba dam. There is a small lake behind the dam, and that's where Samuel Andanje, a young Kenyan research associate with the Kenya Wildlife Service, directed us to the scarred male and his harem of five females. They were part of a pride of twenty-three lions, said Andanje, who spends his nights locating the animals by their roars and his days tracking them in a Land Rover.

Shortly after the male had taught Rob the rules, the females, with the cubs in tow, moved off toward the lake to drink. They made a fine sight in the golden afternoon light, walking slowly through the dun-colored grass with movements that suggested water flowing. Scarface remained behind, to guard the buffalo carcass from jackals and hyenas. As the sun lowered, the lake became a wildlife magnet. Two hippos wallowed in the middle. On one side, a dozen elephants, creased hides reddened by dried mud, were drinking through the great straws of their trunks. Along the shore where the lionesses and cubs crouched, their tongues lapping, sacred ibis pecked the mud with their long, curved beaks: a bird of simple colors, black and white, sharply delineated, and called "sacred" because it symbolized the Egyptian god Thoth, who toted up the pharaoh's good and evil deeds in the Book of the Dead.

We learned that from Clive Ward, who is fifty-five years old and tall and spare, with the face of an ascetic and a clipped way of speaking that sometimes leaves the words trapped in his mouth. Like the fifty-one-year-old Iain, he had guided safaris for years, and is an alpinist and rock climber by avocation. He and Iain have led countless parties of trekkers up Mount Kilimanjaro and Mount Kenya, and as climbing partners, have scaled most of the world's major peaks. Over the years, they have developed a relationship that seems to combine war-buddy comradeship with the easy familiarity of an old married couple; they bicker now and then, and needle each other, but beneath the bickering and needling, you sense an abiding bond knit on sheer rock faces and icy crags and long, hot tramps through the African bush.

Clive's disquisition on sacred ibis was followed by a series of throaty grunts from the male lion, which wasn't a commentary but a call to the females and cubs to return. As they padded soundlessly through the grass, we left—it was growing dark—and came upon a lone lioness, lying at the junction of the road and the two-track that led to camp. She didn't move as the Land Rover approached, nor when we turned onto the two-track, passing within six feet of her. She seemed to regard the intersection as hers, and of course it was.

The big storks roosting in the branches of dead trees in the Voi riverbed looked ominous in the twilight. Up ahead and across the river, waterless now in the dry season, the glow of kerosene lamps and a campfire made a more cheerful sight. Iain believes that you don't need to practice being miserable, and his safaris hark back to the stylish roughing it of a bygone age: commodious wall tents with cots to sleep in, a large, communal mess tent to eat in, outdoor showers with warm water in collapsible buckets suspended overhead, portable privies in canvas enclosures, laundry service, and a competent staff, including Kahin, Simon, Kamal, David, and two camp workers, who do the cooking and camp chores. On an open fire, Kahin, the cook, whips up meals equal to anything served up in Nairobi restaurants, and you wash them down with South African reds and Australian whites, making you feel pretty *puka-sahib*.

After dinner, we sat around the campfire on folding chairs, under the stars, and once, when the wind turned, heard lions roaring in the distance. The sound inspired Iain to offer a sequel to the tale of his encounter with the charging lioness.

"After she disappeared, I had the feeling that she'd run into camp, so I ran back and told my clients to get in their tents and zip them up, and warned the staff that a lion was in camp. Well, they looked at me as if to say that the old boy had had too much sun, and after I didn't see the lioness for a while, I figured they were right. I was about to tell my clients that they could come on out of their tents, when I turned around and saw six Africans running like hell for the Land Rover, with the lioness running alongside them—not after them, but alongside them. The men leapt up to the roof in one bound—if Carl Lewis had been competing against them, Carl Lewis would have lost. I think that old girl was very confused—she'd started off chasing a waterbuck, ended up in a camp full of people, tents, vehicles—things she'd never seen—and must have wondered, 'How did I get into this mess?' She ran out, but stopped at the edge of camp and stayed there all day. Just sat there, like the lioness we saw a little while ago."

"What good did zipping up the tent flaps do?" I asked. "She could have shredded an eighth of an inch of canvas if she wanted to."

"Lions don't like entering dark, enclosed spaces," Iain explained. "That's why it's important to keep the flaps closed at night. Only last August, in Zimbabwe, there was a young Englishman, son of an earl, on a camping safari. Seems there was a lot of drinking going on, and after the party, he went into his tent and fell asleep without closing the flaps. Sometime during the night, a lioness got close to his tent. He woke up, and scared as hell, ran out. Lions like things that run, same as any cat. She chased him, right into a mob of other lions, and when they got through with him, I don't think there was anything left."

This was not a bedtime story to tell in lion country. When my wife and I went to our tent, we not only secured the flaps, we zipped up the covers to the mesh ventilation windows—and could barely breathe the stifling air. I wasn't encouraged by Iain's assurance that lions did not like entering dark, enclosed places. Didn't the man-eaters of Tsavo barge into the tents of the construction crews to grab their meals? Maybe the workmen did not close the flaps, I thought. My sole armament was a K-bar, the ten-inch trench knife issued me when I was in the marine corps in Vietnam. It rested in its sheath on the night table next to my cot, but it seemed to me that the best thing I could do with it in the event of a lion attack would be to fall on it and save the lion the trouble.

"*Jambo*," David called softly from outside our tent. *Jambo* means "hello" in Swahili.

"*Jambo*," we answered and got up and dressed by lantern light. After breakfast, and with light erasing the last morning stars, we rolled out to the Aruba dam to look for Scarface and his family.

They were not where we had left them. We drove along slowly, looking for pug marks in the soft, rust-colored earth, until we heard a deep, bass groan that ended in a chesty cough. It was so loud we thought he was only fifty yards away. Leaving the road, we set off in the direction of the sound, bouncing over a prairie of short, dry grass tinted pale gold by the early morning sun, Clive, Rob, and I standing on the seats with our heads poking out of the roof hatches.

"Ah, there he is," said Iain, at the wheel.

"Him all right," Clive seconded.

I spend a lot of time in the woods and am not bad at spotting game, but I had no idea what they were talking about.

"It's the ears, you look for the ears sticking above the grass when you're looking for lion," Iain said, and drove on, and then I saw them, two triangles that could have been mistaken for knots in a stump if they hadn't moved. We were twenty or thirty yards away when he stood up, with a movement fluid and unhurried. Ugly-handsome Scarface went down a game trail at the leonine version of a stroll, then up over a rise and down toward a marsh, its green swath spread between the tawny ridges. We stayed with him all the way, keeping a respectful distance. He was one big boy, and if he were a man-eater, this is what he would do after he killed you. Flay off your skin with his tongue, which is covered with small spines that give it the texture of coarse-grained sandpaper and are used to bring nutritious blood to the surface; bite into your abdomen or groin, open you up. And scoop out your entrails and internal organs and consume them, because they are rich in protein, your liver especially; and savor your meatiest parts, thighs and buttocks, followed by your arms, shoulders, and calves, cracking open the smaller bones for their marrow. The larger bones would be left for the hyenas, which have stronger jaws. Vultures and jackals would dispose of your face and scalp and whatever scraps of flesh remained, so that, a few hours after your sudden demise, it would be as though you had never existed. There is a terrible thoroughness to the mechanics of death in Africa and we are not exempt.

Scarface led us right to his harem, and then, after posing on a knoll, he moved off into the marsh, the lionesses and cubs following soon after.

"That's that for now," said Iain. "Have to come back in the late afternoon. Let's look up Sam and try to find the rest of this pride."

Andanje led us to a remote stretch of the Voi, and we followed his white Land Rover through *Commiphora* scrub, bristling with thorns. I mentioned the *bomas* Patterson's laborers had constructed, and how the lions had found ways through them, with the canniness of trained guerrillas infiltrating an enemy's barbed wire. Four-footed killers with above-average IQs.

"I don't doubt but that they had the whole thing totally wired," Iain remarked. "The difference between people and animals is that we can see the big picture, and figure out how to survive in any environment, but within their area of specialization, most animals are as smart as we are, maybe smarter." He paused, chewing over a further thought. "Take a look at this country. It's sparse and harsh, there aren't any huge herds of wildebeest, like the kind you get in the Masai Mara, the Serengeti. Tsavo lions have to take what they can get, whatever comes along. I'm convinced that they have territories they know as well as you know your backyard, with their ambush places all staked out. They're clever. They know where to be and when."

An interesting observation, I thought. It reminded me of something I'd read, to the effect that because a human being's one big advantage over a predator is intelligence, the lion that hunts man has to sharpen its wits rather than its claws to be successful. But the lions that Patterson encountered may have had keen wits to begin with, to survive in their environment, and honed them further as they grew more experienced, stalking their big-brained, bipedal quarry.

We found no lions, and by 10:30, the quest was hopeless. It was close to a hundred degrees, and the cats were laid up, deep within the thickets. In the late afternoon, we returned to the marsh near the Aruba dam. There, Scarface's harem lolled with the cubs on the grassy ridge overlooking the marsh, where a solitary bull elephant grazed. Iain parked about thirty yards from the lions and we began observing and photographing. There wasn't much action. The cats did nothing but lie around, mouths half open, eyes half shut, their ears flicking every now and then.

"I'm afraid what you're seeing now is typical lion behavior," said Iain. "This is what they do twenty hours out of twenty-four. Conserve energy."

Later, as the sun dropped below the Chyulu Hills and a blessed sundowner began to blow, the lions stirred. A small herd of Grant's gazelle daintily walked down into the marsh to graze, and the biggest lioness, the dominant female, raised her head and fastened her gaze on them, exactly as my wife's pet cat raises his head when he sees or hears a mouse crawling through our pachysandra beds. Twelve pounds or 250, a cat is a cat is a cat.

"She's looking for a slight limp in one of the gazelle," Iain observed. "Any sign of weakness, but gazelle isn't a lion's favored prey. They're so fast and there isn't much meat on them, so it's hardly worth the effort. Lions are lazy hunters." Gesturing at the marsh, he returned to the theme of feline intelligence. "A lot of thought went into choosing this position, above the swamp and with most of it upwind, so they can see or scent almost anything that comes along. It's perfect buffalo country. The sun's lowering, they're rested, and they'll be getting hungry soon."

But a kill would happen out of our sight, because the lion is a nocturnal hunter, its round pupils adapted for night vision, aided by a white circle below the eyes that reflects light back into them.

When we were about a quarter of a mile from camp, Iain and Clive spotted the female that had occupied the road junction the night before. She was with two very young cubs, hardly bigger than house cats. Her tawny hide looked gray in the twilight, and she walked so quietly on her cushioned paws that she seemed insubstantial, a wraith in the gathering darkness.

She was the last of the Aruba pride that we would see, though we searched for them diligently for the next two days. Elephant were abundant, along with Cape buffalo, giraffe, gazelle, impala, waterbuck, baboon, and zebra; the bird life would have kept the entire Audubon Society happy—from big tawny and bateleur eagles to midsize hornbills to small golden pippets that flew from the bushes like dabs of butter with wings—but no lions. On our fourth morning in Tsavo, Iain's staff struck the tents, in preparation to moving it to this "walking safari" campsite at a place called Durusikale, on the Galana River. If you are to experience the Africa of Isak Dinesen and Denys Finch-Hatton, then you have to do it on shank's mare; "safari," after all, is a Swahili word derived from the Arabic for "to travel on foot."

Roused at 4:30 A.M. by David's *"Jambo,"* we breakfasted under the Southern Cross, and then drove northward, down a road paralleling a river called the Hatulo Bisani, where we had seen a large herd of Cape buffalo the day before. It was Iain's theory that a lion pride might be trailing them. During the long rains of April and May, the Hatulo Bisani would be a torrent; now, with a mere trickle flowing between wide swaths of bright green sedge, it resembled a river of grass. Egrets stood silent vigil on the banks. A goliath heron, a shorebird five feet tall, rose from an island with slow flaps of its huge gray wing.

We found fresh pug marks in the road, followed them for a while, then lost them when they angled off into the scrub. A short distance ahead, the buffalo, maybe six hundred of them, grazed in the riverbed, their gray-black bodies looking like boulders from a distance. Iain's theory seemed to be holding up, but before he could stop and kill the engine, the buffalo heard it and bolted as one great mass of tossing horns, heaving backs, and lunging legs that surged up over the steep bank, across the road in front of us, and onto the sere plains beyond, where the stampede stopped and the dominant bulls turned to glare at us through the risen dust, river mud glistening on their flanks.

We sat there, eyeball to eyeball with one of the biggest, strongest, fiercest animals in Africa, and also one that helps explain why Tsavo lions are so big, and why they're likely to turn man-eater. Cape buffalo are the most numerous of Tsavo's herd animals, and lions prey on them. Lions elsewhere do so only when deprived of easier game, and only in large bands; no average-size lion can take down a fifteen-hundred-pound Cape buffalo single-handed. In other words, the lions of Tsavo are big because their favored prey is big, and because the dense, brushy country compels them to hunt in small groups. Still, hunting buffalo is a risky business, no matter how hefty a lion gets. Recently, Andanje found a lion stomped to death by a buffalo. More frequently, the cats suffer broken bones and puncture wounds; they then naturally turn to easier prey, like livestock and the people who tend them.

Tom Gnoske and Dr. Julian Kerbis-Peterhans, members of the Field Museum research team, have discovered an interesting twist to such behavior: a lion that becomes a man-eater because it's injured doesn't go back to its traditional prey even after it recovers. Eating people, Gnoske said, "is an easy way to make a living."

Intriguingly, one of the Tsavo man-eaters had a severely broken canine tooth with an exposed root. The tooth was well worn and polished and the entire skull had undergone "cranial remodeling" in response to the trauma, indicating that the injury was an old one. It's in the record that at least one man-eater had been prowling about Tsavo before Patterson arrived with his bridge-building gangs, in April 1898. A railroad surveyor, O. R. Preston, lost several members of his crew to a man-eater near the Tsavo River early in 1897. When Preston and his men searched for remains, they found the skulls and bones of individuals who had been killed much earlier. There is no proof that an injury was the lion's "motive" for turning man-eater, but it's a plausible explanation. He might have been kicked in the jaw by a buffalo and lost a tooth; he stuck to preying on humans after the injury healed, having found out how safe and convenient it was. The arrival of the railroad workers, packed into tent camps, must have struck him as manna from leonine heaven.

But what about his partner, who was in prime health? The Field Museum researchers speculate that an epidemic of rinderpest disease may have played a role. In the early 1890s, the disease, likely to have been spread by cattle imported from India, all but wiped out domestic cattle and buffalo. With its usual prey eliminated, the starving lion had to look to villages and construction camps.

Another, more disquieting explanation lies elsewhere, with the elephants of Tsavo.

We turned off the Hatulo-Bisani road and started down the Galana River road, toward the campsite, some thirty miles downstream. Partway there, we stopped to climb one of the Sobo rocks, a series of sandstone outcrops, to scan for game with binoculars and reconnoiter our route—the plan was to walk from Sobo to Sala Hill, at the eastern border of the park. The Galana, fed by melting snows on Mounts Kenya and Kilimanjaro, showed a brassy brown as it slid slowly between galleries of saltbush and doum palm toward its distant meeting with the Indian Ocean. Out on the scorched, rust-colored plains beyond the river, a procession of elephants were migrating to the river to drink and cool themselves in the midday heat. Postponing our lion quest for the moment, we returned to the Land Rover and cut cross- country toward the herd, drawing close enough to count the animals,—about sixty altogether, the calves trotting alongside their mothers, a huge matriarch out front, other old females guarding the flanks and rear.

We were looking at part of what would be called a miracle if it were not the culmination of so much effort, courage, and determination on the part of many people, from internationally known conservationists like anthropologist Richard Leakey to anonymous Kenyan park rangers who died or suffered wounds fighting elephant poachers. The *shifta*, as the poachers are sometimes called, are mostly ethnic Somali tribesmen from Kenya's desolate northeast, with a reputation for banditry and viciousness. In the 1980s, satisfying a huge demand for ivory in the Far East, they reduced Tsavo's elephant population from twenty-five thousand animals to forty-five hundred. The slaughter did not end until the Convention on International Trade in Endangered Species, goaded by Leakey and other conservationists, passed a worldwide ban on ivory trading in 1989. Poaching in Tsavo had dropped dramatically since, and the elephant herd has grown to ten thousand.

Iain and Clive are elephant enthusiasts. After they saw the herd shambling toward the Galana, they took us to a spot on the river where we had a good chance of observing the animals at close hand. We picnicked in the shade of a tamarind tree, with a broad, sandy beach in front of us. Half an hour later, the elephants arrived, within one hundred yards of where we sat. They came on down with a gliding, stiff-legged gait, which looked deceptively slow—they were actually covering ten to twelve feet in a single stride. The marvelous thing was how silent they were, passing through the saltbush with barely a rustle to enter the river. It seemed to us that we were beholding Tsavo's wild soul made flesh.

With cat-burglar creeps, we positioned ourselves on the shore and watched and photographed for almost an hour. It was a wondrous sight. The animals' ears flapped, big as a dinghy's sails; tails switched, trunks curved into their mouths or bent back to spray their heads with water. An incredible organ, the elephant's trunk; it contains forty thousand separate muscles and serves as the hand that feeds the elephant, as a nose, a drinking straw, a built-in shower, and a weapon, all in one.

Matriarchs had taken up sentry positions, covering the four points of the compass. The calves were thoroughly charming as they rolled in the river and submerged themselves. With the wind blowing into our faces, the herd was unaware of our presence, though the matriarch facing upriver sometimes appeared to sense that something was out of ordinary; she would look our way and raise her trunk overhead and swing it back and forth—an olfactory periscope scanning for scent of danger. She never acted alarmed, and that was good. Bull elephants make false charges, but when a matriarch comes at you, she usually means to carry the thing through.

"The usual way an elephant kills a human being is not to stick and stomp," Iain said, "but to knock you down, then kneel on one knee and lean its forehead into you and crush you to death."

Tsavo elephants have all the reason in the world to fear and hate people. Slaughtering them for their ivory is a very old story, going back as far as ancient times, and the caravans that once passed through Tsavo laden with tusks may hold another explanation for the man-eating tendencies of Tsavo lions.

Dr. Chapurukha Kusimba, an anthropologist, grew up in Kenya with the story of the man-eaters and Patterson's epic hunt for them. Now an American citizen and assistant curator of African archaeology and ethnography at the Field Museum, he joined the Tsavo lion research team in 1994. Kusimba studied the traditional caravan routes from the interior to the coast, and learned that the caravans carried slaves as well as ivory. As mentioned before, the Tsavo River was an important stop, where the traders rested their camels, refreshed themselves, and restocked their water supplies before moving on. However, Kusimba believes they disposed of unnecessary cargo first: captives too sick or weak to travel farther were abandoned to die.

With so many corpses around, predators in the vicinity had an abundance of people to feed on, the theory continues. The scavenging likely started with hyenas and then was taken up by lions. From there, it wasn't a big step for the cats to go after living people. That possibly explains the myths about "evil spirits"; the men who mysteriously disappeared from the caravans' campsites had been seized not by devils but by lions. The slave and ivory caravans had passed through Tsavo for centuries, and that leads us to the disturbing aspect of the theory. *Panthera leo* is a social animal, capable of adopting "cultural traditions" that are passed on from generation to generation. If a lioness is hunting people, her young will grow to regard them as a normal part of their diet, and pass that knowledge on to their young. The upshot is that Patterson's man-eaters may have done what they did not because they were handicapped by injuries or because their traditional prey had been wiped out, but because they came from a man-eating lineage so long that an appetite for human flesh was ingrained in them. Stalking and devouring the "paragon of animals" wasn't the exception, but the rule.

That's just a theory, you understand, only a supposition, but the kind to make you wake up at two in the morning if you're in a tent in lion country, and to hear the pad of a lion's paws in every little rustle outside; to mistake your wife's deep breathing for a lion's; to picture him creeping up on the thin canvas that separates you from him, and to know that he isn't there out of curiosity or because he smelled the food in the cook's tent or because he winded a zebra herd beyond camp and is only passing through, but because he's scented *you* and *you* are what he's after; the kind of supposition to make you imagine the horror of what it's like to feel him bite down on your ankle or shoulder with his strong jaws and then drag you out and run off with you, wonderful, indispensable you, apple of your mother's eye, and you screaming and scratching and kicking and punching, all to no avail, until he releases his grip to free his jaws to crush your windpipe, snap your neck, or drive his tusks through your skull, and the last sensation you have is of his warm breath in your face.

Such were my waking nightmares that night, and they were not unreasonable. Maybe a hankering for human meat *was* coded into Tsavo lions' genes. After all, man-eating did not end with the deaths of Patterson's rapacious two. There had been an outbreak in the Ngulia Hills, in what's now Tsavo West National Park, as recently as the 1950s. Closer to home, in the temporal sense, there was the cattle herder taken by a lion near the park borders in July 1998.

And yet, only that afternoon, I had been as captivated by a lion as Joy Adamson had been by Elsa. We had left camp on a game drive, and rounded a bend in the road a few miles downriver, and suddenly she was there, walking purposefully ahead of us. There was nothing beautiful about her; old scratches and cuts marred her skin like sewn rips in a threadbare sofa, and her ribs showed, though not in a way to suggest starvation so much as a spare toughness. If the sleek pride lions of the Serengeti are the *haute-bourgeoisie* of the leonine world, Tsavo lions are the proletariat, blue-collar cats that have to work hard for a meager living. I recalled Iain's description of Tsavo as a land intolerant of fools and unforgiving of mistakes. The lioness blended right into such a landscape; she looked neither tolerant nor forgiving, which is not to say that she looked menacing; self-possessed, rather, and unflappable, and very focused on getting to wherever she was going.

We trailed her, but she was never alarmed. Now and then, she threw a sidelong glance at us, just to check on our distance or our behavior. If we edged too close, she simply angled away, maintaining a space of perhaps fifteen yards. A lady with a mission, she went on through the bristling *Commiphora* with the steady, unflagging pace of a veteran foot soldier, keeping the river on her left. The river showed blue under a cloudless sky and eddied around sandbars, on one of which a big crocodile basked, its gray-green hide reflecting the slanted sunlight.

After she covered some two miles, the lioness began to call with low grunts. We figured she was trying to locate her pride, but if they answered, we did not hear them. Another quarter of a mile, and she stopped on a rise and called more loudly—a sound that seemed to come from her belly instead of her throat, part moan, part cough. *Wa-uggh, Wa-uggh.* In a moment, two cubs, a male and a female, bounded from a saltbush thicket a hundred yards away. They leapt on their mother, licking face and flanks, and she licked theirs.

With her cubs following, the lioness retraced her steps, and we again followed. The wary cubs often stopped to stare or hiss at us, but their mother kept walking without a break.

Iain speculated that she had stashed the cubs in the saltbush to go hunting or scouting, probably in the company of another lioness. Now, she probably was leading the cubs to the kill, if one had been made, or back to the pride.

It would be good if she led us to the pride; our four-day foot safari was to begin the next morning, and knowing where the pride was would give us an objective. I love walking in the wild, but I love even more walking with a purpose. The lioness pressed on with her journey, and then she and the cubs pulled one of the vanishing acts that seem a Tsavo lion specialty. We looked for ten minutes; then, as suddenly as they'd disappeared, they reappeared, wading across the river. They stopped on a sandbar in midstream. There the cubs gamboled for a while, one mounting its forepaws on its mother's hindquarters and allowing her to pull it along as she looked for a spot to complete the crossing.

"All we need now is background music from *Born Free*," Iain remarked, but I thought of Santiago's dream in *The Old Man and the Sea*, his dream of lions on the beach.

She plunged in and swam a deep narrow channel, the cubs paddling after her. The three climbed the bank and then were swallowed by the saltbush. We were sorry to see the lioness go; for all her scruffy appearance, we had grown fond of her and her self-possessed air. Still, she looked awfully lean, and I said that I would have felt better about her prospects if I had seen her and the cubs reunited with their pride.

"Don't worry about her," Iain commented. "She knows exactly what she's doing, she's in complete command of her situation."

I'm not sure how, in the span of a few hours, I had gone from feeling sorry for a real lion to being in abject terror of an imaginary one. At two in the morning, the rational brain doesn't function as well as it does at two in the afternoon, and you start thinking with the older brain, that cesspit of primeval dreads. Or maybe my heebie-jeebies had been a reaction to another of Iain's bedtime stories, told over another of Kahin's superb dinners: fried eggplant, pumpkin soup, and bread pudding with hot cream.

A wealthy Texas couple and their two sons were on safari with Tropical Ice. One midnight, Iain was awakened by the parents' screams: "Iain! They're here! They're coming in!" He tumbled out of bed, unzipped his tent flap, and saw a lioness walk right past him. Worse, he could hear other lions in the underbrush near camp—and the crunching of bones. Iain shouted to his clients to get on the floor of their tents and cover themselves with their mattresses. More lions appeared, playfully batting the guy lines of the couple's tent, as if to tease the frightened occupants. Their two sons, scared witless but desperate to pee, filled every receptacle in their tent with urine. Iain, in the meantime, ran to get the help of his two armed Masai guards, who had managed to sleep through the commotion. As they approached the thicket in which Iain had heard the hideous crunching noise, they were greeted by growls. The Masai did not live up to their reputation as fearless lion hunters; they fled in panic. It turned out that the lions were guarding their kill, which wasn't a person but a warthog. Iain drove them away merely by clapping his hands—a sound that frightens lions, because no other animal makes it.

The next day, the couple asked to leave the area. Iain agreed. Later, as he was loading the Land Rover, and as the woman was packing her suitcase, he saw what he termed "a horrifying sight." A lioness was sauntering alongside the tent, which was open at one end. As calmly as he could, Iain told the woman to come out, but not to run, and get in the car. She had no sooner jumped in and shut the door than the lioness rounded the corner and walked into the tent. Had the woman still been inside, the lioness would have killed her. "Maybe not eaten her," Iain added, reassuringly, "but definitely killed her because she would have tried to run."

Dangers imagined are always worse than dangers confronted. I was in good spirits the next morning, and actually looking forward to facing a lion on foot, if for no other reason than to conquer my fear. To protect us, Iain had contracted two K.W.S. rangers, Adan and Hassan, who were armed with Belgian FN semiautomatic assault rifles. Dressed in jaunty berets, camouflage uniforms, and combat boots, they looked more like commandos than park rangers. Only foot safaris with armed guards are allowed in the vast area north of the Galana, mostly because *shifta* are still active there, and likely to hijack or ambush a vehicle full of tourists.

I hoped that Adan and Hassan would not imitate the behavior of the Masai in Iain's story. If they did, we didn't have much else in the way of self-defense—my trusty K-bar; Iain's Gurkha kris, a souvenir from a trek in the Himalayas; and Clive's Masai short sword, called a *simi*. African lore and legend is full of stories about strong men who have killed lions with knives, but lions weren't the only dangerous game we might encounter. The saltbush forests easily conceal elephant, Cape buffalo, and the hippopotamus, which kills more people in Africa than any other animal. Since Tropical Ice started running safaris in 1979, Iain's guards have rarely had to fire over the heads of elephant, and never shot a lion, but they have had to kill six hippos, which are very territorial and very aggressive.

With Hassan on point and Adan as rear guard, we waded warm, silty Galana to the north side, Iain instructing us to stay close together so we sounded not like seven average-size things but like one big thing—an elephant—to deter crocodiles. We saw one of the reptiles, a nine- or ten-footer, a quarter of an hour after we'd forded. Alarmed by our approach, it crawled quickly away, its plated tail sweeping behind. We continued upriver, toward the Sobo rocks, and ran into a dozen hippos, entirely submerged except for the tops of their dark heads and their piggish, protruding eyes. They tolerated our photographing them for a while, but when we crept closer, one big bull lunged from the water with astonishing speed for so cumbersome a creature, his cavernous mouth open and bellowing. Only a warning, which we heeded by moving on.

The morning was overcast and breezy. An African fish eagle glided over the Galana, while a fan of pale gold sunlight spread through the clouds to eastward. By ten o'clock the air was hot and searing—reminiscent of Arizona in July. But we had the whole immense wild to ourselves, because most modern tourists are unwilling to walk miles in triple-digit temperatures, and too timid to confront wild creatures on foot. What a difference to observe game on their own terms. To photograph them, we had to read the wind as the hunter does, and practice stealth and keep our eyes peeled for the slightest motion. We stalked up close to a band of Cape buffalo, and a small elephant herd, and the experience was far more satisfying than driving up to them. Sweating, exercising caution and bushcraft, we *earned* the right to bag them on film.

We were on the last mile of the trek when we found pug marks in the sand, leading straight along the shore toward a grove of doum palm some three hundred yards away. They were deep and well defined, that is, recent. Iain and I fell into a discussion as to how recent. Clive, looking ahead with the naked eye, said they were very recent, because two lions were laid up under the palms. Clive pointed, and Iain and I raised our binoculars.

"It's a log," I said, "a big palm log."

Iain concurred.

"I am telling you, lions," Clive insisted, peevishly. "Two bloody lions. One's maned, too."

Then Adan said, "Lions, one hundred percent," but he spoke a little too loudly. The log lifted its head.

My binoculars framed an atypical Tsavo lion, a Metro-Goldwyn Mayer lion with a golden mane, lying in the shade with his companion and gazing straight back at us. With the palms overhead, the scene looked biblical.

The easterly wind favored us. We began a stalk, heading up over the embankment to approach the lions from above, Rob and I with our cameras ready, Adan with his rifle at low port, prepared to shoot if necessary. Hassan's was braced on his shoulder, the muzzle pointing backward at the rest of us. Iain, directly behind him, pushed the rifle barrel aside. Hassan shifted the FN to his crooked arms, holding it upside down as if he were cradling a baby, and sauntered along like a man strolling in Hyde Park instead of in Tsavo, with two big lions just ahead. A less-than-inspiring guard. I decided to grab his rifle if I had to.

We filed along a game trail between the saltbush and the riverbank, closing the distance. The idea was to capture an image of lions up close and personal and while on foot. All right, what was the difference between a picture taken from a car and one taken on foot? I don't know, only that there seemed to be a difference. Was it necessary?

Was it stupid? In today's America, where every red-blooded American boy and girl wants to be a dot-com entrepreneur and what used to be called "manly courage" is considered atavistic, the moral equivalent of a prehensile tailbone, I suppose it would be considered unnecessary, stupid, and, worst of all, unprofitable. But listen to the ancient Roman stoic Epictetus: "Reflect that the chief source of all evils to man, and of baseness and cowardice, is not death, but the *fear* of death. Against this fear, then, I pray you, harden yourself; to this let all your reasonings, your exercises, your reading tend." Still true, I'd say. The point of life is not success in e-commerce, or in any sort of commerce; it is to be brave; it is to master fear of death, which is the genesis of all fears. And one of the exercises by which you steel yourself to that fear is to confront something that could break your neck with a swipe of its paw.

I don't wish to exaggerate the emotions of the moment. None of us was trembling. We were apprehensive instead, in the old sense of the word. We *apprehended,* in a state of heightened awareness, alert to every sound and movement. Coming abreast of the palm grove, Iain walked in a crouch, and we followed suit, trailing him and Hassan over the lip of the embankment to look down into the pool of shade beneath the trees. I raised my camera.

I hate to end this episode on an anticlimatic note, but the lions were gone. They must have fled at the sound of our voices, though we never saw them move. We could not find their tracks. It was as though they had dematerialized.

The next day, we planned to head downriver, in the hope, if not the expectation, of seeing the lean lioness and her cubs once again.

The two elephant skulls, relics from the poaching days, humped out of the grass like white boulders. A plover had built its nest in one of the eye sockets. Ahead lay a pile of fresh elephant dung, flecked with undigested grass and seeds, which hornbills feed on and then spread across the savanna with their own droppings. Elephants are the architects of Tsavo's environment; eliminate them and everything changes, and not for the better. A very old rhino skull was nearby, a memorial to an ecological holocaust—man-made, of course—and a reminder of the fate that nearly befell the elephant, and might still, if the ivory ban is lifted. When Iain's mother and father emigrated to Kenya from England in 1956, rhino were so abundant that Iain and his brother used to count them on family vacation drives from Nairobi to Mombasa. Leslie, my wife, remembers seeing more than a few of the animals in 1972, when she took a five-week safari through Kenya, Uganda, and Tanzania (a then-twenty-three-year-old Iain Allan had guided her and her group up Mount Kilimanjaro). Today, rhino in Kenya are more rare than bison in the American West; in two decades, they were poached almost to extinction for their horns, which were ground up into medicinal and aphrodisiac powders for sale in the Far East, or used to make dagger handles coveted by oil-rich tribesmen in Yemen and the Arabian peninsula. A rhino restoration program is currently under way in Tsavo, with a few surviving animals held in a protected release area, but Iain said he had not seen one in the wild for fifteen years.

Two hours into the trek, we found evidence of an old lion kill: the skull and horns of a big Cape buffalo, resting in the grass beside a *lugga,* or dry streambed. Iain and Clive poked around, studying the area like homicide detectives.

"Probably an old bull, alone," said Iain. "The lions were down in the *lugga,* behind that big bush, two to three of them. They sprang at the buffalo from the side, just as he was about to come down the bank."

But that was all we saw of lions that morning. By eleven o'clock, with my shirt soaked through with sweat and my eyeballs feeling sunburned, we crossed back to the south side of the Galana, where Simon picked us up in a Land Cruiser (it had replaced the ailing Land Rover; Tsavo is tough on trucks, too). We learned from Simon that we need not have walked eight miles to find lions; they had found us. Only forty-five minutes after we left, four males appeared on the north side of the river, almost directly across from camp. Simon thought they had moved off.

I took a nap after lunch, took some notes, then sat shirtless and shoeless in my camp, my baked brain a perfect tabula rasa. Iain appeared, walking fast over the Bermuda grass. Gesturing, he told us in a whisper to follow him to his tent, and to be quiet. The four lions had reappeared.

With cameras and binoculars, we ran on tiptoe and squatted down. Across the river, between two and three hundred yards downcurrent, two of the four were crouched on the bank, drinking. Their hides so matched the sand and beige rock that they seemed made of the same stuff. I put the binoculars on them. They lacked manes, and I would have thought they were females, but their size suggested otherwise. Thirst slaked, one turned and padded up the bank, and it was clear that he was a male. He disappeared into a clump of doum palm; the second drank a while longer, then joined his friend. A moment later, the first lion emerged to walk slowly into the saltbush behind the palms, the other following shortly afterward, and then a third.

"See how relaxed they are?" said Iain, softly. "They're not acting as if they're aware we're here. If they are, and they're this casual about it, we may have some major problems tonight."

Now the fourth lion showed up, just as I got out of my seat to fetch my field notes from my tent. He caught the movement and stopped, turning his head to face in our direction. I eased back down, carefully raised the binoculars, and had the unsettling impression that I was staring into the lion's face, and he into mine, from a distance of, say, ten yards. Crouched low, the joints of his bent forelegs forming triangles, his shoulders a mound of muscle, sinews and tendons twisting like aircraft cable under his skin, he was so still that he could have been a carving. Like the others, he had no mane.

No one knows the reason for this trait. It is thought by some that it evolved in Tsavo males because a mane is a liability in the thick, thornbush country. Another theory is that pride lions on the plains sport manes as symbols of power and health to attract females and warn off rival males. A mane would be useless for those purposes in Tsavo, where vision is often limited to a few yards. However, bald male lions occur through sub-Saharan Africa, though they tend to be found most frequently in harsh, scrub-bush habitats similar to Tsavo's. What's really intriguing is that some experts in leonine behavior believe they have identified a historical trend in man-eating, which can be traced geographically to such environments. Their findings are preliminary, but if they are correct, maneless lions could be more likely to prey on humans.

Take the "Man-eater of Mfuwe," which devoured six people in Luanga National Park, a bushy region of Zambia nearly a thousand miles from Tsavo. It was shot by Wayne Hosek, a California investment analyst and sportsman, in September 1991. Four feet even at the shoulder and ten feet, six inches from its nose to the tip of its tail, it weighed five hundred pounds—the biggest man-eating lion on record. It had no mane.

The nature of the environment, the size of the lion, the absence of a mane—Hosek's trophy fit in with the theories. I reflected on that, gazing at the big fellow across the river. He crept down to the edge of the bank, lowered his head, and drank, pausing to look at us again. He then leisurely climbed back up and lay down in the shade. If he was concerned about us, he didn't show it.

"What did you mean, if they know we're here and are casual about it that we could be in for problems tonight?" I whispered to Iain.

"They won't attack, but they could come into camp."

He didn't say what led him to make so confident a prediction, and I didn't ask.

After dinner, we sat around the campfire and were entertained by Clive, a yarn-spinner and a terrific mimic of Australian accents and British brogues. Afterward, Iain, who has an encyclopedic knowledge of contemporary pop music and is an avid reader of literary fiction, talked rock groups with Rob and books with Leslie and me. In the middle of this erudite discussion, the lions began to roar from across the river. It was a sound like no other, deep and resonant.

The finish line for the previous day's walk was the jump-off point for the next. Driving there, we saw two of the lion quartet on a beach, quite a ways off, but they were soon gone. From eight in the morning till noon, we trudged ten miles to Sala Hill, rising as a perfect pyramid out of the savanna, but could not find the pride the four males and the scruffy lioness belonged to.

We made a more concentrated effort the following day, beginning at the spot where we had seen the female and cubs cross the Galana. Distinct pug marks were printed in the fine sand near a stand of doum palm. The strong sundowners in Tsavo scour animal tracks pretty quickly, so the prints must have been made the previous night or early in the morning. There were more on the sandbar, where the cubs had cavorted with their mother three days earlier, and on the opposite bank. One set of tracks led us into the saltbush, and to a lion's daybed—a patch of flattened grass and dirt—but we lost them farther on, where the earth was hard as pavement and covered with foot-high yellow grass.

"You can see why that dumb movie called them ghosts," Iain said, referring to *The Ghost and Darkness*. "They're always in ambush mode. They stay hidden, come out to hunt and kill, then hide again. They *are* ghosts."

His commentary was borne out a little farther upriver, when we struck the track of the two males spotted from the car the previous day. Again, we followed it, again we lost it. The lions could have been anywhere or nowhere. As Adan pushed into the saltbush, his rifle at the ready, I compared Tsavo lions not to ghosts but to the Vietcong: masters of concealment, of hit and run, showing themselves only when they chose. I was beginning to appreciate what Colonel Patterson had endured a century ago. It was an adventure for me to track these lions, but I would not have wanted to be charged with the task of finding and killing them.

We continued upriver, splitting up for a while, with Iain and Hassan tracking on the land side of the saltbush corridor, Clive, Adan, Leslie, and me on the river side (Rob was at park headquarters, photographing Kusimba and Sam Andanje). The sand was almost white and crunched underfoot like snow on a subzero day. More lion tracks vanishing on broad terraces of sandstone fissured so symmetrically they appeared to be man-made. Joining up again, we went on. Still, no lions, then Adan found another set of prints.

"These are very new," whispered Iain, pointing at one. "This is now."

A dry wind blew through the acacia, the palm fronds rattled. A sand grouse, flushing five feet away, made me flinch. Great predators can make their presence known, even when they aren't seen or heard. When such monarchs are near, your senses quicken, for the simple reason that your life may depend on it. I had experienced that keenness of perception several times in Alaska, coming upon grizzly tracks, and once in Arizona, crossing the fresh prints of a cougar while I was quail hunting, but I'd never experienced it as deeply as in those haunted thickets of Tsavo. But there was something else as well. To walk unarmed in the lion's kingdom demands a submission not unlike the submission required of us in the presence of the divine, and it graces those who walk there with the humility that is not humiliation. I was acutely aware of being in a place where I, as a man did not hold dominion, but had to cede dominion to a thing grander, stronger, and more adept than I.

Iain stopped suddenly, wrinkled his nose, and said, "Smell that?"

I shook my head. My sense of smell was the one that had not been heightened; I suffer from allergies. In fact, my nose had started to run, and here's an interesting factoid: one of the things I'm allergic to is cats.

"A kill. There's something dead, rotting in there," said Iain, gesturing at a thicket.

Then the wind eddied a bit, and I caught it—a stink a little like skunk, a little like week-old garbage.

Adan and Hassan pushed into the saltbush, while we who were unarmed waited in the open. When the two rangers emerged, several minutes later, they reported they had found nothing except hyena and jackal tracks, indicating that the carcass, wherever it was, had been abandoned by the lions and was now the property of scavengers.

The trek ended at the palm grove across from camp, where the four males had laired up. A lot of pug marks, dark stains in the sand where the lions had urinated, but nothing more.

The next day was just as fruitless, as far as lions went, but we did see a wild rhino, breaking Iain's fifteen-year record. The day after, we ended up in the saltbush where the lioness had stashed her cubs. We made our way through, not talking, watching where we stepped, looking for tracks, then entered a grove of old doum palm.

"Make a perfect movie set, wouldn't it?" Clive whispered. The trunks of the high trees were worn smooth, where elephants had rubbed up against them, and the lanes between the trees were like shadowy halls, some blocked by flood-wrack from the rainy season: barricades of logs and fronds, behind which a dozen lions could have lurked unseen. We expected to hear a low, menacing growl at any moment, an expectation that was not fulfilled until, making a circle, we came out of the trees and reentered the saltbush. The sound wasn't a growl, however; more of a loud grunt or bellow.

What happened next happened all at once. A cloud of dust rose from behind a thicket, Adan whipped around, leveling his rifle, and Iain said, "Get behind me!" to Leslie and me. Just as we did, certain that we were about to be charged by a lion, an elephant appeared, not twenty yards to our right. It was a young female of some two or three tons, shaking her head angrily, her ears flared. She stomped and scuffed the earth, then started toward us. Adan fired a shot over her head to scare her off. She stood her ground and let out a trumpet, her ears flaring again, dust rising from her feet, dust spewing from her hide as she tossed her great head back and forth. Iain yelled to Adan in Swahili. He fired again, and for an instant I thought he'd shot her—some trick of light made a puff of dust flying from her shoulder look like the impact of a bullet. In the next instant, as the female ran off, I realized that he'd put the second round over her head.

Iain lit into Adan, all in Swahili, but it was plain that the ranger was getting a royal dressing-down. I couldn't understand why.

"Rangers are supposed to know that you don't have to shoot at an elephant to scare it off," Iain explained. "That female was old enough, about fifteen, to have seen other elephants shot by poachers. You had to have been here in the eighties to appreciate it. Elephants are traumatized by the sound of gunfire. They're very intelligent animals, and it's not necessary to fire over their heads. A hand clap will do it, or just waving your arms. What we try to do on a foot safari is to observe without disturbing the animals, and move on, without them ever being aware that humans are around."

Before heading back to Nairobi, we made a pilgrimage to the "Man-Eater's Den." Colonel Patterson's discovery of this cave in the Ngulia Hills, northwest of the railroad right-of-way, was the coda to his story, and our visit to it shall be the coda for this one.

After Patterson had eliminated the two "brutes," as he called the lions, work resumed on the Tsavo River bridge. While waiting for a shipment of construction materials he took a break to explore some rocky hills near his camp and to do some recreational hunting. He was in a dry riverbed, pursuing a rhino, when he spotted something that stopped him cold:

"I saw on the other side a fearsome-looking cave which seemed to run back for a considerable distance under the rocky bank," Patterson wrote. "Round the entrance and inside the cavern I was thunderstruck to find a number of human bones with here and there a copper bangle such as the natives wear. Beyond a doubt, the man-eaters' den!"

After taking a photograph (which is printed in *The Man-Eaters of Tsavo*), he left his find, and from that day in early 1899 until recently, its location was lost to history. Patterson's characterization of it as a lion's den has aroused controversy and skepticism among naturalists and zoologists for a century: lions are not known to be denning animals (the tale of Daniel in the lion's den notwithstanding).

In 1995, as part of its Tsavo lion research project, the Field Museum team decided to find the cave and determine if it really had been occupied by lions. That year and the next, Dr. Kusimba, Dr. Kerbis-Peterhans, Gnoske, and Andanje made extensive searches southwest of the Tsavo

River bridge—the direction Patterson said he'd followed on his excursion. Nothing was found until March 1997, when Gnoske, after rereading Patterson's descriptions and comparing them to the landscape, realized that Patterson's directions had been way off: the "rocky hills" mentioned in the book were not *south*west but *north*west of the bridge.

The day after making that determination, Gnoske, Kerbis-Peterhans, and Andaje found a cave in a shady riverbed only a mile from the bridge. It perfectly matched the one in Patterson's photograph. The man-eater's den had been rediscovered after ninety-eight years.

But *was* it a man-eater's den? For two years, the team sifted through the dirt to recover human bones and examine them for tooth marks; if there were any, the researchers could determine if they had been made by lions, hyenas, or leopards. They looked for the copper bangles and artifacts Patterson had seen, as well as for human teeth, to distinguish between Asians and Africans; Asian teeth would be all but incontrovertible proof that the victims had been the Indian railway workers.

The result of all that work was surprising, and a little disappointing. Kusimba's conclusion is that the legendary cave never was a lion's den nor any sort of den, but in all likelihood a traditional burial cave of the ancient Taita people, who once inhabited the Tsavo region.

When Rob was photographing at park headquarters, Kusimba took him to the cave. Now Rob would show it to us. Entering the gate to Tsavo West, we drove on to an abandoned airstrip and parked. Iain and Clive, who had never seen the cave, were as eager for a look as Leslie and I. So, with Rob in the lead, the two guides became the guided. After thrashing around for a while, we came to a ravine. Rob shouted from up ahead, "Here it is!"

And there it was, with a corridor between two big boulders leading beneath an overhang and into a cavern. A fig tree spread its branches above, its roots clinging like tentacles to one side of the entrance.

"Well, I don't think it looks so fearsome," said Iain, who doesn't have a high opinion of Patterson, considering him to have been an imperial martinet, a so-so hunter, and something of a grandstander.

I agreed that the cool, shady spot was almost idyllic. But we were there on a magazine assignment. We were not trying to build a bridge in the African wilderness and, at the same time, hunt down two clever cats that were using our workforce as a fast-food restaurant. To

Patterson, with his memories of his workers' screams, of his servant's gruesome remains, of the tense, interminable nights waiting with his rifle, the cave would have appeared "fearsome." And given the ignorance about lion behavior that prevailed in his time, it was understandable why he mistook a burial cave for a man-eater's den. Imperial martinet or not, he did pretty damned well with what he had.

That said, I did find Patterson's characterization of his adversaries as brutes and outlaws objectionable. I recalled our second to last morning in Tsavo, as we sat in camp and watched a zebra herd warily come down the far bank of the Galana to drink. They had been waiting on the ledge above the river for a long time, suffering from what Iain termed "the paradox of survival." The animals were parched, but feared that a lion or crocodile was waiting for them at river's edge, for lions and crocs know that zebras must drink eventually. And so, the whole herd stood still, gazing at the river with what seemed to us equal measures of longing and dread, until the desperation of their thirst overcame their fear. They did not rush down with abandon, but watered in orderly stages. A dozen or so animals would drink, while the others waited their turn and the stallions stood watch. If one group got greedy and took too long, the stallions would let out a series of loud, sharp brays. It was a strange, distressful sound, falling somewhere between a whinny and a bark.

Even a layman should not anthropomorphize, but to me, the stallions seemed to be saying, "You've had enough, get a move on, we don't have much time." In a way, I identified with them. They were lion prey, and out there, so was I; but that recognition did not offend my sense of human dignity. The offense was to my human pride. Nothing wrong with pride, except when it becomes excessive and denies others, whether men or beasts, the right to their pride and dignity. If I had been in Colonel Patterson's boots, I would have pursued the lions with as much determination after all, his first responsibility was to finish the bridge and protect his workmen's lives—but I don't think I would have regarded the lions as savage brutes violating some law of heaven. If anything, they had been obeying the fundamental law of all creation, which is survival.

To realize that I shared something in common with the wary, anxious zebras was not degrading, but merely to acknowledge my true place in nature where nature is wild, the stage on which the drama of predator and prey is played out.

dark skies of sudan

2 0 0 1

There is the Africa tourists know—elephant herds, tawny lions, torrents of wildebeest surging across the Serengeti—and then there's the Africa passing twenty thousand feet below, the Africa Africans have to live with, boiling with intractable civil wars, oppressed by kleptocratic regimes, suffering from hunger and epidemics: all the biblical curses and probably a few the Bible's authors hadn't thought of.

Sudan, the biggest country on the continent (as big as the U.S. east of Mississippi), has all those afflictions in proportion to its size. One million square miles of misery. The mostly black southern Sudanese, either Christian or animist, have been fighting the Arab, Muslim northerners, who rule this vast country, for thirty-six of the forty-six years since independence from Great Britain (a decade-long armistice that ended in 1983 was nothing more than a long intermission in this colossal tragedy). More than two million people have died, if not from bombs and bullets then from the famines and disease spawned by the conspiracy of war, drought, and flood. The United Nations classifies southern Sudan as a region in a state of chronic emergency, and has been sending food, medicine, clothing and other assistance into the south for a dozen years.

It's routine, a way of life, and this flight, Foxtrot-12, is a routine airdrop of food, sixteen tons of maize. The superannuated C-130 Hercules, once owned by Southern Air, the CIA's Central American airline, now belongs to TransAfrik, a cargo carrier on contract to the U.N. It flies out of the dusty, flyblown, rubbish-strewn Kenyan frontier town of Lokichokio, headquarters for the U.N. aid operation Operation Lifeline Sudan.

The bush pilots who deliver humanitarian aid into Sudan are a varied lot, ranging from shady buccaneers to airborne do-gooders to workaday aviators like the skipper of Foxtrot-12, Captain Bob Potyok, a fifty-nine-year-old Canadian and a veteran of African skies.

"Ethiopia, Rwanda, Angola, Sudan, all the fun spots," the mustached six-footer quips, smoking a cigarette as we wing westward through broken clouds. He adds quickly that that he prefers the term "blue-collar pilot" to "bush pilot," because the latter denotes some seat-of-the-pants throttle jockey

Bush or blue-collar, what all these flyboys (and girls) have in common is a willingness and an ability to fly in conditions that would give your average commercial airline pilot chest pains. Landings at dirt airstrips in the middle of nowhere, no control towers (except for the one at Loki), no ground radar or beacons.

Airspeed two hundred knots. The clouds part, revealing Nile River tributaries coiling back on themselves, and tree-speckled savannas and malarial swamps. Gradually, the C-130 descends from its cruising altitude, down to a thousand feet. Below are dome-shaped mud-and-wattle huts, the brindle backs of cattle, a robed herdsman, and ahead, a big white X marking the drop zone. An airdrop is not a simple maneuver. At an altitude of only seven hundred, the Herc has to be slowed to "stall plus twenty," meaning twenty knots above stall speed, and its nose brought up precisely eight degrees, turning the plane into a kind of airborne chute.

The altimeter winds downward, a thousand feet, eight-eighty, Potyok turning tightly to make his pass, one hand on the wheel, the other on the throttle levers. In the first-officer's seat, Capt. J. B. Ramos, a fifty-four-year-old Filipino, watches Potyok's performance. This is a "check flight" for the Canadian, a kind of examination, and Ramos, with twenty thousand hours of experience flying Hercs, is his examiner.

The DOOR OPEN light flashes on the instrument panel. Away aft, the rear hatch drops, revealing a square of sky, against which the two loadmasters, tethered to the plane by static lines, stand silhouetted. The cargo bay is filled with two long rows of pallets, piled high with white sacks, marked with WFP for "World Food Program" in blue letters. Potyok pulls back on the wheel, adjusts the flaps. The huge plane's nose tilts upward, the loadmasters jerk the restraining hooks, and half the load tumbles out, the sacks falling like giant snowflakes.

Potyok makes a tight turn to check the drop. It's on the money. Another pass, and again the nose goes up, Potyok calling to the load-masters through his radio headset, "Commence drop, go, go, go!" And the second half of the load slides out, the pallets rattling on metal rollers.

"Load away," the chief loadmaster informs the pilot as another blizzard of maize falls through the sky.

The second drop is as accurate as the first. This particular crew is proud of its record: a ninety-eight per cent recovery rate, meaning that only two per cent of its cargoes miss the DZ.

Potyok throttles up, the Herc climbs to cruising altitude and heads back for Loki, the crew eating lunch as the autopilot takes over. The whole operation has been slightly more exciting than a delivery by United Parcel Service, which suits Potyok and Ramos just fine. In their profession, an adventure usually means a catastrophe, or something close to it.

With her short, blond hair, fair complexion, and brilliant smile, Heather Stewart could easily be a hostess at a Sussex garden party. In fact, she is the premier bush pilot in Kenya and Sudan, a direct spiritual descendant of Beryl Markham, the pioneering aviatrix who captivated Hemingway and wrote *West with the Night*. It's difficult to believe that Stewart is sixty-one years old; she not only looks much younger, she lives like someone half her age, piloting small planes into a war zone three or four times a week, across hundred of miles of wild country.

I returned to Africa two weeks ago, interested in fliers like her and Potyok, who endure hardships and take risks to save the Sudanese from the scourges of war and nature—and sometimes from themselves. These aviators don't *have* adventures—discrete episodes of excitement in otherwise humdrum lives—their daily lives *are* an adventure, one with an ostensibly noble purpose. I wondered why they did what they did. Were they secular missionaries who delivered food, medicine, and clothing instead of the Word of God? Were they motivated by the allure of danger—or of making a good buck? (Relief work pays much better than you might think, with food monitors earning sixty thousand dollars a year, skilled pilots up to twice that.) Not surprisingly, I've discovered that most were people who hoped to satisfy the needs of conscience and pocketbook simultaneously—doing well while doing good. I'm also here to investigate sinister rumors that some pilots, under the guise of delivering humanitarian aid, are smuggling arms and ammunition to the Sudanese rebels, collectively known as the Sudanese People's Liberation Army (SPLA).

Potyok and his crew gave me a look at Sudan from high altitude, but if I really want to understand the world of relief pilots, I'm going to have to get a view of Sudan from the ground—if I can find a relief plane that has room for excess baggage like a journalist. So far, I've been bumped off one flight into Blue Nile province, scene of some recent heavy fighting, and another flight into Jonglei province has been scrubbed. That's why I'm talking to Stewart. I've been told that if I'm going into Sudan, then she's the one who can get me there, the one I want behind the controls. Accept no substitutes.

We are sitting beside the swimming pool in the compound Stewart built as living quarters for the expatriate fliers and relief workers based in Lokichokio. There are several such compounds, but Trackmark Camp (Trackmark is the name of Stewart's aviation company) is considered the Ritz of the lot. With its bar and pool, its stone-walled bungalows and hibiscus, it's an oasis in what is otherwise a squalid settlement of Turkana tribesmen: tin-roofed shacks and shanties, crowded warrens of tukuls that look like umbrella tents made of twigs and straw. Scrawny goats and emaciated cattle wander the dirt streets, the air stinks of human and animal shit, garbage festers every-where, under reefs of flies. Loki, as it's known, sits beneath the Mogila Hills, on a thornbush plateau in Kenya's harsh, drought-stricken northwest. It's as dangerous as it is filthy. I've been warned not to leave the compound at night. The Turkana are avid bandits, mostly because the drought has decimated their herds and made them desperate. Only the day before, a car carrying four people was ambushed not far from town. The driver was killed, the passengers robbed, right down to their shoes. To make matters even more tense, the Turkana are at war with a neighboring tribe, the Toposa, and nightly gun battles provide back-ground noise to conversations around the expat bars. This is not the Kenya that the Kenyan Tourist Bureau advertises abroad.

Stewart is sometimes called "All-Weather Heather," a nickname created more for its rhyme than to intimate that she'll fly through thunderclouds. She's a careful pilot, meticulous about maintenance, because she can't afford not to be. Flying into dirt airstrips where runway lights are as rare as whiskey in a Shiite household provides enough excitement without the additional thrill of an engine failure caused by negligence. There is also the chance the airstrip might be under fire. Just finding the right one is a trick—Stewart still navigates by dead reckoning. Follow your compass. Check your speed, calculate your time, figure out where you are, pray that you're right.

Her meticulous approach to preparation hasn't always inoculated her to the unpredictability of flying in Africa. She's experienced the usual bush pilot woes—flat tires, flat batteries, radios that break down, villagers siphoning paraffin-based aviation fuel from airstrip drums to light their lamps—and some unusual woes as well.

"One time, I was flying three C-130 Hercules pilots, an American, a German, and a Belgian. We were going to different airstrips to see which were suitable for a Hercules. We got to a town called Akabo. No one had flown there for ten years. The strip looked dry and landable, but there was only a dry crust on top, and underneath, black cotton soil. I was flying a Cessna 402, its nose wheel and undercarriage weren't suitable for rough airfields, and we got stuck." She says this in the offhand manner one might use in describing, say, a fender-bender in a parking lot. "We couldn't take off and no one could come in. We had no food except some biscuit, and we drank river water, purifying it with tablets. I radioed for a food and water drop, but it was three days before anyone could get anything to us."

The airstrip had been the scene of a recent battle in which SPLA rebels had driven off the government forces, she says. "There were thousands of mosquitoes and the heat was terrible and there was always the fear that government forces would come back and attack. There were many dead bodies lying about, and you can imagine what that was like. The German was a survival expert, but then he got bitten by a scorpion and was in a great deal of pain. The plane with the food and water dropped morphine, and we shot him up with so much of it that he got stoned. Finally, one of the Catholic missions was able to get a helicopter to us. I stripped the radio from the Cessna, and we got out. It was quite good to change my clothes and have a bath."

Like Markham before her, she is a product of the British Empire. Though born in England, she was raised in Nigeria and came to Kenya on a visit when she was eighteen, married a much older army officer, bore two children, got divorced, caught the flying bug on a bush flight to Lake Turkana, married a second time, had two more children, and earned her pilot's license—all by the time she was twenty-five. Five years and one more child later, she was flying white hunters into Sudan—good years she says now, staying in hunting camps for a week or more, floating down the Nile in river barges, in search of lion, elephant, and antelope.

After a decade as a company pilot for foreign firms—"Quite boring," Stewart says—and a stint flying for film director David Lean (*Lawrence of Arabia*), she took to delivering khat into Somalia. The mild narcotic is legal there, and is the drug of choice among the teetotaling Muslim Somalis. She had a couple of kids in school in England, and needed the money, but this was the 1980s and Somalia was devolving from a country into a congeries of warring fiefdoms. One day, she was refueling her plane at a Somali airfield.

"I never had enough fuel for a round trip, you see, and I had to get out on the wing with jerry cans. Well, a gun battle between warlords broke out then, and there were bullets whizzing all around.

"I finished up and got in the cockpit—my plane had six bullet holes in it, and a bullet passed right through the cockpit, past the back of my head. Missed me by that much"—spreading her thumb and forefinger—"That made me think, so when somebody said, 'Go fly in Sudan, they really need people there,' I went. It was safer than Somalia and more predictable."

Which, I think, speaks volumes about what Somalia was like.

Stewart and an American bush pilot, Jim Gaunt, helped establish the Lokichokio airfield for the U.N. in 1989, the year she founded Trackmark. At that time, she says, almost wistfully, "It was just me and my airplane." That year marked two other, larger beginnings: the current Islamic government in Khartoum seized power in a coup and declared the war in the south to be a jihad, and the United Nations inaugurated its humanitarian airlift. During the past twelve years, the government has pursued policies nothing short of criminal. It denies aid to southern Sudan's victims of hunger and disease and drops cluster bombs on churches, missions, and defenseless villages, massacring thousands of people and driving thousands more from their homes, into concentration camps or into the bush. It has even revived an ancient practice: squadrons of Arab horsemen are sent to raid southern towns, where they kill the elderly and men of fighting age and capture young women and children to sell into chattel slavery. The slaves are beaten, branded, and often forced to convert to Islam.

On its part, the U.N., through its World Food Program, UNICEF, and dozens of nongovernmental organizations under U.N. auspices, has delivered a tonnage of aid that exceeds the amount flown during the Berlin airlift in 1948. There is a catch, however: an agreement the U.N. negotiated with Khartoum when the relief effort began. Under its terms, U.N. and U.N.-sponsored flights out of Lokichokio must file advance notice with the Sudanese government, which then gives or withholds clearance to land.

Whether it gives or withholds, the government often benefits from this arrangement, because food, clothing, and medicine are weapons in Khartoum's arsenal. With prior knowledge of where an aid flight is to land or airdrop supplies, it can dispatch militia units to seize them. The SPLA rebels control vast parts of the south. In response, the government frequently prohibits relief flights from landing in SPLA-dominated regions or in areas where it's trying to starve the southerners into submission. The U.N.'s compliance with the agreement has created a kind of vacuum of mercy that's been filled by a number of maverick operations that work outside the U.N. umbrella. Renegade aviation companies, teamed up with privately funded nongovernmental organizations, deliver their cargoes to the no-fly zones in defiance of Khartoum's warnings that their planes will be shot out of the sky. The pilots and crews call it "flying on the dark side." Some pilots on these missions file false flight plans or no flight plans at all, to reduce the risk of being shot down or being captured when on the ground.

Stewart has flown on the "light side," ferrying supplies to approved airstrips on U.N. contracts, but she also flies on the dark side for groups beyond the pale of U.N. oversight. In her early days, she did a lot of flying for Catholic missionary priests in Sudan's Western Equatoria province. Stewart would take off before dawn on the two-hour flights, land, throw camouflage netting over her aircraft, and leave at night, guiding on a flashlight held by someone standing at the end of the runway. To honor her efforts, the missionaries brought her to Rome for a private audience with Pope John Paul. This good Protestant woman knelt and kissed his ring, but, to make sure all religious bases were covered, she later flew the archbishop of Canterbury on a tour of south Sudan.

These days, she ferries other kinds of Christians who are on Khartoum's hit list. One group is Christian Solidarity International, a Zurich-based organization that redeems Sudanese slaves, buying them back from their former masters through middlemen, and then setting them free. The government of Sudan has responded by putting a price on the heads of two of its leaders, an American human rights activist, John Eibner, and Baroness Caroline Cox, a member of the British House of Lords; when Stewart flies them on redemption missions, she takes off from super-secret locations inside Kenya—there are too many Sudanese spies in Loki.

Though Stewart says she strives to stay neutral and to avoid "getting caught up in the glamour of the cause," she confesses that she flies medevacs for wounded guerrillas when called upon. "I always make sure to carry a jar of Vicks with me," she says airily. "I put a little in each nostril. The stench of gangrene can be overwhelming in a small plane."

On other occasions, her passengers have been John Garang, the SPLA commander in chief, and his staff officers and bodyguards. "There are all these big guys with guns on your plane, and when you land, more guys with guns, all over the place. It's flying dangerously, it's quite a buzz, really. I'd much rather do that than fly a bunch of fat tourists to look at lions."

She volunteers that there is one thing she won't do for the SPLA— deliver weapons. "I've been asked to but I don't," she says. "Not for moral reasons. It would be reported if you flew arms, you'd get known for that, and people wouldn't fly with you, because it's too big a risk. I've flown contracts with the U.N., and I would have lost all that work if I were known as a gunrunner."

By this time, I've confirmed that those rumors of gunrunning relief pilots are true, and I ask Stewart why she thinks they do it. "They do it for the money," she answers crisply. "If they say it's for any other reason, it's just bullshit." But with reflection, she concedes that there may be other motives as well. "They like to think they're getting away with something. What is forbidden is always more attractive."

The gunrunners themselves offer more complex reasons for taking such huge risks. It can be argued that Khartoum turns a blind eye to unauthorized flights like the kind Stewart makes into no-fly zones. The government may be reluctant to carry out its threat to shoot down aircraft carrying grain or vaccines or blankets, for fear of adding to

Sudan's reputation as a rogue nation. So most renegade aviators fly not so much on the dark side as in a gray zone, not quite "legitimate," not quite outlaws. But those who smuggle arms to the SPLA operate in what is unquestionably the contrabander's night, where the world of the missionary meets the world of the mercenary and men who are a little bit of both, for the love of the southerners' cause or the love of money or the love of risk or the love of all three, have decided that doing the right thing means more than helping to feed Sudan's hungry, heal its sick, clothe its naked.

I met two of them in Nairobi, and they gave me a glimpse into the shadows.

Through a haze of cigarette smoke, I watched a shaky video image of an Antonov descending out of the morning light, its nose wheel reaching for the airstrip, a red scratch on the face of the savanna. As the Russian-built cargo plane rolled to a stop, her twin turbo props churned up a maelstrom of laterite dust that caused the men waiting on the ground to turn their heads aside. There were about twenty of them, all dressed in jungle-green camouflage and armed with AK-47s, except for two who wore pistols and the scarlet berets that identify high-ranking officers in the SPLA.

The officers approached the aircraft after the engines shut down and the five Russian crewmen filed out the door. The Russians were flying for Relief-Link Limited, a company owned by my chain-smoking host, a Kenyan named Patrick Butler, but better known to his compatriots as "Papa Bear" for his bulk: he's six foot one and over 250 pounds, with powerful arms, a tree- stump neck, and a torso like a fifty-gallon drum. We sat watching the video in a house in an upscale Nairobi neighborhood near Relief-Link's office. Papa Bear and a freelance American flier named Dale Roark had been tutoring me about the relief effort in Sudan, liberally seasoning the facts with piquant observations about the war, the guerrillas, the Sudanese government, and the United Nations. They hoped this video of an actual gunrunning mission might illustrate the points they were trying to make.

Roark and Papa Bear became friends in the 1990s, when they worked together in another relief airline called 748 Air.

Butler's grandparents migrated to Kenya from the Seychelles Islands. With most of the world's races in his ancestry—white, black, and Asian—he has a burnt-sienna complexion, and is the eternal outsider, a man without a tribe in a country and society where tribe means everything. In a boyish voice that doesn't seem to belong to someone his size, he speaks of his commitment to the people of southern Sudan with a battered but still passionate idealism that belies the image of the gunrunner as sleazy merchant of death. There is something special about the southern Sudanese, he says, something that draws you in and compels you to do more than supply them with food, medicine, clothes.

"You see guys out there who've been fighting since they were fourteen and who can tell war stories all day that will curl your hair, but put a piece of ice in their hands and they're amazed. They've never seen or felt ice, they've never seen water turned to stone."

Roark, also a big man, though not as big as Papa Bear, would choke if you suggested that he was an idealist. He has elevated cynicism into something like a personal religion. He has no use for do-gooders of any stripe, considering himself a mercenary pilot who will fly for anyone, so long as the money's right. Once, back in 1973, he taught math and metalworking at an inner-city high school in Oklahoma City, because he wanted to help underprivileged kids, a lapse that the fifty-three-year-old pilot of fortune now blames on smoking too much bad dope in his youth. He quit teaching after two years, he says, in a southwestern drawl as thick and down-home as redeye gravy, "Because I realized I hated kids."

His evolution from world saver to cynic is, however, of more recent vintage. He describes it with a litany that is also a partial résumé of his flying career:

"Back when I was flyin' for the contras in Nicaragua, my mama would write and ask me, 'Dale [he pronounces it DAY-ull], what are you doin'?' I'd write her back and tell her, 'Mama, I'm flyin' good to the good and bad to the bad.' Later on, when I was flyin' photo-mapping missions in the Gulf War, which we fought for those useless Kuwaitis, I'd tell her, 'Mama, I'm flyin' good to the good and bad to the bad, but it sure is hard to tell the difference.' A while later, when I was in the war in Yemen, I told her I was flyin' good to the good and bad to the bad and there wasn't any difference. And now that I've been in Africa, I tell her, 'Mama, I'm flyin' bad to the bad because they're all bad.' "

There is a zest to Roark's jaded view of life in general and of Africa in particular. When he says that flying aid into Sudan accomplishes nothing except to give "high-paying jobs to third-world thugs," he seems to delight in the futility of it all. After listening to him for a while, I'd begun to wonder if his cynicism wasn't a tad artificial; not exactly a coat of protective armor around a vulnerable heart, but, rather, a prophylaxis against sentimentality. He's the kind of guy who wants to make sure that he never has any illusions, and God knows, foreigners who come to Africa with good intentions are full of illusions, which Africa inevitably crushes because Africa isn't kind to people with good intentions.

At any rate, Roark's actions often belie his words, because he is a walking contradiction. To begin with, he's a cowboy who likes to claim he's an Indian. Born and raised on a farm in western Oklahoma, he's mostly of Irish ancestry but gets a chuckle out of flashing a card proclaiming him a member of the Southern Cheyenne tribe, and he'll tell you with a barely discernible wink that he's descended from a Cheyenne woman who had been with Chief Black Kettle's band when it was attacked by Custer on the Washita River in 1868. Politically, Roark is a composite of a libertarian and a conservative Republican; but he once flew the Grateful Dead on tour and befriended Jerry Garcia, not exactly an icon of the Right. In keeping with his contrary nature, he has taken hair-raising chances on behalf of the southern Sudanese, despite his claims that he's allergic to altruism. In 1996, he and one other pilot were the only aviators willing to defy a Sudanese government blockade and fly food, blankets, and medicine to victims of a devastating flood in a town called Pochalla, on the Ethiopian border. For several weeks, risking ground fire as well as the hazards of landing at a dirt airstrip hemmed by floodwaters, Roark flew more than fifty missions, often in a dangerously overloaded plane. The head of one nogovernmental aid agency told me that hundreds of people owed their lives to Roark and the other pilot.

Still, Roark insisted that he hadn't stuck his neck out because his heart bled for the victims. Was it for the money? I asked. He shook his head, saying that the money was good, but not that good. Then what on earth was he doing here? His glance sliding off to the side, he fingered the bill of his baseball cap and grinned sheepishly. "Every morning I wake up wonderin' what I'm doing here. I honestly don't know."

Later on, I turned to Butler for an answer, but his wasn't much better. He saw no end to the crisis, no hope for peace. That was when he urged me to see the video of a mission he called "Operation Rescue," which had taken place only two weeks before I arrived in Nairobi.

The airfield where the Antonov had landed was near the town of

Yei, an SPLA stronghold about fifty miles north of the Uganda border, Butler said, and then identified some of the dramatis personae: "The captain's name is Alexander, and the first officer is Igor. That one, wearing the sunglasses, is Commander Gre [pronounced gear]. . ." Butler gestured at one of the rebel officers shown in the video. ". . . and the one next to him is Commander Weir. They're briefing Alex on the situation. It will be his decision to fly in or not."

After a few moments, the two commanders shook hands with Captain Alex. The tape cut to a guerrilla radioman, speaking into his field radio in the Dinka dialect. Most rebels belong to the Dinka tribe.

"Okay, so now Alex has agreed to fly the stuff in and the radio operator is telling the men that it's on the way," Papa Bear translated.

The camera panned to the edge of the airstrip and lingered, almost lovingly, on the stuff: seven tons of assault rifles, machine guns, mortars, mortar shells, rocket-propelled grenades, anti-tank mines, and small-arms ammunition in metal boxes stacked like bricks. I can't say that I was shocked to learn that the gunrunning rumors were true, but I was surprised that the two men were willing to show me clear documentation. It was the next best thing to being an eyewitness.

On screen, the rebel soldiers haphazardly loaded the weapons and ammunition into the Antonov, while Butler told me that the hardware had been brought across the border from Uganda by truck. This was where things really got complicated, so much so that Butler had to pause the video and explain the situation twice before I understood it.

Disunity, he said, is the curse of southern Sudan; there is not only a good deal of intertribal conflict, but *intra*tribal feuds and antagonisms are common as well. The weapons had been destined for SPLA forces operating on the west side of the White Nile. They generally got the lion's share of military hardware because Commander in Chief Garang was a Dinka from the west side of the river. Commanders Weir and Gre, however, were Dinka from the east side and directed operations there, as well as in the Nuba mountains. The Nuba is a remote, contested region that straddles northern and southern Sudan and controls land routes between Khartoum and the southern Sudanese oil fields. At the time the video was being shot, a Nuba town called Atar was under attack by government militia forces comprised mostly of turncoat Nuer tribesmen. At Atar, the Nuer militia outnumbered and outgunned the SPLA defenders. Commanders Weir and Gre felt that their men were more in need of the weapons and ammunition than Garang's, and so hijacked the shipment from their boss.

The video rolled again, showing the airstrip at Atar, hundreds of miles north of Yei. Low hills rose in the background; in the foreground, the Antonov was parked at a skewed angle at the very end of the runway, which had turned out to be three hundred meters shy of what the fully loaded Antonov needed to land. Captain Alex, in a nifty piece of bush flying, had avoided running off the airstrip into the surrounding scrub by ground-looping his plane: revving up one engine while throttling down the other, which causes the aircraft to make a U-turn.

Mortar or artillery fire thumped in the distance.

"They were very close," said Butler. "There was fighting on the airstrip only thirty or forty minutes later. If the Antonov had been delayed, the plane, the crew would have been overrun."

A couple of men were slashing the grass and brush to lengthen the runway so the plane could take off, while a platoon of guerrillas unloaded the cargo. These fighters were lean as underfed cats, and nowhere near as well turned out as those at Yei—the very image of ragged bush rebels. Several were armed only with spears.

"That's how desperate they were—" Butler again, his voice rising"—When the Nuer fight, there is no surrender. The Nuer will chase you into your house and under your bed to kill you. The Nubians were going to fight the Nuer militia with spears! It's better to fight and die, because there is nowhere to run."

As the weapons were distributed, village women ululated in celebration, their strange, warbling cries mingling with the muted thud of shellfire. Guerrillas shouted and embraced Captain Alex and his crew, then lay down their spears and ran off toward the front with their new AK-47s, RPD machine guns, mortars, and rocket-propelled grenades. In a twinkling, their mode of warfare had passed from the Bronze Age to the modern.

"That's what draws you in—you see the joy on their faces when a plane lands with cut flowers and canned sardines," Butler went on, explaining that planes flying gun runs carry weapons as "cut flowers" and ammunition as "canned sardines" on their cargo manifests.

As a code word, the latter made some literal sense—the ammo boxes did resemble oversize sardine cans—but the former seemed an odd designation for rifles and mortars. Roark cleared that up for me.

"Cut flowers are the gift that keeps on giving," he drawled.

And what happened at Atar? I asked as the screen went blank. The story had a happy ending. The gift that keeps on giving gave the rebels the means to fight off the militia attack. The town and its airstrip remained in SPLA hands. It was one very small triumph in a very long war, a triumph that Roark and Butler readily admitted was meaningless as far as the big picture went.

"Martin Luther King said that people with good intentions but limited understanding are more dangerous than people with total ill will." Butler, sipping the scotch I had brought him from the duty-free shop in London, was waxing philosophical. "When I first got into this business, I thought the U.N. and all the nongovernmental organizations were people with good intentions who didn't understand what the people really needed, like arms to defend themselves instead of medicines and tools they didn't know how to use. So I got involved in shit like this. I thought these SPLA guys were going to kick ass and liberate the south, but now, we've got Africans fighting Africans, and I realize it's hopeless."

Well, video or no video, I was no closer to answering my earlier questions. If anything, I had more. If the war was pointless, why help to perpetuate it by supplying weapons? If the southern Sudanese were third-world thugs who fought each other as much as they fought the government, why arm them? It had to be the money, right? How much did Relief-Link earn from a gun run like the one I'd just seen? Seventeen thousand dollars, Butler replied, but added quickly that his company had yet to be paid for the mission. Then Roark chimed in: just a few days ago, he had delivered six and a half tons of small-arms ammunition to Garang's forces, but he hadn't seen a dime. It was not unusual for the SPLA to renege on its bills, Roark added.

"Why are you guys telling me all this?" I asked.

"We knew you'd find out sooner or later," Butler replied amiably, "so we thought it would be better if you heard it from us first. We want you to know that we don't do it just for the money."

I politely suggested that I did not believe him. On average, an aid flight grosses between eight and ten thousand dollars. From an economic standpoint, it made more sense to fly in seven tons of weaponry for seventeen thousand than seven tons of sorghum for half that, even when you factored in the bonuses paid to air crews for the extra risks. And the risks of running guns into Sudan were so high that I didn't see how they could be run without a wholehearted commitment to the southerners' cause, or the hope of making a big, fast buck, or a little of both.

Then there were the knotty moral questions. A lot of relief agencies are catering a war: food intended for civilian mouths often ends up in the bellies of SPLA fighters. It's also true that rebels wounded in the conflict are treated at the International Red Cross hospital in Lokichokio. Are feeding the guerrillas and binding their wounds morally distinct from arming them? The line seemed awfully fine, yet it was there, and men like Butler were willing to cross it.

"You see things like at Atar—men with spears fighting men with guns," he said, "and you know you can't walk away. You see people who've survived massacres, you see hospitals bombed with chemical weapons, and you get roped in. You identify with the cause."

Roark, stretched out on the floor, looked at Papa Bear and then at me, and made sure to guard his reputation as a cynic with no allegiances.

"Patrick's got Sudan," he said. "Me, I'll fight any war."

Later that night, Roark and I had a drink at the venerable Aero Club at Nairobi's Wilson Airport. He filled in the blank spots in his biography and confessed he'd personally flown dozens of gun runs when he was with 748. He and a young American aid organizer, Kevin Ashley, set up the air-relief company in 1997. For Roark, it was one more episode in a career more checkered than a chess board.

He's a mustang. The word derives from the Spanish *musteno*— stray—and Dale Roark never did run with the herd of housebroken, nine-to-five males. It would be easier to imagine Clint Eastwood portraying Oscar Wilde than to picture Roark holding down a regular job or driving the kids to soccer practice. Even his fellow bush pilots, not a domesticated lot, think he's something of an outrider. Joe Peters, a Kenyan who is Butler's partner in Relief-Link, recalls the time he flew back from a mission with Roark.

"We were at twenty-one thousand feet, coming up on a helluva thunderstorm. What you're supposed to do is fly around it, but Dale said, 'Aw, hell, let's fly through it,' and we did. We were bouncing all over the place, and then the wings and the props started to ice up. I was flipping switches like mad, getting the pumps going full blast. When we flew out of the cloud, there was still ice on the wings, so Dale put her into a dive and down we flew into warmer air and melted the ice. Dale was laughing all the way."

Roark has flown in every kind of plane from Piper Cubs to 727s, logging so many hours that he's stopped booking them. He's crashed several planes and walked away. He's also crashed three marriages, and walked away from their wreckage as well. He's been shelled or shot at in more than one country, from the Congo to Somalia. At the controls of a 727, he rescued French civilians from Rwanda, two weeks after the Hutus started their genocidal campaign against the Tutsis.

"We had to taxi under mortar fire," he remembers. "There were at least three hundred dead Tutsis all around the terminal, and from what I heard about the way the Tutsis treated the Hutus, they deserved what they got."

As that comment suggests, Roark's opinions are so outrageous that he probably would draw grimaces from the producers of *Politically Incorrect*. But he makes no apologies, and like all good cowboys, he doesn't ask permission. A few years ago, after he crashed a plane in the Nuba mountains, he was summoned to the American Embassy in Nairobi.

"They told me I was prohibited from flying into the Nuba. They said they didn't need a dead American up there. I told them to go fuck themselves."

His father flew P-38s in World War Two and taught Roark to fly in a 1947 Piper Cub, out on the vast plains where Oklahoma rubs shoulders with the Texas Panhandle. At fourteen, he had a paper route, like a lot of American boys, except that he flew his in the Piper Cub, delivering the *Daily Oklahoman* to isolated ranches and farms. He did not get his pilot's license until he was seventeen, by which time, he says slyly, "I'd already bought and sold a couple of airplanes."

After taking a degree in aeronautical engineering at Oklahoma State University, Roark earned a master's in aviation education. His anomalous stint as an inner-city schoolteacher followed, then a string of aviation jobs. He flew crop dusters, flew for Haliburton in the Oklahoma and Texas oil fields, and delivered cargoes to Southern Air, the CIA airline that supplied the Nicaraguan contras. He flew for United Parcel and Emory, for NATO in Egypt and Chad, for the Saudi Arabian air force during the Gulf War, and for Executive Outcomes, the South African mercenary outfit.

Listening to his professional history, I figured that Roark would have to be 150 years old to have done all he claimed. I wondered how much of it to believe, but other pilots told me it's all true, if a bit embellished.

In the mid-1990s, Roark teamed up with Kevin Ashley. A tall, fair-haired Californian whose bland good looks belie a passionate temperament, Ashley had been a food monitor for the U.N.'s World Food Program, bitterly disillusioned with the organization's supine acceptance of Khartoum's rules. He became a gadfly around U.N. headquarters in Lokichokio, urging his superiors to drop their policy of artificial neutrality and take sides. When they didn't, he quit, and then found a mission for himself in the Nuba mountains.

The Sudan government was then fully embarked on its jihad to bring the entire country under Islamic law, but its motives in subduing the Nuba were more economic than ideological. To protect the oil fields south of the mountains from a potentially hostile population, Khartoum had ordered a campaign of systematic terror bombing to drive the Nubians out. Tens of thousands streamed into "refugee centers" that were really concentration camps; the rest fled deeper into the hills, where they faced starvation and epidemics. Ashley found stark naked villagers living in the Stone Age. His zeal inflamed, he decided to become their savior.

With his contacts in the various relief agencies, he could easily obtain supplies. What he needed was a plane, and a pilot, to fly them in, and he found both in Dale Roark. The nomadic Oklahoman had just ferried a Gulfstream-1 to Nairobi from Texas.

The trim, Gen-X crusader and the beefy, cynical, middle-age flier made as odd an odd couple as ever shared space in a cockpit, but they worked well together. Beginning in mid-1996, they flew just about every conceivable thing to the beleaguered Nubians: seed, farm implements, blankets, wheelbarrows, oil presses, soap, shirts, dresses, sandals, grain in fifty-kilo sacks. They hauled in Bibles for religious aid groups, and, once, two miles of snow fence.

"The people made cigarette paper out of the Bibles," Roark told me with a sardonic grin, obviously enjoying the picture of the gospels going up in smoke. One more confirmation that Africa is no place for anyone who believes in anything too strongly. "But the snow fence really worked. There's not been a road snowed in southern Sudan since then. Now the wheelbarrows were another thing entirely." He stretched every syllable of the last word as if it were a rubber band—*en-taa-yer-lee*—then removed his hat, ran his fingers through his brown hair, and let his eyes wander off into their habitual sidelong gaze. "I come in there one time and saw these women, with the wheelbarrows all loaded up, but not pushin' 'em. They were *carryin'* 'em on top of their heads."

Because Lokichokio was infiltrated by Sudanese government spies, Roark and Ashley flew out of Wilson and filed fictitious flight plans. They spoke to no one about what they were up to. Despite their precautions, they had some close calls. The most memorable came when they landed at a Nuba airstrip soon after a government offensive had gotten under way. Mortar shells began to burst at the far end of the runway. Ashley and a handful of Nubians frantically pushed and pulled the cargo out of the aircraft while Roark calmly counted the incoming rounds: fourteen. Shellfire on the airstrip—for Roark, it went with the territory.

Then he and Ashley learned of a government scheme to bribe a Muslim tribe in the Nuba to turn against its infidel neighbors. The intelligence convinced the pair to change the nature of their cargoes.

"They were bringin' supplies in a Toyota Land Cruiser," Roark said. "We figured that if the rebels could ambush them, they could seize the Land Cruiser and the supplies and then have a vehicle for themselves. The rebels didn't have much—the ones who had guns sometimes didn't have but two rounds of ammo per man, so I flew a load of rifles and ammunition into them, and they seized the vehicle, they did it, but"—again the wary, off-center glance—"when I come back a while later, I found the lug nuts off the wheels, pieces of the transmission scattered all over. It didn't a last month."

He was taking a lot of chances and wasn't making all that much, after paying his fuel and maintenance expenses. When he was approached to help Laurent Kabila, the Congolese rebel leader, overthrow Mobuto Sese Seko, Roark and another American named Dan Calley formed two corporations in Uganda, Busy Bee and Knight Air, and began ferrying Kabila's troops to and from the battlefronts. When that contract was finished, Roark was back in the money—he says that he and Calley cleared $900,000 thousand dollars out of a gross income of $1.8 million—and returned to flying in Sudan. With the help of an old mercenary buddy from Executive Outcomes, Roark bought an aging Hawker-Siddley 748 that once belonged to Queen Elizabeth's fleet of private planes. Ashley was brought into the deal. The odd couple formed 748 Air Services in February 1997.

While the Hawker flew missions in Rwanda and Somalia, Roark's G1 was back in service in the Sudan, delivering supplies for Concern and Goal, two Irish NGOs, and for Norwegian People's Aid, or NPA.

Sometimes you save lives by filling bellies, sometimes by giving people the means to defend their lives. Truck convoys carrying arms and ammunition rumbled across the Ugandan border under cover of darkness to the Sudanese town of Chukudum. Roark picked up the loads at the airstrip, then flew them north on seven-hundred-mile journeys, over the jungles of the far south, over the immense flatlands and marshes of Eastern Equatoria into Jonglei province, crossing the White Nile near the river port of Malakal before winging on into southern Kordofan, where the Nuba Mountains rose out of the scrubby plains.

Once again, considerable pains were taken to conceal the clandestine missions, not only from the Khartoum government, but from Kenyan and U.N. authorities as well. To put a buffer between 748 and the arms-smuggling operation, Roark sometimes leased planes from it to his dummy Ugandan corporation, Knight Air, and flew the weapons under its flag. The funds for the lease, he says, were channeled through the Ugandan Ministry of Defense, which also was the source of the weapons.

Some of the arms flights made as much as eighteen thousand dollars, some did not make a cent. Roark showed me a shareholders' report for 748. It was thick as a phone book for a small city, with numerous entries listing the date and income for every flight the company made in 1998. He marked off which were gun runs, and after several came the notation, "Not Paid."

"You really didn't make a dime?" I asked, incredulous once again. By this time, we'd moved from the Aero Club to his apartment. "Or were you trying to hide the income?"

Roark shook his head.

I said, "Then you must have had other reasons."

He twirled his sunglasses in one hand—another of his nervous habits.

"These U.N. pilots, filing their flight plans twenty-four hours in advance with Khartoum, they're playing Mother, May I? There's two kinds of pilots flying in Sudan, those who defy the government of Sudan, and those who don't."

That remark was as revealing as Roark was likely to be. He ran guns into Sudan because there were people, inside the country and out of it, who said he couldn't do it. No other reason. End of story. But a memento hanging on a wall suggested that he cared about the people of the Nuba and southern Sudan more than he liked to admit. It was a carved wooden water gourd, with these words painted along its edge: "Our Thanks and Gratitude To Capt. Dale for his great deeds to Safe [sic] and Assist Us—The people of the Nuba Mountains."

I reflect on all this as I sit with Heather Stewart beside the pool in Trackmark Camp. So I've seen Sudan from above, seen it in a video, but have yet to set foot in it. Can she help me out? She makes no promises, but says she'll see what she can do.

Today, the day after speaking with Stewart, I'm offered a chance to spend some time on Sudanese soil, in a town called Panyagor, some three hundred miles northwest of Loki. What brings me there further illustrates just how mixed up the war in Sudan is. Would that it were merely a conflict between Arabs and black Africans, Christians and Muslims. As Butler and Roark told me, it's also a war of southerners versus southerners, ancient tribal feuds elevated into savage ethnic battles. Nearly ten years ago, Riek Machar, the SPLA's second in command, fell into a bitter dispute with Garang over how to run the war. Machar is a Nuer tribesman, and the Nuer have warred with the Dinka for generations. Machar ultimately broke with Garang and formed his own faction of the rebel army, which was eventually armed, supplied, and encouraged by the Khartoum government to fight Garang's. In 1991, his warriors attacked Garang's hometown of Bor, burning it to the ground, committing unspeakable atrocities, and driving the people it didn't kill into the bush.

I am to tag along as sixty-four of those people, after years of exile in refugee settlements, return to Panyagor, which was caught up in the Nuer rampage. A lumbering Antonov-32, piloted by a cheerful Russian who will give only his first name, Valery, takes off from Loki, lands at Natinga, just inside the Sudanese border, and loads its passengers, mostly women, children, and elderly of both sexes. One boy carries a Chicago Bulls duffel bag; a tall man sports a baseball cap that says JESUS IS THE WAY.

Crowded into the plane's cargo bay, which is also crammed with a half ton of maize, the refugees sit quietly, stoically, though the small children start to cry as the overloaded Antonov rumbles down the dirt landing field, groaning, rattling, straining to get airborne. Eyes stare blankly out of coal-black faces as the plane wings up to twenty thousand feet, then over desert and swamp and savanna until it touches down at Panyagor, a tight cluster of domed huts behind a bamboo stockade.

The refugees file out, returning to the home they haven't seen for almost a decade. Relatives and friends swarm to greet them, but the reunion is surprisingly subdued. The Dinka are not demonstrative by nature, and I suppose this, in addition to the suffering they've endured, accounts for the suppressed emotion. Lanky SPLA guerrillas, some so tall they almost have to duck when passing under the Antonov's wings, saunter about, AKs slung over their bony shoulders. A Dinka official, Elijah Malok, profusely thanks Captain Valery and his five-man crew. "This is a great thing, and we are grateful to all who made this possible," Malok proclaims, his six-foot-eight-inch frame looming over the average-size Russian. Meanwhile, the Antonov's navigator, Vladimir, goes to pet a yellow bird attached to a string on a young boy's shoulder. The bird bites his finger.

Valery and Vladimir work for Skylink Aviation, one of the maverick outfits that flies to places the government has declared off limits. Since Panyagor is one of these, we don't stay on the ground long enough for me to learn much beyond what I've already come to know: oftentimes, the south Sudanese are their own worst enemy.

When I get back to Loki, Stewart has returned from a grueling mission in which she flew solo about four hundred miles to Rumbek, a Sudanese town west of the Nile, where she picked up a Catholic bishop and two missionary priests who needed to be taken to another town to start a new mission. On the heels of a three-hour return flight through rainy-season storms, through treacherous downdrafts over the Didinga Hills and on into the hot currents swirling over Kenya's northern desert, she is showered and coiffed and having dinner with me at Trackmark Camp. She tells me that the Rumbek flight was especially important at this time, because Trackmark badly needs the revenue.

The thing to understand about the aid business is that it is a *business,* and for bush pilots who own their own aviation companies, it's not all daredevil soaring on silver wings into the African wilds.

Only a couple of years ago, at the height of the Sudan crisis,

Trackmark had fourteen airplanes, either owned or under lease, twenty-two pilots, and a large ground staff. Stewart built an office at Wilson Airport in Nairobi and another in Loki, and then became a part-time hotelier when she set up Trackmark Camp. Today, though, the company is down to three airplanes and four pilots. The problem is the unpredictability of the relief business, aggravated by corruption, a social virus endemic to Kenya. Trackmark's U.N. contracts have dwindled drastically, steered, Stewart says, to a South African company by former high-level U.N. manager who went to work for the rival firm.

"You see what he did—he said to those South Africans, 'Give me a job with you and I'll see that you get contracts from the U.N.' It's disgusting."

For now, Trackmark is hanging on because it has retained its U.N. radio call sign, which allows it to fly cargoes for nongovernmental agencies operating under the U.N. umbrella but not for the World Food Program. If the company loses its call sign, it will have to rely strictly on contracts from the maverick aid groups, and they wouldn't provide enough business to keep Trackmark out of the red.

The next day, I learn that Norwegian People's Aid needs 1.2 tons of medical supplies flown to their hospital in Chukudum, a Sudanese town not far over the border. I need to get into Sudan. Heather Stewart needs business. So I charter her to fly me and the supplies. I am a relief worker for a day.

Sitting beside her in the copilot's seat, I watch Stewart cross-check her GPS against the navigation sheet. She gets a pressure reading from the Loki tower, adjusts her altimeter, and requests clearance for takeoff. The fourteen-seat Caravan rolls down the runway, and leaves the ground at eighty knots. Most planes seem to labor to get airborne, shuddering and roaring against gravity, but the Cessna rises so effortlessly it feels as if we're riding on the back of a hawk. Our first stop is to be a refugee camp, Kakuma, which is in Kenya, a short hop from Loki. We are to pick up an old friend of Stewart's, Marianne Fitzgerald, who has been working with the refugees for the past two years. It's early afternoon, and as the heat rises from the scrub desert below, the ride gets bumpy. We follow a winding riverbed bordered by trees, the only green in sight, and then the black ribbon of the highway that leads to Nairobi, hundreds of miles away. Stewart is giving her friend a lift because she can't leave the camp by road. It's ambushed by Turkana bandits.

Kakuma is a sprawl of tin-roofed barracks and Turkana huts surrounded by thornbush *bomas*. Sixty-five thousand refugees, some Ethiopian, some Somali, but most Sudanese, are crammed in there, awaiting visas and documents for emigration to the U.S. and Europe. As we descend over a mission church near the camp, Stewart smiles and lets me know that she has a bad-girl side.

"I fell madly in love with the Catholic priest here some time back, and to say hello, I used to buzz the mission, coming back from Sudan."

We land smoothly. A woman alongside the runway bows her head and holds on to her straw hat against the prop wash. Marianne Fitzgerald could be Stewart's sister—a blond, blue-eyed woman of a certain age who doesn't look it, a daughter of British colonials. After she's buckled into one of the passenger seats she tells me that she lobbies Western governments on behalf of the refugees. Some are former Sudanese slaves who escaped captivity or were redeemed from the masters, not all of whom were Sudanese Arabs. Some of the slaves were sold to buyers in Chad and Libya. Africans captured by mounted Arab raiders, led away into distant bondage. What happened to the twenty-first century? It isn't here yet, it may never be.

We return to Loki, have lunch at Stewart's camp, then drive back to the airfield for the flight into Sudan. Marianne, a woman of adventurous temperament, is going along for ride.

We bank over the Moglia Range, then bear westward into a sun tarnished by a late afternoon haze. The land below is a patchwork of red and tawny spotted with green. The winding galleries of trees mark the rivers, but there is no water in them and the slopes of the mountains northward are fissured and brown. Far ahead loom the Didinga Hills and Sudan. Our destination gives the mission a certain dash: Chukudum is in a prohibited zone. We're flying on the dark side. . .

Stewart takes notes on a pad strapped to her right thigh—she'll use the information to fill in her log later on. We're at 10,400 feet, cruising at a 120 knots through a canyonland of cumulus.

"Visibility's awful, isn't it," she says in her best BBC voice.

It sure is; the haze looks like the smoke from a forest fire. We are in Sudan now, and receive a lesson in the unfairness of God and nature. Kenya, only sixty miles away, is starved for moisture; the Didinga Hills below are lush and green, the rivers sparkle, a rain cloud sweeps the horizon. Stewart flies around the highest ridges, to avoid getting caught in a downdraft, then begins her descent. The Cessna soars over rocky crags that rise, like temple towers, from the jungled hillsides. A rainbow shimmers over a bright green valley. It does not make an arch but a full circle, a gigantic, glittering ring of color. It's easy to see why Stewart loves what she does.

The airstrip is a scar on the valley floor. Now we can see tukuls showing through the trees, farm fields, a road, and, on a plateau below a rocky pinnacle that lends a fortresslike appearance to the place, the brick buildings of a now-abandoned Maryknoll mission. As she lowers the wheels, Stewart tells me that last year, only minutes after she took off from this same landing field, a Sudanese air force plane came over and dropped fifteen cluster bombs. A little something to think about during my stay.

Stewart's landing is a "greaser," not a bump, just a sweet smooth roll over the hard-packed dirt. A squad of SPLA soldiers appear out of the bush. A Land Cruiser and a flatbed truck are parked nearby, on a rutted road.

It's getting dark, and we quickly off-load the supplies—latex gloves, syringes, surgical instruments, antimalarial medicine—and pile them into the truck. Stewart and Marianne work alongside us, then say so long, climb back in the cockpit, and wing off. In a moment, the Caravan is a white, model airplane against the green hills. One moment more, and it's gone.

Less than two years ago, Chukudum was a thriving town, or as thriving as a town can be in southern Sudan. The Maryknoll sisters ran a primary and secondary school at their mission station; Catholic Relief Services was active here. Norwegian People's Aid, with equipment that had been flown in by Dale Roark among others, had built a 120-bed hospital. But Chukudum was also an SPLA stronghold, and was bombed several times, menaced by government militia in the garrison town of Kapoeta, thirty miles to the north. Khartoum's forces almost did not need to lift a finger—once again, the southern Sudanese did their work for them.

The SPLA troops in Chukudum, then commanded by a man named Bior Ajaong, were mostly Dinka, who by all accounts did not behave like liberators but like an occupying army, alienating much of the local population. Enter another SPLA officer, Peter Lorot, a Didinga tribesman, who was sent to Chukudum in January 1999 on a recruiting mission. Lorot did not like what he saw and told Ajaong that he was taking command. Ajaong replied that he would do such thing without orders from higher echelons. Lorot stood firm—he wasn't going to argue, he was taking over. Ajaong charged him with mutiny and sent a captain and several men to arrest him. Lorot, knowing that mutiny in the SPLA meant a firing squad, shot the captain to death, then escaped with several hundred followers to Kapoeta, where he defected to the Sudanese government. They armed and trained Lorot's band, and ordered him to attack Chukudum, which he did in April, shelling it with mortars, raking it with machine gun fire from the surrounding hills. Although his militia was beaten back, the fighting was so ferocious that the Maryknoll missionaries fled and never returned. The mission schoolteachers, the staff from Catholic Relief Services, and most of the townspeople did likewise. But the Norwegians remained.

I hear this dismal tale from two people. One is a forty-two-year-old man named Alfred Lothia, chairman of the parish youth group and in charge of a campaign to clean up the wreckage and rebuild the mission. The other is Major William Lokirimo, the new SPLA commander in Chukudum. He was assigned to replace Ajaong and to repair relations between the guerrilla forces and the populace. Both he and Lothia were very anxious to persuade me that the troubles were over; they wanted word spread to the Maryknolls and to the relief organizations that it was now safe to return.

I spend three days in Chukudum, watch Lokirimo's men train, and then attend Mass in the church, where the pews are logs laid down on the floor and broken beams hang from the ceiling. The dome over the altar has been blown out, and through it the congregation can see the sky and the hills behind the mission. The choir is very good, singing hymns in the local dialect to a drum rather than an organ. Because there is no priest, the Eucharist cannot be given, but the rest of the ceremony is presided over by a deacon. In the middle of his sermon, the congregation on one side of the aisle suddenly stirs; people jump up and begin to bolt; others mill around, seemingly in a panic. One man raises a stick over his head and swats at something on the floor. A few people gather in a circle and stomp their feet. I am mystified, and wonder if the deacon's homily has angered his parishioners. Then the man with the stick dashes to one of the side doorways and throws the stick outside. Something is coiled around it—a puff adder.

The things you see in southern Sudan will turn your stomach when they don't break your heart. I tour the hospital the next day. The long, low, mud-brick bungalow is doubtlessly better than no hospital at all, but I would not want to be a patient in it. It is dim and foul-smelling, tuberculosis victims cough and hack, mixed in with other patients because there is no isolation ward for them. Starving children stare at us with wide, expressionless eyes, a twenty-year-old boy lies dying of liver cancer. There are bullet wounds, snakebites, and malaria, and in the yard outside, an orderly in a green smock holds an electrical sterilizer over a campfire to cleanse surgical instruments; faulty wiring, he explains, shorted out the sterilizer coils. Nearby, forty or fifty people in tribal dress hover over cooking fires in the shade of tamarind trees. They are the relatives of patients, and the yard is the only place they have to stay. In the pediatrics ward, bare-breasted women, marked with ritual tribal scars, nurse their sick infants. A few of these women, we're told by the chief nurse, walked through the bush for six days to get here.

I am shown the X-ray facility. It's a round, mud-walled building that resembles a tukul. Inside is a fairly new Siemens X-ray machine, a table, a lead shield, all the accessories. Only one thing is missing, the British-trained technician tells me: film. The hospital has not had any X-ray film for eight or nine months. I am thinking about all those guns that were flown into and out of Chukudum. My God, couldn't someone have brought in X-ray film?

How gratifying it would be to report that all is at should be: the southern Sudanese, united shoulder to shoulder to fight an oppressive regime. The United Nations, with total lack of self-interest, pours in aid to the suffering victims. How gratifying it would be to report that all is black and white, that there is no corruption, gunrunning, self-defeating tribal warfare. Poor, bleeding Sudan. I recall the puff adder in the mission church. The serpent in the garden. It's too symbolic to be symbolic.

I receive a radio message from Stewart late on the third day. She has flights coming up for tomorrow and the day following, so she must pick me up now. She says will land at precisely 5:25 P.M. It's now 4:00 P.M. The airstrip is six kilometers away and Chukudum's two vehicles are not available. I heft my pack, and escorted by seven guerrillas, hoof it out at a brisk clip. I know Heather. I know that if she says she'll arrive at 5:25, she'll be there at 5:25. We make it with time to spare. A wicked thunderstorm is forming to the south and west: jet-black clouds, rain so dense it looks solid, lightning that blazes horizontally, like huge tracer bullets. At 5:23, the Caravan appears off to the north. Now we'll see if All-Weather Heather lives up to her name. She brings the plane in, more medical supplies are off-loaded, and we take off, climbing eastward over the hills just as the storm rolls over the airstrip like an ocean wave.

return to tsavo

2 0 0 1

We were awake before dawn, the Southern Cross shining brilliantly in a sky as black as when we'd gone to bed. After a hurried breakfast in the mess tent, Craig Packer and I left camp in a Land Rover, bumping down a dusty road that appeared as a trail of white ash in the headlights. A pair of hyena eyes glowed back at us from out of the dense underbrush crowding the roadside. Full daylight had arrived before we reached our destination, the stark Ndara Plains. There, we turned right at a junction, passed a dry water hole, and rounded a bend. Craig braked to a quick stop. Fifty feet away, three male lions lay by the road, and they didn't appear to have a hair on their heads. Noting the color of their noses (leonine noses darken as they age, from pink to black), Craig estimated that they were six years old—young adults.

"This is wonderful!" he said, after staring at them for several moments. "This is what we came to see. They really *are* maneless."

Tall, lean, with a black beard slightly tarnished by gray, Packer is a professor at the University of Minnesota's Department of Ecology, Evolution, and Behavior, and arguably *the* leading expert on the Serengeti lion, the majestic beast that roars at you from the MGM screen and appears in soundless photographic books about Africa, its head mantled in fur. He and Peyton West, a Ph.D. candidate who has been working with him in Tanzania, were agnostics on the subject of Tsavo's maneless lions, suspecting that the animals were adolescents mistaken for adults by amateur observers. The trio lying beside the road that morning converted the two skeptical scientists.

I'd joined them on a twenty-three-day research expedition, drawn back by the magnetism of Africa, by the memory of the wilderness I'd walked with Iain Allan and Clive Ward almost a year and a half ago. The expedition was mostly Peyton's show. Thirty-two years old, she had spent several years in Tanzania, compiling the data she needed to answer a question that ought to have been answered long ago: why *do* lions have manes? It's the only cat, wild or domestic, that displays such ornamentation. Now she was attacking the riddle from the opposite angle. Why do Tsavo lions *not* have manes? ("Manelessness" is a relative term, covering the spectrum from the complete lack of a mane to a partial one.) Does environmental adaptation account for the trait, or are the lions of Tsavo, as some people believe, a distinct subspecies of their Serengeti cousins?

Those animals have been under continuous scientific observation for thirty-five years, beginning with George Schaller's pioneering work in the 1960s. Though Tsavo is Kenya's oldest and largest national park, its lions have hardly been studied, which partly accounts for the legends that have grown up around them and, over the years, encrusted into fact. Not only do they *look* different, they *behave* differently, displaying greater cunning and aggressiveness. "Remember too," the *Rough Guide* to Kenya warns the adventure traveler, "Tsavo's lions have a reputation for ferocity." Their fearsome image, you'll remember, goes back to 1898, when that infamous pair of males devoured Colonel Patterson's railroad workers and inspired him to write *The Man-Eaters of Tsavo* nine years later. The lions' notorious reputation annoys some scientists.

"People don't want to give up on mythology," Dennis King told me one day. The British-born zoologist has been working in Tsavo off and on for four years. "One of the myths is of the rogue beast, the cattle-killer, the man-eater. I am so sick of this man-eater business. Patterson made a helluva lot of money of that story, but Tsavo's lions are no more likely to turn man-eater than lions from elsewhere."

But tales of their savagery and wiliness don't all come from sensationalist authors looking to make a buck. Safari guides and Kenya Wildlife Service rangers tell stories of lions attacking Land Rovers, raiding tent camps, stalking tourists. Tsavo is a tough neighborhood, they say, and it breeds tougher lions.

How much of that folklore is true? Can it be verified or denied through scientific methods?

Thomas Gnoske and Dr. Julian Kerbis-Peterhans, the two researchers from Chicago's Field Museum of Natural History I'd interviewed after my first trip to Tsavo, published an intriguing hypothesis was advanced last year in *Swara*, the journal of the East African Wildlife Society: Tsavo lions may be a feline "missing link" between the unmaned cave lions of the Pleistocene *(Panthera spelea)* and modern lions *(Panthera leo)*. The Serengeti variety is the most evolved of the species—the latest model, so to speak—while certain morphological differences in Tsavo lions (bigger bodies, smaller skulls, lower jaws identical to those of the rare Asiatic lion) suggest that they are closer to the primitive ancestor of all lions. Their greater size makes them more able to take down the predominant prey animal in Tsavo, the Cape buffalo, one of the strongest, most ill-tempered animals on earth. It often kills the lion that meant to kill it, or severely injures him. And a wounded lion *is* more likely to turn to cattle and humans for food.

Craig and Peyton had serious doubts about Gnoske's and Peterhans's idea, but admitted that Tsavo lions pose a mystery to science. To tackle it, they had come equipped with an arsenal of tools: a pair of life-size dummy lions that could be dressed in manes of varying sizes and colors (to test behavior in controlled circumstances); an infrared camera that measures body heat and converts the measurements to digital images (to test levels of heat stress); electronic altimeters and thermometers, GPS (to mark locations of prides); night-vision scopes', and tape recordings of various animal calls (to summon lions from their lairs).

They brought their resources to bear on the trio discovered by Craig and me. Later that day, we returned to Ndara and found the three doing what lions spend most of their time doing—nothing. They lounged in the bushes, flicking at flies with their tails. They had been christened Baby Huey (the largest), Meathead (whose jutting jaw gave him a stupid expression), and Fur Boy (the smallest but the owner of the most hair: sparse side whiskers and a furry "bib"). Peyton was going to run an experiment using techniques developed in the Serengeti, where she found evidence suggesting a correlation between a luxuriant mane and masculine vigor. She and Craig didn't expect the same results with the three Ndara males, because Fur Boy's inferior size indicated that he was the youngest, but when the recorded roar of a female lion was broadcast through a speaker mounted on the roof of Peyton's Land Rover, Fur Boy was the first to set off toward the sound. The other two stood side by side, then followed and caught up. Fur Boy, however, pulled ahead and won the race. Oval pupils dilated in the gathering dusk, he looked for a lioness but found only a Land Rover occupied by a female of the wrong species.

In any event, he and his companions had behaved as Serengeti lions would have in the same circumstances.

"That's the thing about our science," Craig exulted. "We can make things happen. It would have taken years, just by observing things as they happen naturally, to see what we saw tonight in minutes."

In science as in life, pride goeth before the fall. The next experiment, four days later, failed.

In the interim, we'd discovered that Baby Huey, Meathead, and Fur Boy belonged to a male coalition that included a fourth male, which we found devouring a maggot-infested buffalo carcass with a lioness near Aruba dam. We called him "Burr Boy" because of the burrs matting his scruffy side whiskers, and he was courting his female dining companion, "Melinda," while a second lioness, an old one with rounded teeth, "Granny," had joined the group.

Peyton was hoping for an opportunity to test another of her hypotheses: like a peacock's tail, one of the purposes of a lion's mane is to attract females. (In Tanzania, experiments appeared to show that lionesses preferred males with longer manes.) Back at camp, she dressed the dummy lions in two different hairstyles, adorning one with a Serengeti-style mane, the other with the short crest and whiskers of a typical Tsavo lion. Now what she needed was for the two females to distance themselves from the distracting presence of the four males.

Finally, the chance came. Melinda and Granny were by themselves, dozing in the shade of thornbushes. The fake lions were trucked out to Aruba in a covered trailer, then set on the ground side by side, about twenty feet apart, with photographer Bob Caputo's remote camera between them to record what happened. Peyton and Craig played a tape of a dying wildebeest, a doleful sound. The point was to get the females' attention. Once they were afoot and moving toward the groans, they would spot what would appear to them as two males guarding a kill. Then we would see which they attached themselves to: if the maned one, that would be a good indicator, though not positive proof, that a good head of hair draws females, even females accustomed to the "bald" males of their home range.

For a while, the scientists' magic trick seemed to be working. The lionesses were proceeding warily toward the dummies—females usually are cautious when strange males appear—but this pair were especially shy. Halfway there, they stopped, lay down, and never moved another inch. When darkness fell, we packed up. Neither Peyton nor Craig had ever seen anything like it in the Serengeti.

"Well, it looks like Tsavo remains a mystery within a riddle wrapped in an enigma," Craig quipped.

Two days later, Bob returned from a scouting trip to Aruba and reported that he'd spotted Burr Boy all on his own, bedded down behind the earthen dam. A solitary male provided an excellent opportunity to test how a male reacts to mane length in rival males. The dummies were re-coiffed, the first with a long, blond "wig," the other with a short one. Peyton had run this experiment seven times in Tanzania, and every time, the live lion approached the dummy with the smaller adornment, leading her to hypothesize that another purpose of a mane is to send a message to males; the more prominent it is, the stronger is its possessor, telling potential rivals, "I'm no one to mess with."

We set up alongside the Aruba lake, in the splendid light of a late East African afternoon. A hen plover and two chicks, each hardly bigger than a locust, pecked grass seed at the shore. A sacred ibis flew low over the water, a winged spear of black and white, while a pair of hippopotami wallowed, one giving a cavernous yawn—it looked as if you could park a Volkswagen in its jaws. In the far distance, a herd of elephant proceeded at a stately pace toward the water hole. The idyllic scene was shattered when Peyton switched on her call of hyenas on a kill. It sounded like Hell's own choir accompanied by a madhouse glee club: a demoniacal medley of groans, cackles, giggles, howls, and shrieks. As unpleasant as it is to human ears, the racket hyenas make when devouring prey is an irresistible summons to lions, telling them that there is food to be had, ready to eat. Just drive the hyenas off and take the meat for yourself.

In a few minutes, Burr Boy's head appeared above the berm. He started forward, but instead of finding a pack of hyenas and a more-or-less free meal, he saw what looked like two invading males. He approached with utmost care, amber eyes riveted on his adversaries, nostrils twitching to pick up a scent. An arresting sight, all that golden muscle flowing in the golden light, but I wasn't too impressed with his intelligence. In the Land Rover with Peyton, I whispered that he ought to have figured out by now that the two creatures in front of him, scentless, motionless, and silent, were decoys.

She pointed out that confrontation with a rival male or males is the biggest event in a lion's life; he can't afford to be anything but extremely cautious, the consequences of rash action begin so catastrophic: eviction from his pride, serious injury, even death.

"If you were in a dark alley and some guy pointed an authentic-looking toy pistol at you and said, 'Give me your wallet,' what would you do, even if you suspected the gun was fake?" she said.

Burr Boy, now within five yards of the dummies, crept toward the one with the shorter mane, lowering his head and circling around to its side, which is something lions always do around a strange male. Facing one eyeball to eyeball is sure to provoke a fight.

Craig and Peyton were satisfied. Eight times in a row, the last time here in Tsavo, a lone male approached the dummy with the sparsest mane, calculating that it was the lesser of two possible evils. As far as behavior went, the evidence was tipping toward a similarity, rather than a difference, between Tsavo and Serengeti lions.

But why do they *look* different?

Craig was working on a few ideas. Tsavo's heat was central to one. Noontime temperatures often approach, and sometimes exceed, one hundred degrees. We had seen lions reacting to the climate—panting constantly, lying on their backs with their legs spread, like giant house cats on an August afternoon. Readings from the infrared camera had indicated wide body temperature variations between their upper and lower parts, leading Craig to speculate that much of the lions' energies were devoted to keeping cool, leaving little left over to grow a mane. The Serengeti is higher and cooler than Tsavo, so the males there can develop their distinctive ornamentation without paying too high a price.

Craig's observations in South Africa's Kruger National Park inspired another thought. Kruger is also a harsh, penurious place, with a scant supply of prey animals. The lions there attain full body size at the same rate as Serengeti lions, but coalitions of bachelor males often spend several years on their own, killing large prey like buffalo and giraffe, before they're ready to take over a pride. In the Serengeti, rich in food, the period of nomadic bachelorhood is much shorter. Tsavo's environment is rougher even than Kruger's.

"You don't get twelve-point bucks in marginal habitat," Craig remarked. "It could be that conditions here are such that it won't allow males to express what's in them genetically until they're older."

In so many words, extreme heat and a scarce food supply turn Tsavo males into super-annuated adolescents.

A third notion was more exciting from a field biologist's point of view: Tsavo lions really are genetically different. Craig thought the best way to determine that would be to capture a male cub from Kruger, another from the Serengeti, and a third from Tsavo and raise them in identical conditions. If all grew manes at roughly the same rate, then we could say that Tsavo's environment explains manelessness. If not, then we would have a good indicator of significant genetic variation.

To test the heat-stress theory, Peyton needed to make further studies of males with the infrared camera, preferably males with some sort of mane. We had located a large pride not far from camp, near a place called Ndololo, but we'd seen only lionesses, cubs, and juveniles. The pride must be led by one or two adult males, and she went in search of them one morning, with me tagging along.

I had found lion research to be more routine than I'd expected—hours and hours of boredom punctuated by moments of sheer boredom, waiting for the lazy beasts to do something. I was shortly to learn that the work can be otherwise.

We bounced along a narrow, rutted track bordering the Kanderi swamp and the Voi River, hornbills flying past with plaintive cries. We found a place where the undergrowth thinned out, affording us fairly broad views on both sides of the road. Peyton played the hyena tape, and as the hideous wails and howls echoed across the landscape, we scanned with binoculars.

"Ohhhhhh shit!" she shouted. "Holy shit!"

In almost the same instant came the trumpet blasts of elephant. My head snapped around to see nine of them charging us from out of the scrub: three calves and two adolescents behind a phalanx of four matriarchs, coming on at a stiff-legged run, throwing up dust, ears flapping like barn doors in a gale, tusks glinting in the early light. Evidently, the racket had gotten on their nerves as well. They were a hundred yards away at most, a distance they halved in about two seconds, which was when the lead matriarch ceased trumpeting and lowered her head to let us know that the threat displays were over. This was the real thing. She came straight for us with a terrible singleness of purpose. Her tusks could easily pierce the Land Rover's thin aluminum skin, and with a little help from her friends, maybe without it, she could overturn the vehicle and stomp on it until it looked like a flattened beer can and we looked like—well, I didn't care to think about *that*. With admirable *sangfroid,* Peyton switched off the tape recorder and started the engine. We took off as fast as the road would allow, meaning not very fast, certainly not fast enough to suit the matriarch. We hadn't gone far before she, followed by the rest, thundered through our parking spot. Eight of the elephants carried on, but the old girl, with astonishing agility, turned abruptly and chased us down the road. She was not about to let a good tantrum go to waste.

Peyton stepped on the gas. The matriarch continued in hot pursuit, like a traffic cop chasing a speeder. Finally, satisfied that we'd been well and properly seen off, she halted, and with a parting scream and a final toss of her great head, turned back to rejoin the others. The herd shambled off, now as calm as they'd been enraged—a beautiful and magisterial procession against an eastern sky going from bright orange to peach to primrose.

After a silence, Peyton said, "I'm really scared of elephants. I've gotten to know lions so well that I don't feel frightened of them. Maybe it's a false sense of security, I don't know, but I'm irrationally scared of elephants."

I assured her that in the moment just passed, her fears had been perfectly reasonable.

We composed ourselves and doubled back to see if the hyena call had stirred any lions out of hiding. I doubted we would see a one; if the call had drawn them in, they would have been scared off by the elephant charge.

"Stop!" I yelled.

There, forty, fifty yards away on the riverbank, posed as if for a family portrait, was the Ndololo pride, eleven altogether, but once again, all females, cubs, and subadults. Peyton turned off road and eased toward them. We recognized the old female and the lioness with the injured hip. They were not "tourist" lions, and before Peyton could identify the others, they nervously stole away, across the dry riverbed. It was steep-sided, twenty to thirty feet deep. Looking for a drift so we could cross and follow them, we drove slowly along the near side, the

Land Rover lurching into and out of hidden potholes. We spotted another lioness, who was pregnant, and followed at a discreet distance.

"Look! The males!"

Peyton pointed ahead. They lay in the grass, two of them, both maned, sparsely but maned nonetheless, the one black, the other blond. The lioness vanished into the brush beside the riverbed in classic Tsavo fashion—she was there and then not there—but the males stayed put for a while, allowing Peyton to count their muzzle spots and make note of their ear notches (another point of identification). Then they rose and padded away, and both were by far the best-looking males we'd seen so far, fully mature and in prime condition, with sleek, tawny-gray coats, deep chests, shoulders striated with muscle. Four hundred fifty pounds, each of them. We trailed them, bumping over deadfalls concealed in the grass, and found them resettled nearby; but they moved again, crossing the Voi to dissolve in the deep scrub beyond. We found a drift and crossed the riverbed, the Land Rover in low-range four-wheel drive and canted at a forty-five-degree angle, climbing the bank on the far side.

The black-maned lion had found a cozy bed in the shade. Peyton focused her still camera and imitated a hyena's whoop to get him to raise his head. It was then that I recalled the ranger's story about the big male that had attacked the mini bus, the pregnant female must have been the lioness he'd been mating with, and recalling that black-maned lions tended to be dominant, I figured the culprit was the one in front of us. I hoped he didn't object to having his picture taken. Another whoop, but the lion didn't cooperate. Just then, two juvenile elephant appeared, browsing under a tamarind tree only yards away, on my side of the vehicle.

"Guess what's going to happen in a few seconds," I whispered.

Sure enough, Mom hove into view, probably one of the matriarchs who'd come at us like Hannibal's cavalry. It was simply amazing and unsettling how something so big could show up so quickly, with barely a sound. She cast an ominous stare in our direction, flapped her ears, shook her head, and we didn't need a translator to interpret her body language. Off road, in close country, there would be no escaping a charge now. Peyton put the car in gear and we left. The lion also wanted no part of the matriarch. As he vanished into the undergrowth, we saw, through a corridor in the ranks of *Maeva triphilia*, eight lionesses and cubs file past, like cars crossing an intersection. Then they disappeared. The entire pride had become invisible, cloaked in the thick greenery. We pressed on for another quarter of a mile. Apparently, Peyton meant it when she said she wasn't afraid of lions. I was. The vegetation was so thick that branches screeched against the windows. The lions could have been anywhere from three feet to a mile away, but if the testy male was hiding in one of those thickets and decided to repeat his performance with the mini bus, one of us would get a paw in the face before we saw it incoming. I was all for calling it quits, but didn't want to interfere in Peyton's research and kept my anxieties to myself.

We entered a lovely, shady grove of tamarind, trunks rust-red and polished from elephants rubbing up against them. We'd both drunk too much coffee. Peyton got out to pee and asked me to keep a look-out for lions. When she was finished, she did the same for me, but fear overcame shame and shyness and I stood pissing right beside my door. It was now past nine and already hot and Peyton decided it was time to call it a morning. Wonderful, I thought, but didn't say it.

Ten minutes of slow, cautious driving (there were pits in the ground two and three feet deep) brought us back to the drift. As we started down, the right wheel banged into a ridge of dried mud hard as curbstone. Peyton's foot was jarred off the clutch, killing the engine. She turned the key to restart it. Not even a click. Another turn and still nothing. It was like we were in a motorless car.

"Ohhhh, shit," Peyton said. That was becoming the watchword of the day.

We tried the lights. They didn't work. Peyton turned on the radio to tell our companions about our predicament, assuming the VHF could reach them. No matter. The radio didn't work.

"That bump must've knocked a battery cable loose," she speculated.

A stalled car on a steep incline deep in the bush, with a herd of temperamental elephants and a pride of fourteen lions close by. I didn't relish climbing out to check the battery, but relished much less the idea of walking seven kilometers—over four miles—back to camp.

"Okay, pop the hood hatch and I'll have a look," I said.

"It's under your seat."

We got out and pulled off the seat. Everything had been direct-wired to the battery—the GPS, the electronic altimeter, the radio, along with several other gizmos, and I looked down at a linguine of wires. After detaching them and the cables, we cleared the battery posts and re-attached everything and again tried to start the car. The silence told us that a long, hot, dangerous hike was probably in our immediate future. Wishing to avoid that with all my heart, I looked down the riverbank, which formed a ramp some sixty to seventy-five feet long to the riverbed. I made a suggestion: while I dug out the ridge blocking the right wheel, Peyton would stay in the driver's seat, keeping a lookout for lions, elephants, or any other dangerous wildlife. I would then push the Land Rover, and as it rolled downhill, she would try to jump-start the engine.

I untied the shovel from the roof rack, took a long, careful look around, and got to work. Ten minutes and a gallon of sweat later, we were ready to try. I got behind the vehicle and pushed with all my strength. The Land Rover wouldn't budge. More shovel work followed, with Peyton lending a hand by chopping at the ridge with the jack handle (although I would have preferred she stick to her sentry duties). I tried once more, really putting my shoulder to it. How heavy was a Land Rover anyway? It was as if I were trying to push a semitrailer.

"Parking brake off?" I called.

She said it was, and then suggested that she get out and help me push. I pointed out that if the vehicle ran away on us, we would lose our only chance to get it started again; so I pushed a third time and maybe got two inches of forward motion out of it. Peyton joined me, stating that the incline didn't look too steep; if we left both doors open, we could jump in as the car rolled gently down, and then she would try the jump start. She could not have weighed more than 115 or 120, but she was stronger than she looked, because, with her shoving on right side and me on the left, the stubborn thing started to roll. We'd misjudged the degree of incline, however. The Land Rover sped toward the river bottom, both of us dashing after it. I made quite the hero of myself by tripping and falling when my sandal wedged into an exposed tree root. Just as I hit dirt, I heard Peyton whoop like a cow-girl and glimpsed her, leaping onto the running board and swinging herself inside. The vehicle bounced into the riverbed. A lovely puff of oily smoke burst from the tailpipe, and I heard the still-lovelier rattle of a running diesel.

"You are quite the young lady." I said when I got back in.

"Major bush girl." She flexed a bicep, then graciously added, "But it was team effort," then let out a laugh. "That was just totally awe-some!"

There is nothing so stimulating as to be shot at without effect, Winston Churchill had written while covering the Boer War. Tsavo had just shot at us without effect, and Peyton was stimulated. I wasn't; deeply relieved, rather. I guess that's one of the differences between being thirty-two and fifty-nine.

Three days later, Craig and Peyton spotted the Ndololo pair again, and tracked them a long way before losing them in the Kanderi swamp, less than a mile from camp. The striking lions didn't deserve charm-ingly condescending nicknames, so we called them "Othello" and "Prince Hal." Setting aside the infrared camera tests for the moment, Craig decided on another experiment with the dummies, by dressing one with a black wig, the second with a blond. Peyton's work in the Serengeti had shown that when threatened by two invaders with dark and light manes, lions choose to attack the latter, which suggested that a dark mane is a sign of strength, light a sign of weakness. Othello and Prince Hal, being dark and blond themselves, would provide ideal sub-jects to test the theory one more time.

Two hours before dusk, we set off into the Kanderi. The dummies were placed in the usual way, side by side, with twenty-odd feet sepa-rating them. A female lion's roar blasted through the speaker on Craig and Peyton's vehicle. On the third try, as daylight faded, Othello and Prince Hal appeared, stalking up from behind us. Every movement was sure and purposeful as they approached in a rippling of sinew and mus-cle. Using every bit of cover and concealment they could find, they slipped through the underbrush with barely a rustle, disappearing, re-appearing, disappearing again.

They circled around and crept toward the invaders, Othello lead-ing the way. He crouched in the tall grass, while Prince Hal, slightly behind, stood upright. What a sight he made, there in the dying light, facing the interlopers. He hunkered down, and Othello moved forward a pace or two before he crouched again. Prince Hal followed suit. Creep, look, crouch. Suddenly, Othello let out a throaty cough, then a rising, resonant roar, followed by a series of grunts in diminuendo. *Wauugh-aaraRRRAR-UNH-unh-unh-unh.* As this fell off, Prince Hal sounded his call, *Wauugh-aaraRRRAR- UNH-unh-unh-unh,* and Othello moved for-ward. The stars and a quarter-moon came out, and if it had not been for their light, we would not have seen him make the decisive move. With Prince Hal backing him up, he skirted around to the light-maned dummy's side then gave it a good sniff. On the radio, Craig told us to switch on our engines and headlights, because, in a few seconds, his expensive decoy was going to be knocked over and torn to bits. We did as we were told, and the two lions ran off into the elephant grass. Peyton and Craig could not have been more delighted.

Craig had to return to Tanzania the following morning. The rest of us remained in Tsavo for the next ten days, ranging from arid eastern half to the green, western hills that looked out toward the ice-crowned peak of Mount Kilimanjaro, seventy miles away. Did the expedition unravel the mystery of Tsavo's maneless lions? No. Before he left, Craig told me such a project would take two to three years. Only then will the lions of Tsavo come out of the shadows of legend and into the light of scientific knowledge. I'm not entirely sure that will be a good thing. I'm one of those people Dennis King doesn't care for, reluctant to surrender the myth. I cling to the image of Othello and Prince Hal, roaring in the African night, beautiful in some terrible way, incarnations of all that's left in our world of the wild and the unknown.

ASIA

the enfield and the koran

1 9 8 0

On the Pakistani side of the Khyber Pass, along the road that climbs and twists to Torkam on the Afghan frontier, painted stone tablets add splashes of color to the brown Khyber hills. They stand singly in some places; elsewhere, they cluster like tombstones in a crowded graveyard, odd-looking symbols chiseled on their facades: crossed sabers and crossed rifles, wreaths, crowns, and banners bearing names like DORSETSHIRE and GORDON HIGH-LANDERS. The tablets are not tombstones but markers commemorating the exploits of the British regiments that played in the rougher innings of what a nineteenth-century English officer called the Great Game.

There is another kind of memorial on the Afghan side of the border, at a place called Gondabak. It is a stark beige-colored hill, no different from all the other stark beige-colored hills except for the extraordinary number of human bones that have been found under its rocks by the people who look for such things. The bones are all that is left of the 44th Foot, which formed the rear guard of a British and Indian army retreating from Kabul in 1842, the last year of the First Afghan War. At Gondabak, the regiment made one of those last stands that later provided raw material for historical novelists and the Hollywood illusion factory. But it was the real thing for the 44th on that winter's day nearly a century and a half ago: Afghan tribesmen overran the regiment, massacring forty-five hundred troops and twelve thousand camp followers and sparing only a handful. One of them was told to return to India and inform Her Majesty's colonial government that the Khyber Pass could be very hazardous to an Englishman's health.

News of the disaster stunned the British; a punitive expedition was mounted and the defeat avenged; but Afghanistan never became part of the empire upon which the sun never set. That is why the Afghans still sing about the battle, why they talk about it in such detail that you would think it had been fought only yesterday. It was their best inning of the Game, the time when they played the opposition to a shutout.

What was the Great Game? The officer who coined the phrase did not live long enough to explain precisely what he meant by it: an Uzbek emir beheaded him while he was on a diplomatic mission in the area now known as Soviet Central Asia. Rudyard Kipling, who died in bed at a respectable age and who popularized the phrase, portrayed the Game in terms of intrigue and high adventure in his novel *Kim* and his short story "The Man Who Would Be King." In these and other tales, Kipling created literature from an idea the British politicians of his day regarded as axiomatic: that an expansionist Russia, pushing south through Turkestan, meant to use Afghanistan as an invasion route to the subcontinent and the warm-water ports of the Arabian Sea and the Persian Gulf. In that sense, the Great Game was understood to mean the rivalry between two imperial powers battling for control of Central Asia.

Whatever the Game was—intrigue, adventure, geopolitics, or merely subject matter for celluloid spectacle—its main arena was Afghanistan, a country almost as big as Texas, half of it desert, the other half covered by mountains so high you can look *down* on thunderstorms from the peaks and passes. In response to real or imagined threats, the British invaded the country three times—in 1883, 1878, and 1919—and fought enough skirmishes in between to keep several generations of generals in medals, to make journalistic and political reputations (Winston Churchill was a war correspondent in one Afghan campaign), and to give Kipling plenty of background for his poems and stories about the North-West Frontier.

For the Afghans, the wars against the British were just another chapter in a very long history of resistance to foreign domination. They have fought any number of men who would have been their kings: Greeks under Alexander the Great, Mongols, Scythians, Arabs, Englishmen. The Russians had a go at it in the early eighteenth century and were stopped by the Afghans at a place called Darband in 1725. They made another attempt in Napoleon's time, but their army could not conduct such a long-range campaign and was withdrawn. From then on, the Russians relied on subversion, avoiding direct conflict with the Afghans, whom a Western military analyst described to me as "the most ruthless practitioners of mountain warfare in the world." As any newspaper reader now knows, that long-standing policy ended in December 1979, when a Soviet army of nearly one hundred thousand men began rolling into the mountains of the Hindu Kush to crush a rebellion by Muslim tribesmen against a Marxist government that had taken power in Kabul with considerable help from Moscow.

The invasion revived the Great Game. If Kipling were to return to the North-West Frontier today, he would find enough similarities in the situation to give him a sense of déjà vu and enough dissimilarities to leave him a little bewildered. The old fear of a Russian thrust toward India and the Persian Gulf has been reawakened, but that fear now resides in Washington, not London. Afghan rebels are again sniping from the hills (often with weapons their grandfathers carried in Kipling's day), but they are sniping at an enemy equipped with the lethal technology of the late twentieth century—Mi-24 helicopter gunships, Mig-23 jets, and T-62 tanks.

I went to Afghanistan in early May, a few days before the Soviets opened an offensive in Kunar and Nuristan provinces, which lie just over the Pakistani border. I landed in Peshawar, the capital of Pakistan's North-West Frontier and the city where the eight major Afghan rebel factions maintain their headquarters. My object was to cross the frontier clandestinely with one or another of the insurgent groups. "Doing a Dan Rather" is what it's called by reporters covering the war, although the CBS newsman was not the fist correspondent to slip into Afghanistan, just the most famous and the most photogenic. A reporter's dolling himself up like a Moslem tribesman and sneaking over the border sounds like something out of a bad movie, but with Afghanistan closed to Western journalists it was the only way I could get into the country.

I learned in Peshawar that the Afghans are very liberal when it comes to punctuality. They have elevated the late arrival and the broken appointment to an art form, so I was not just surprised but delighted, stunned, amazed, when Tamim knocked at my door in the Khyber Inter-Continental at 7:20 P.M., only twenty minutes late. He was wearing baggy trousers, sandals, and horn-rimmed glasses that made him look not so much like a guerrilla as like what he'd been before the war began: a student of civil engineering. He looked around the room with a nervousness I thought was caused by the atmosphere of the hotel, a standardized plastic palace that wouldn't have looked out of place if it had been moved to Dayton. Walking in, Tamim began to examine my dresser like a man searching for a hidden microphone.

"Where is the *kibli?*" he asked, referring to the arrowlike symbol that points in the direction a Muslim must face during prayer. "All these rooms have a *kibli*. They're usually attached to this furniture."

That was the cause of his anxiety. It was time for the prayer before sunset, and my room lacked a *kibli*. I went to the balcony, saw where the sun was setting, and told Tamim to face the wall against which the couch stood. This he did, spreading a bath towel as a prayer rug.

Turning around, I saw Tamim in the mirror above the dresser, kneeling and bowing, praying with an unselfconsciousness no longer possible in the secular West. Faith is one of the few things the rebels have going for them. At its worst, it is a faith that can quickly degenerate into a mindless, murderous fanaticism; at its best, it is a force that gives the insurgents the spiritual strength to face Soviet planes and tanks.

"We have two choices: to become Russians or to fight," Tamim had told me earlier. "This is our way; to fight and become martyrs for our faith. We'll fight with or without the help or other countries. But if we lose in Afghanistan, eventually you will face the same problem: to fight or become Russians."

He was twenty-six years old, had learned his English while studying in Kabul, and was now a spokesman for his faction, which was called Jamiat-Islami. It was his job to answer questions from that curious, not-always-honorable fraternity of men who earn their living by covering wars in distant places. I had met Tamim two days before while making my rounds of the various rebel headquarters, trying to find a group willing to smuggle me over the border. A previous attempt with Hisbi-Islami, the largest insurgent group, had turned into a comic misadventure that was less the stuff of Kipling then of *Flashman,* George Fraser's spoof of imperial heroics in Afghanistan.

Dressed in my Muslim-tribesman costume (the disguise was necessary to get me through the numerous checkpoints the Pakistanis had set up in the frontier areas), I had ended up in an Afghan refugee camp at Miran Shah, a town west of Peshawar and about twenty miles inside the Pakistani border. My cover had been blown when I'd started photographing four Russian gunships that, by accident or design, were dropping bombs well inside Pakistani territory. It seemed a good story: the Soviets were attacking a neutral country. The Pakistani security men who'd spotted me didn't think so. They arrested me and after finding that I didn't have government permission to travel in the frontier provinces, packed me off to Peshawar under guard. I was not returned to my hotel, which is the usual procedure the police follow when they catch a newsman mucking around where he doesn't belong. Instead, I was taken to the headquarters of the North-West Frontier constabulary, where two hard-eyed, no-nonsense young men said they suspected me of being a Russian agent who had slipped into Pakistan to stir up trouble among restive tribesmen. Like many American correspondents, I'd grown accustomed to accusations that I was working for the CIA; but this was the first time I'd been charged with playing for the other team. It was only after hours of interrogation, during which I answered questions of the how-many-home-runs-did-Babe-Ruth-hit variety, that I convinced them I was a patriotic American with no ties to the KGB.

Next day, like a salesman calling on his clients, I paid visits to the seven other guerrilla factions, which are grouped loosely—*very loosely*—under the umbrella of an organization named the Islamic Alliance for the Liberation of Afghanistan. Most of the rebel headquarters are near the old city, in the shadow of a gloomy fifteenth-century fortress that rises above a chaos of bazaars and narrow streets exotic and sinister enough in appearance to convince you that you are indeed in a dangerous place. I found Jamiat-Islami's offices in a row of storefronts on a street where horse-drawn rickshaws jousted with Hondas and Toyotas. At the entrance, a sentry carrying a Kalashnikov rifle gave me a body search. Another escorted me down a gangway to a courtyard surrounded by rooms where guerrillas recently returned from the front lay on straw mats, their feet dirty and callused, their rifles stacked in a corner. (One look at those Mausers and Lee-Enfields told you that if the CIA is arming the rebels, as Tass would have us believe, it is doing so by raiding antique gun shops.) "*Mujahideen*" is what the guerrillas call themselves; depending on who is translating, it means either "freedom fighters" or "holy warriors."

I was ushered into the political information office, where several men lounged on the floor. Removing my shoes, I walked in and joined them. They served me tea, for the Afghans, like most Muslims, put great store in treating guests hospitably. One of the men asked whom I wished to see. I told him I was looking for Tamim, whose name had been given to me by another correspondent. He said to wait: and while I waited, men drifted in and out of the room or sauntered aimlessly in the courtyard. The place had none of the snap and bustle you expect of a military headquarters. The general atmosphere was the same as that in the other offices I'd visited—casual disorganization.

That is, in fact, one of the weaknesses of the Afghan resistance. To this disorganization, add disunity. The mujahideen are, for the most part, feudal warriors who value personal honor and bravery but who have almost no comprehension of the fact that success in modern warfare requires collective action. The Islamic Alliance for the Liberation of Afghanistan is an alliance in name only; it suffers from the fragmentation that afflicts many revolutionary movements, though not for the usual ideological reasons. As far as their political philosophies go, you can say of the rebel factions what George Wallace said of Democrats and Republicans: there isn't a dime's worth of difference between them. They all espouse some form of fundamentalist Islam. The splits in the resistance have been caused by its leaders, gray-bearded chieftains who have lived long enough to acquire enemies lists longer than Richard Nixon's and who have found in the war a good reason for raising private armies with which they can settle old scores. To put it another way, the Afghans have a penchant for blood feuds, and they often tangle with one another when they aren't fighting the Russians. The day I arrived in Peshawar, a bomb exploded in the building occupied by Jamiat-Islami, killing fourteen people. The guerrillas blamed it on Soviet agents, but Western and Pakistani intelligence sources said a rival Afghan group had set off the bomb.

Tamim entered at last. Folding his legs under him, he sat down. After we'd exchanged courtesies, he made a plea for help: "We are not like the Vietcong. They had assistance from two superpowers, China and Russia. We're alone. Why doesn't America help us?"

I couldn't answer him. Tamim responded with a vow that the Afghans would fight to the last man and the last bullet, regardless.

"Our faith is the strongest barrier against Communism," he said, with a nod to a banner hanging on a wall. It read:

OUR MOTTO: ALLAH IS OUR FINAL GOAL. PROPHET MUHAMMAD OUR ULTIMATE LEADER. JIHAD OUR WAY. MARTYRDOM FOR THE FAITH OUR GREATEST DESIRE.

"The Russians have good weapons. We don't. But we have it in the heart, and we capture weapons from the Russians. And when they get out of their tanks and fight us man to man, we always win."

Tamim neglected to mention that the Russians seldom leave their tanks for that very reason; but he was obviously sincere in his belief that bravery, faith, and the Enfield rifle are a match for the T-62 tank and the Mi-24 gunship.

With all that said, I asked Tamim about the chances of slipping over the border with some of his men. After reflecting a few moments, he suggested a trip to Kunar province, which would require five to eight days' travel. A party of guerrillas was planning to leave for Kunar the day after tomorrow. He would contact me at seven o'clock on the following evening.

Now in the hotel room, Tamim finished his prayers and sat on the couch. Lighting a cigarette, he announced rather dramatically: "You will be leaving for Kunar in the morning. A Pakistani security man is always outside our headquarters at seven, so you must be there before then to change clothes. Do you have everything?" I said I did and showed him my kit: the long shirt, baggy trousers, round Chitrali cap, and capelike blanket worn by Afghan tribesmen; a canteen, hiking boots, a camera and camera bag, and a small, lightweight mountaineer's pack containing a sweater, a change of socks and underwear, notebooks and pens, a Swiss Army knife, and a first-aid kit. Tamim approved of everything, the medical gear especially. "You might need that," he said. "We don't have any doctors."

We were seated beside a dirt path, gazing at the mountain marking the frontier we had just crossed into Afghanistan. Mahmud Hezrat rose, adjusting the pack he had fashioned by wrapping a blanket around his belongings and supplies, then looping and knotting the tag ends into shoulder straps. It weighed thirty or forty pounds, but the thinly built Mahmud carried it with the ease of the old mountain man he was.

"Yusef, stand," he said, meaning that our rest was over. Except for certain military phrases, "stand" and "sit" were the only English words he knew. He did not call me by my first name because he could not pronounce it; I'd told him to address me by my middle name, Joseph, which comes out "Yusef" in Pashto, the predominant language of the Afghans.

I stood slowly, as did Steve Bent, a twenty-one-year-old British freelance photographer who had decided to come along. We were both wiped out after climbing over the mountain that stands between Afghanistan and Bedjauer, the Pakistani border town where we'd spent the night. Six thousand feet up, six thousand down.

Ten of us had crossed the frontier that morning: seven teenage mujahideen, all unarmed and carrying sacks of flour, clothing, and rifle ammunition; Bent and I: and the nominal leader, Mahmud Hezrat. He was about fifty, with the large nose and high cheekbones of a Pathan (the dominant ethnic group in Afghanistan and northern Pakistan) and a vague mustache that made him look like a taxi driver who cheats on fares. He wasn't like that at all but utterly trustworthy, the only fighting man in the bunch. The other seven, as far as I could tell, were raw recruits who had never seen action.

Below the mountain, our small column moved down a dirt track beside a riverbed that was dry except for a trickle of brown water idling down its middle. Terraced wheat fields rose in alternating bands of green and gold on both sides of the river; mud-walled villages stood atop the hills above the fields, these hills climbing toward still-higher hills that rose to meet the Hindu Kush, a great blaze of white far in the distance.

It was a beautiful country, but the fields and villages were nearly deserted. You didn't need to be a military expert to figure out why: Kunar province, this part of it anyway, was a free-fire zone. Mahmud described the destruction in the tone of a park ranger naming species of plants for nature lovers. Pointing at a huge hole blasted out of a mosque, he said, "Roosie tank." At two craters yawning in the middle of the road: "Roosie bomb." At a house with its roof blown off, its timbers charred: "Roosie rocket." At a row of smashed houses on the far side of the river: "Roosie helicopter." Then, sweeping his arm back in the direction from which we'd come: "*Majer, majer.* Pakistan," meaning that the people had fled to the refugee camps across the border. My immediate impression was that the Russians were playing the Great Game with new weapons but in the same old way. Give the wogs a whiff of grapeshot and make 'em run.

By midafternoon we had been on the move nearly eight hours, and an old bullet wound in my leg, which I'd suffered four years earlier while covering the Lebanese civil war, was hurting like hell. Bent and I were parched, hungry, drenched in sweat, and exasperated by the language barrier, which made it impossible for us to find out why we were sailing off into the wild blue without a rifle among us, where we were going, and how long it would take us to get there. We felt a little like captives being led off to an unknown destination.

Sensing our mood and exhaustion, Mahmud took us to a mud-brick house owned by a tall, strongly built mujahid named Posli Akhbar. I dubbed him "the gay guerrilla" because, to abbreviate a long story, he showed an extraordinary affection for Bent and me. Put up in Posli Akhbar's guest room, a dark, dirty hovel abuzz with flies, we were fed a lunch of bread, goat's milk, and tea. Then we collapsed on beds made of woven straw and slept through the afternoon.

In the evening, we made a determined effort to find out from Mahmud where we were headed. The conversation was conducted in pidgin English, pidgin Pashto, and sign language. An hour of this produced some answers. Mahmud showed us an envelope with Pashto script on it: it was a sealed message from Jamiat headquarters to a man named Sher Rahman, whom he described as a *turjoman,* a field commander. Mahmud was a courier. Rahman's position was less than two days' march away, at a place called Kattar. After the message was delivered, we would spend a day or two with Rahman's men, see a bit of the war, and then hike back to Pakistan. I felt reassured; there was a purpose to this expedition, after all. I was also taken with the idea of delivering a message to a guerrilla chieftain. Sher Rahman. It was a grand name, something out of Kipling. We never did find him.

The rain clouds sweeping down from the mountains made the Kunar River look like a ribbon of liquid lead. Flecked with the white of the rapids, it swept past us with a low, steady roar. Some distance to the northwest, where the sky was still clear, a squadron of Russian gunships skimmed over a ridgeline, then nosed down out of view. A few minutes later we caught the rumble of bombs and the short, sharp bursts of rockets. Crouched among the boulders on the riverbank, we listened to the bombardment, scanned the skies for helicopters flying in our direction, and waited to board the raft for the river crossing. That, not the Soviet gunships, was my immediate concern. The current boomed along at a good ten or twelve knots, but the raft was the sorriest jury-rigged lash-up I'd ever seen—nothing more than a few logs and lengths of scrap lumber tied to inflated goatskins and steered with two oars made of flat boards tied to poles with old rope. But it was the only way the guerrillas could get to the other side; the ferries downstream at Chigaserai and upstream at Shegul were in Russian hands.

One of the boatmen—actually a boy of no more than fifteen—finished blowing up the goatskins with a bellow and waved us aboard.

"Bismillah ar-rahman, ar-rahim," Mahmud said as we shoved off and spun into the current, the fast water lapping over the skins, the boatmen heaving on the oars, Now the other mujahideen joined in the chant. *"Bismillah ar-rahman, ar-rahim."* The words mean "in the name of God the all-merciful, the all-loving-kind," and are spoken by Muslims before any important or dangerous undertaking. They are equivalent to the Christian sign of the cross.

The boatmen got the better of the current and swung the raft at an angle across the river. When it bumped against the opposite bank, the rebels opened their arms wide and cried, *"Allahu akhbar"* (God is great).

We scrambled up a cliff to where a dirt road ran through a mile-wide stretch of flat, open country broken by stone fences. It was the closest thing I'd seen to an actual battlefield since we'd crossed the border. Fresh tank tracks corrugated the road. There were old Russian fox-holes ringed by rock parapets, a few burned-out trucks, and scattered bits of spent flares and ammunition. Warning that the fields were sometimes shelled and that armored columns often patrolled the road, Mahmud told us to move quickly. Move quickly we did, Bent loping on his long legs while I hippity-hopped on my gimpy one. Mahmud led us on, running in short sprints, then dropping low to look around, then running again. The other seven, by contrast, sauntered along behind us, filled with the ignorance of death that is one of the privileges of youth.

When we stopped to catch our breath, I told Bent, "I'm sticking close to the old man from now on."

"Why's that?" the Englishman asked in his tough Manchester accent.

"Did you see the way he moved? He's not interested in dying for Islam. He wants to stay alive. That gives us a lot in common."

Getting to our feet, we half ran, half walked into a gully, then climbed a trail to the outskirts of a village named Shinqaluq.

It was an Edenic spot, with pink wildflowers growing at the trailside, wide-spreading chinar trees for shade and concealment, and a cold spring from which Bent and I could fill our canteens. Three mujahideen armed with collectors' pieces were sitting near a small cave they used as an air-raid shelter. It came in handy a few minutes later, when two gunships appeared over a low ridgeline a quarter mile away. They came on not with the rapid *wap-wap-wap* of American Hueys but with a throaty growl, flying straight toward us at low speed and at an altitude of no more than five hundred feet. We scrambled for cover. The cave could hold only two or three men; the rest of us crouched or lay flat under the trees. We could hear the measured throb of the rotor blades as the helicopters flew directly overhead, their slowness suggesting the leisurely confidence of predators with no natural enemies.

It was obvious that these Russian pilots weren't afraid of anything the mujahideen could do to them. And with good reason. The guerrilla beside me was aiming his rifle at the aircraft, and I thought, *"Jesus Christ, don't shoot that damn thing and draw their fire,"* when I saw that his gun was a breechloading Martini-Henry. Stamped on the receiver were the initials v.r.—"Victoria Regina"—and the date of manufacture, 1878. Happily, the choppers flew on. The pilots either did not see us or, if they did, decided we weren't worth the waste of ammunition. We waited for several minutes to make sure they gone for good; then Mahmud shouldered his makeshift pack and spoke the words I was already tired of hearing: "Yusef, stand."

At Kattar, which we reached a day and a half later, a band of guerrillas told us that Sher Rahman had packed his bags. He had been blown out of his position by the Russian bombardment we had heard while crossing the Kunar, and had fled into Nuristan, on the far side of a mountain with the haunting name of Nungalam Tangasaar. It rose some ten or fifteen miles away, all eleven thousand feet of it, its peak white above the timberline. Nuristan is the modern name for Kafiristan, the land where Kipling's Daniel Dravot would have been king; and though a small part of me was curious to see it—its inhabitants are a fair-skinned people who, according to a legend too marvelous to be true, are descendants of a lost legion of Alexander the Great—the larger part of me was not so curious as to want to undergo an eleven-thousand-foot climb.

The march from the Kunar River had been an ordeal for Bent and me. There seemed to be only two directions in eastern Afghanistan: up and farther up. The Russian troops owned the roads and they owned the river valleys, forcing the mujahideen to stick to the high country.

From Shinqaluq we traveled up a ravine to the foot of a dark mountain called Pandasaar. There we rested in the house of a bearded elder and again ate flat, pie-size loaves of bread washed down with goat's milk.

It was a killing six-hour trek up the eight-thousand-foot Pandasaar. Through chinar and wild mulberry trees on the lower slopes, through walnut and hazel higher up, we climbed a trail that was steep enough in places to make our thigh muscles quiver. At sunset we reached the summit, too drugged with fatigue to appreciate the view, then slogged down a short distance to a wretched little village of pine-log huts.

Our night camp was the local mosque, a drafty shack with an open doorway and paneless windows. While Bent and I stretched out, our thin blankets not much protection against the wind, Mahmud and the others sat around the fire talking to a few local guerrillas, men whose faces had the color and texture of the leather bandoliers that crisscrossed over their chests. The mujahideen seemed indefatigable. I saw then how smart the Russians were to fight this war with helicopters and tanks. The toughest infantry in the world would be no match for the Afghans in these mountains.

In the morning, peppered with tick bites, we started down the other side of Pandasaar, walking quickly over an upland meadow into the shelter of a pine and cedar forest when two Mi-24 gunships buzzed close by. A few miles off ten more choppers were clearly visible against the white of the distant mountains. One by one, they dipped down to strafe some valley far below. We could not see the bombardment, but we heard it—a low, rolling rumble.

The trail led us through the pines, then past empty villages where water coursing down chutes made of hollowed logs turned mill wheels that creaked on uselessly because there was no one to put grain into the mills; past fields where goats grazed with no one to heard them; past files of refugees, the children carrying chickens and teakettles, the women burdened with infants slung papoose-style over their backs, the men bent double under enormous bundles of rugs, blankets, and odd bits of furniture. One very old man hopped along like a crippled bird, using two tree branches for crutches. The Russian bombardment kept echoing through the mountains with a sound that made me think of oil drums rolling through a tunnel.

"*Khali,*" Mahmud said, using the Arabic work for "empty." Then, "*Majer, majer.* Pakistan."

His reaction to what the Russians were doing—emptying Afghanistan of Afghans—wasn't clear from his flat tone of voice. It was very clear when you looked into his dark, deep-set eyes, in which the tension between fury and sorrow created an intensity that seemed capable of burning holes through a man.

On the trek down Pandasaar, we not only saw the effects of Soviet methods but felt them—in our guts. We had eaten nothing since the previous night. So when we reached Kattar and heard that Sher Rahman had fled to Nuristan, Bent and I hoped Mahmud would give up the chase. He didn't. We went on, into a deep gorge where a river flung itself against the rocks, roaring so loudly that we had to shout to make ourselves heard, then up and up a narrow trail until the sound of the river diminished to a whisper.

Small bands of guerrillas, who seemed to be wandering the countryside aimlessly, passed us along the way. They greeted us with calls of "*Salaam aleikum*" (Peace be unto you) and fed us a mishmash of contradictory information. Sher Rahman had been killed in the bombing. Sher Rahman lived. Sher Rahman had fled to Kabul, not Nuristan. No, Sher Rahman was still in Kunar, in the village of Gumbier, with an army of four thousand mujahideen.

Off we trekked to Gumbier, where we found not four thousand rebels but four. They were sitting outside the house of a local commander, a proud, dignified-looking man with a thick black mustache, a bullet-studded bandolier, and bad news. Sher Rahman had definitely gone to Nuristan; he had established a new outpost at Amirat, a village in the Weygul River valley on the far side of the mountain called Nungalam Tangasaar. To reach Amirat, we would have to scale the mountain by way of a pass below the peak; we would reach the village late the following afternoon, Allah willing.

The mustachioed chieftain put us up for the night. Bread, goat's milk, tea. Bent and I were hungry to the point that we could hardly eat, tired to the point that we could not sleep. Lying on the wicker cots, we listened to some distant shelling and to the guerrillas talking among themselves. We understood very little, of course, but a few words from the English lexicon of war kept cropping up in their conversation. And it occurred to me that these isolated mountaineers had been talking about other things not long ago—about marriages and tribal disputes and crops and livestock and local scandals. Now it was "helicopter," "bomb," "tank," "rocket."

The pass over Nungalam Tangasaar stood at nine or ten thousand feet, where the air was thin and cold. Even with the sun high, we could see our breath and the steam rising from our bodies. Looking down past a meadow covered with yellow wildflowers and Parnassus grass, down to the dark green timberline, I felt rather pleased with myself for having made it up the mountain. More than pleased—exhilarated. We had begun the ascent at four in the morning and had finished it around noon, Bent and I sucking the air as greedily as thirsty men drink water.

From atop the pass, where the summit pointed upward like a huge white spike above us, we gazed down on Nuristan, on all the wooded ridges, steep ravines, and glass-clear streams tumbling into the Weygul valley, beyond which more ridges rose toward mountains whose peaks were almost as bright as the sun. It was the kind of country that does the same thing to your heart as the sight of a woman you love passionately; but just to remind us that we weren't on some hike in the Bavarian Alps, a formation of Mi-24s appeared, silhouetted against the white mountains. The helicopters swooped down and began to strafe the Weygul.

This attack did not end after an hour or two; it went on all afternoon. Around four, after we had passed through forests where the pines looked a thousand years old, we started down a steep hillside toward Klaigul, a Nuristani village of flat-roofed houses built in tiers against a cliff. A stream rushed beneath it toward the river, above which helicopters circled and dived. Smoke from their bombs rose in columns over the villages hugging the banks of the Weygul. We could hear tank cannons and the helicopters' mini guns, which fire so rapidly that a single burst sounds like the explosion of a drag racer's engine when the starter's flag goes down. Sometimes a guerrilla's machine gun fired five or ten rounds in reply; this told me that the mujahideen had great fire discipline or, more likely, did not have enough ammunition. Even if they had had enough, it would have been virtually useless against the

Mi-24, one of the wonders of late-twentieth-century death engineering. The gunship's armor plating makes it a flying tank, invulnerable to all but the heaviest anti-aircraft fire; it is armed with a conventional machine gun in the nose, an undernose mini gun (which shoots six thousand rounds per minute), 128 rockets, as many as four bombs carried in wingtip pylons, four air-to-surface missiles, and electronic sensor packs for accurate rocket firing in bad weather or rough terrain.

Watching those helicopters flying at a speed and altitude no American pilot would have dared in Vietnam unless he'd had a death wish, listening to the pitifully brief bursts from the rebel guns, I thought, "This isn't a war, it's a Russian training exercise."

We did not see them at first; they were below us, lazing along almost at treetop level over the stream, their green fuselages camouflaged against the ridge on the far side. Rising as the streambed rose, the two gunships appeared suddenly at our eye level and less then half a mile off.

"Kena!" (get down!) Mahmud shouted. The others, Bent among them, ducked under a grove of mulberry trees a hundred feet or so downslope. Mahmud and I were caught on an exposed patch of ground where a few low bushes offered the only concealment. The two of us lay under these, keeping our eyes on the helicopters as they climbed toward the pass. They hung in the air for a moment; then—and I swear this is true, though I know it can't be—the lead chopper seemed to shudder in the excited way a man-o'-war bird shudders just before it swoops down on a school of fish. All right, I was imagining things, hallucinating perhaps—stress and exhaustion do funny things to your brain chemistry—but I can still see that tremor passing through the helicopter the instant before it banked sharply and came down toward us, its rotors flashing in the sun.

Mahmud started to pray. *"Bismillah ar rahman, ar-rahim."* He gestured to me to cover my watch with my sleeve so that it wouldn't reflect the sunlight. Both gunships were closing in now, low enough for us to see the barrels of both the nose gun and the mini gun under the nose. *"Bismillah ar-rahman, ar-rahim."* Mahmud's praying had become frantic, a desperate appeal, a garble of words in which I could only make out *"Allah."* Allah, Allah, Allah. The gunships drifted overhead; any slower and they would have been hovering. Mini guns, rocket pods, bomb racks, sensor packs. The whole nine yards. Six thousand rounds a minute.

A one-second burst would turn a man into something resembling dog food. And if it had to happen, I hoped it would happen that way—quickly. The only thing I wanted less than to be killed in Afghanistan was to be seriously wounded in Afghanistan. The mujahideen are waging partisan warfare on the thinnest of shoestrings. Not enough modern weapons, not enough ammunition, and as Tamim had told me, no doctors. No medevacs, either. The injured are evacuated on muleback or camelback. Few survive the trip out. For most, it is slow death.

Mahmud continued to send up his fervent prayers. The choppers were straight overhead, their turbos making a pulsing whine. I don't know if Allah was listening, but the gunships abruptly made a tight turn and headed back toward the Weygul. That river was as far as I cared to go. Mahmud, however, remained faithful to his mission and led us on to Klaigul, which was a mile farther.

We saw our first Nuristanis there. Some were as dark as the Pathans, but others looked as English as the blond, six-foot Bent. Despite the helicopters buzzing nearby and the bombs falling only two miles away, the local mujahideem commander, a twenty-two-year-old ex-teacher who spoke English, took us into his house and treated us with the usual hospitality. We asked our host if he could help by guiding us to Amirat. He shook his head. The Soviet attack was concentrating on Amirat. It was much too dangerous to go there. If Sher Rahman wasn't dead, he was on the run to somewhere.

That was it as far as I was concerned. We had chased this phantom Rahman for four days, often marching fourteen hours a day. We had gone far enough. Using the local commander as an interpreter, I told Mahmud that. Much to my relief, and Bent's as well, he agreed. Gesturing toward the Weygul, he said that the mujahideen there were finished. He had done the best he could; to go on would be foolhardy. In the morning we would start the return trip to Pakistan.

We ended up back on Pandasaar four days later, with plenty of company. Blankets wrapped around our shoulders against the chill, Bent and I sat awaiting our turn to move. In front of us a file of refugees struggled up a trail toward the crest of the mountain. The men were carrying bundles of mattresses and sheepskins on their backs, bundles that looked big enough to crumple a mule. The women, their silver bracelets and amulets jingling, shambled along, some with infants held to their breasts. Those children old enough to walk walked, as they had been walking since they'd left Nuristan, on bare feet over rocky trails that bit and slashed their skin. They were all going up the mountain: men, women, and kids, the old and the sick, about a thousand people altogether. Bent and I watched, awed by their endurance.

We had left Klaigul and climbed for six hours to another village, where we spent a cold, unhappy night sleeping in a cave. Next morning, with Russian mortar shells thudding in the valley below, the villagers decided they would go with us. They packed whatever could be carried and left everything else behind. One headman ran up to me pointing at a helicopter with one hand and waiving a .303 Enfield cartridge in my face with the other. He shouted in Pashto, but I understood his meaning clearly enough: he and the others were fleeing because those .303s were no defense against the technology and the firepower that the Soviets were throwing at them.

Over the next three days, the original column grew from about a hundred people to a thousand. As far as I could tell, this mass evacuation had not been planned. It seemed as spontaneous as a flash flood, with refugees flowing in from the Weygul and an adjoining rivevalley, the Pech, which had also come under attack. Perhaps a fifth of the column were mujahideen, men who had been designated to guard their clans and families on the long walk to Pakistan. Their presence made the evacuation look like a retreat, and in some ways it was.

We ran from the Russians, then almost ran into them. All during the three-day march from Nuristan we had heard the sound of the Russian bombing behind us. On the morning of the third day, as the column was beginning to climb Pandasaar, that same sound started coming from somewhere in front of us. We were nearing the pine-log village, the one where Bent and I had slept in the mosque a week before, when we passed a mujahideen patrol coming from the direction of the Kunar River. They gave us the worst possible news: Soviet helicopters were attacking the village of Shinqaluq and the ford over the Kunar River; a column of twenty tanks had also moved in to block the crossing point; the tanks' machine guns had opened up on the rafts and had sunk them, killing three guerrillas and four civilians. There were Russians behind us in the Weygul valley, Russians west of us in the Pech valley, and now Russians in front of us on the Kunar The door out to Pakistan had been closed. We were cut off, trapped, screwed.

The leaders of the evacuation decided that we could do nothing but wait it out. It was midmorning of the following day when a young mujahid entered the stable where Bent and I were housed and squatted beside the fire we had built to ward off the high-country cold. He and Mahmud fell into a long conversation, after which the old man looked toward heaven and muttered a prayer. It turned out to be a prayer of thanksgiving. The tanks had moved, Mahmud explained in the usual mixture of pidgin and sign language. New rafts—launches, he grandly called them—had been brought up. There was, however, one Russian position upstream from the crossing point and another one downstream. The plan was to move the column through this opening and ferry the whole lot across under cover of darkness. The operation would have to be completed by dawn, to avoid being spotted by Soviet gunships.

Feeling relieved and anxious at the same time, Bent and I went outside to await our turn. Mahmud approached, carrying a shotgun and a Lee Enfield with a rag tightly bound around the forestock and barrel to hold them together. He handed it to me, explaining that moving a thousand people across a wild river and through Russian lines at night would be a tricky business; he could not guarantee our safety. If things went wrong, we would have to look out for ourselves. I hoped I would not have to fire that beat-up rifle. It wasn't my war, but Mahmud seemed to think otherwise.

"Mujahid," he said, clapping my shoulder with a smile.

The column was organized, more or less, into clan and village groups; along with Mahmud, we had been adopted by the family of a dark-bearded mullah named Gulzada. The four of us idled outside the stable while, inside, Gulzada's youngest daughter baked loaves of flat bread for the trip ahead. His wife and his older daughters huddled nearby, veiling their faces with their shawls. Finally Gulzada shouldered his belongings, and Mahmud turned to me and said, "Yusef, stand."

The flat, upright boulders looked like grave markers in the light of the quarter-moon. Led by Mahmud, we stumbled down a gully toward the Kunar. The sound of distant mortar and machine-gun fire punctuated the steady, whispering rush of the river. Moving out of the gully, we started over a stretch of flat ground crisscrossed by tank tracks. Gulzada and his family trailed behind. We clambered down a cliff toward the Kunar, its waters black except where the rapids caught the moonlight. Below, we found hundreds of people crowded onto a narrow, rock bank.

The ferrying operation was already well under way. Those still waiting their turn raised their hands toward the sky and implored God to grant the others safe passage. It was moving to hear their voices rising in the darkness above the noise of the water, to sense the strength of their hard, simple faith.

The operation went on all night: a thousand people ferried over a wild river on rafts buoyed by inner tubes and inflated goatskins. Our turn came a little after five. It was now fully light, and we would be utterly helpless if any helicopters showed up.

The crossing took only a few minutes. When we got to the other side, I embraced Mahmud and thanked him. He, of course, thanked God. He then took a roll of Afghan currency and paid the boatmen. If courage, honor, and faith are the Pathans' principal virtues, greed is their principal vice. The boatmen were charging twenty *afghanis* per head to take the refugees across.

We saw another, uglier example of Pathan avarice four hours later, on the trail back to Pakistan. The river crossing had split the long column into small bands, and the group Bent, Mahmud, and I were traveling with was waylaid by bandits who lived in the Kunar valley. There were only three of them, led by a vicious young man armed with a Russian machine gun. They were levying a toll on travelers passing through their territory. The mujahideen outnumbered the gang ten to one, and could have shot all three. They didn't because, as Mahmud explained, the bandits' clansmen—dozens of them—would have come down out of the hills and wiped out the mujahideen in revenge.

Mahmud was the only one to ignore the machine gunner's order to move to the side of the trail. Cool-headedly he walked on telling Bent and me to do the same. We hugged the embankment to stay out of the machine gun's line of fire. The young man kept yelling and we kept waving, until we rounded a bend to what I hoped was safety. Mahmud flopped down and in gestures, said that his heart was pounding. From what I could understand of his sign language, he had defied the bandit's orders out of fear that they would have discovered Bent and I were foreigners and held us for ransom. I felt greatly relieved, and grateful, and disgusted. The resistance had enough strikes against it without Afghans' using the war as an opportunity to plunder other Afghans. But then, there are profiteers in every war.

We reached the border two days later, after a hard march. The combined retreat-evacuation had been successful; no one had been lost or injured. Nevertheless, it was a defeat—a small and perhaps temporary one, but a defeat. Five months of fighting had already created a million refugees. Now a thousand more had been added, a thousand more people who would not be there to give the mujahideen shelter, food, and intelligence. It was, I thought, the Great Game in reverse. A century and a half ago, the Afghans had driven out one foreign conqueror; now another was driving *them* out.

And many of those primitive mountain people were leaving the terrors of war for those of a new and alien way of life. I recall Gulzada's youngest daughter, a girl of about ten or eleven, letting out a hysterical scream while we were walking down a road toward the refugee camp at Bedjauer. A pickup truck was coming toward us. The truck was what had frightened her. She had never seen one before.

the coils of memory

1 9 9 9

We are in a village cemetery, among low hills west of Danang, but not all the dead here lie in the ground. Some wing above us, swooping and circling with distressful cries. Leslie mistakes them for birds—they look like plovers, she says, observing their black, brown, and white markings and long slender legs that resemble forked tails when drawn back in flight. She knows a few things about aviary species—she used to work for *Audubon* magazine—and speculates aloud that these birds are making that strange cry, at once mournful and alarmed, because we're disturbing their nesting area.

"Those are the souls of the dead," Thieu says, correcting her identification. "Both Vietnamese and American, and they're crying out their sorrow to the living."

Nguyen Quang Thieu is a poet, but he isn't speaking metaphorically; among the Vietnamese, the threads of the mystical are spun tightly into the weave of daily life, and the supernatural world is as real as the one they can see and smell and touch. Every other village in this land owns at least one ghost; every other family can tell you that they have been visited by an ancestor dead for a hundred years, and the whole country, from the mist-shrouded hills near the Chinese border to the broiling marshes of the Mekong Delta, celebrates *Trung Nguyen,* Wandering Souls' Day, on the fifteenth day of the seventh lunar month. That is when offerings of fish, meat, and fruit are laid at domestic altars and in public temples to mollify spirits made itinerant because they have been forgotten by the living.

I had an encounter with a restless Vietnamese ghost thirty-four years ago, in a village only a mile from where I now stand, among grave markers that look like miniature pagodas. The five of us—Leslie, Thieu, photographer Rob Howard, and Thinh, a guide from the East Asia tourist company in Danang—spent the morning in the village. It is called Hoai Nhon, and it looked much as I remembered it: a hundred-odd houses with thatch and tile roofs clustered along a dirt road, in the shadow of jungle hills I recall by the numbers that designated their height in meters on our military maps: 327, 268, 264. At the southern edge of Hoai Nhon, shaded by old trees, is a long bungalow, made of concrete block and stucco, that serves as the village school. It had the same purpose in 1965, although there were no desks or blackboards or students in it then. Wartime. School was out for an indefinite period.

My thoughts travel back to a night of relentless rain and monsoon wind in mid-December, when a squad of marines from my platoon, my radioman, and I were inside the schoolhouse, smoking our smokes, drying off and resting up after a night patrol. The villagers had warned us to stay out of there at night. Years before, during the French-Indochina War, the local teacher had been executed by Viet Minh guerrillas for his loyalty to the French colonial government, and, the villagers said, his unquiet ghost often returned in the hours of darkness to haunt the scene of his death. We ignored their warning, though not necessarily because we were skeptical about the ghost's existence. With such an abundance of enemies from this world—those flesh-and-blood phantoms called the Vietcong—we needn't worry about those from the world beyond.

But around two in the morning, the schoolhouse door began to rattle and bang. At first, we thought it was the wind, but we quickly dismissed that explanation: the door was shaking as though someone were trying to force his way inside. "Who's there? Who goes there?" the squad leader, a sergeant named Pryor, called out. There was no response. A marine swore he heard someone moving around outside. A second later, the door shook so violently it seemed about to be ripped from its hinges. I drew my pistol, Pryor leveled his M-14 rifle, but we held our fire, because another squad was standing guard on the perimeter outside, and we were afraid of hitting one of our own men. We pulled the bar back and shouldered the door open, but saw no one.

Shining flashlights on the ground, we searched amid the bootprints made by marines for the smaller prints that would have been made by a Vietcong infiltrator. There weren't any.

Next moment, three drenched marines came up to report that they had heard the sound of footsteps in the mud near their foxholes, yet hadn't seen anyone. Pryor and I went back into the schoolhouse, barred the door, and waited for several minutes, testing to see if the wind had been the cause after all. The door didn't budge, and as the wind groaned and the palm fronds rasped and the rain crackled against the roof, we looked at each other but did not say what we thought.

The next day, a villager told us that when he'd left his hut the previous night to relieve himself he'd seen a wraithlike form, drifting down a ravine toward the schoolhouse. Months in the bush had bred within us a certain credulity. Vietnam, we'd learned, was a land where anything could happen, where just about any story was plausible. We were convinced that we had been visited by the Teacher's Ghost.

Nothing since then has changed my mind, which is why I don't believe my wife and do believe Thieu: the souls of the dead, both Vietnamese and American, have taken the form of birds to cry their sorrow to the living. I don't know the names of the Vietnamese dead, but I do know the names of some American dead, sixteen altogether, and the names merge in my memory into a single name, as the faces merge into one face of a young marine who will never know the indignities of old age:

GAUTIER GUZMAN FANKHAUSER FERNANDEZ LEVY
LOCKHART MANNING MUIR PAGE REASONER
SISSLER SIMPSON SNOW SULLIVAN WARNEE WEST.

Their ghosts are here, along with another, and its name is Phil Caputo: the ghost of who I used to be, a twenty-three-year-old rifle platoon leader in the Third Marine Division, a man I am sometimes proud of and sometimes ashamed of, but proud or ashamed, whom I must accept as he was then, a warrior, a killer, carbine in his hand, knife and pistol hanging from his belt, his rucksack and cargo pockets filled with the implements of his lethal trade: hand grenades, smoke grenades, flares, compass, maps in acetate covers with patrol routes and checkpoints and concentrations of preplanned artillery fire marked in grease pencil.

I am here to make my peace with him, and with the biggest ghost of all, the ghost of a past that haunts me still.

I made my peace with my former enemies nine years ago, when I and seven other American veterans who had become novelists and poets were invited to Vietnam by the Vietnamese Writers Union to meet with Vietcong and North Vietnamese army veterans who had become novelists and poets. "We are writers of blood and fire," said one of our hosts at the opening conference in Hanoi, sounding a note of brotherhood. "We saw war with the naked eye, but holding a pen is a thousand times more difficult than holding a rifle."

Danang was where the war began for me, on March 8, 1965, and I had a strange feeling of homecoming when our group of warriors-turned-writers traveled to that crowded, noisy port on the South China Sea. That evening, at a dinner hosted by the local chapter of the Writers Union, a poet named Ngan Vinh made a brief speech and then read one of his works, "After the Rain in the Forest." He was a striking-looking man, tall for a Vietnamese at five feet nine, with a lean, muscular build and a shock of thick, black hair graying at the temples. During the war, Vinh had been a platoon leader like me, commanding forty-two men in the 1st battalion, 40th brigade of the North Vietnamese Army, and his poem was about carrying a wounded comrade to safety after a battle in the monsoon in 1967. The words and imagery—the weight of the man on his shoulders, blood mixed with rain spilling into the mud of the trail—astonished me because they were so like the words and images of a poem I had written in 1966, the first literary work I'd published outside of school magazines. It was called "Infantry in the Monsoon," and it was about carrying wounded comrades in the rain. I mentioned this coincidence to Vinh after the meal. He asked me to read the poem, but I didn't have it with me; nor could I remember more than a few lines, which I recited, at his request. We got to talking, discovered that his battalion and mine had operated in the same valley, southwest of Danang, in early 1966, and though we determined that we had never fought each other, that was close enough. Vinh filled two glasses with vodka and said we had to drink together. We tossed our glasses back, and then Vinh embraced me and said, "You and me, Philip, we are brothers in arms," and that night, June 21, 1990, was when the Vietnam War ended for me.

There remained only one piece of unfinished business. In one of his poems—I forget which—Rudyard Kipling wrote, "We have but one virginity to lose, and where we lost it, there our hearts will always be." I had wanted, in 1990, to return to the battlefields where I had lost that virginity, and where my friends had lost far more—their arms, their legs, their minds, their lives. I made an attempt, got as far as the village of Hoai Nhon, but no farther. An irate village chief turned me back because I did not have the proper authorization to visit the area. Also, no one had notified him that I would be coming, which insulted his dignity and violated protocol. I told him I was in Vietnam at the invitation of the Writers Union, and with the blessings of the government, but that cut no ice with him. There is an ancient proverb in Vietnam: "The emperor's power stops at the village gate."

On this trip, I went to some pains to obtain all the correct documents and imprimaturs, and through the good offices of the Writers Union, made sure the local authorities were told about my visit. Now, wearing the same canvas-and-leather jungle boots I wore over thirty years ago, I am going to walk down the same paddy-dikes that were once exposed to snipers, down the same muddy trails once sown with mines and boobytraps, then through the swales of elephant grass that sawed the skin, and on up into the mountainous jungle beneath whose soaring canopy men with rifles once waited in patient ambush. But I am not on an adventure. This is more in the nature of a pilgrimage, to make peace with myself, yes, but something more. I am thinking, in this instance, of a line Ophelia speaks in Act Four of *Hamlet:* "We know what we are, but know not what we may be." In Vietnam, some cherished image we Americans had of ourselves as a people essentially virtuous came apart. My own flattering self-image was shredded here. I thought I was one thing, and discovered that I had become a person I never wanted or expected to be. I had found a darkness within myself, a kind of evil twin I hadn't realized was in me. I am here to confront him as well, that aspect of my youthful ghost that I am ashamed of.

And so I lead this rather strange patrol that consists of my wife, a photographer, a poet, and a tour guide toward Hill 22, which was a forward outpost that my company, C company, 1st Battalion, 1st Marines, had occupied between November 1965 and February 1966. If there is much that's familiar—the peasants in conical straw hats plowing with water buffalo, or bowing and stooping in the rice paddies; the hamlets shaded by banana palms, and far off to the west, the brooding slopes of a cloud-capped mountain called Nui Ba Na—there is more that's unfamiliar. Flowers for one: bougainvillea, hibiscus, and frangipani, along with scarlet and saffron blossoms I cannot name. Birds for another, not just the birds Thieu identified as grieving souls, but green and turquoise birds, and egrets with feathers as white as angel wings. I do not remember seeing birds and flowers during the war. Had the birds been driven out by the fighting, had the flowers died for lack of tending? Or had I simply not noticed them, my soldier's eyes blinded to beauty? Maybe so. In my Vietnam memoir, *A Rumor of War,* I had written about the peculiar vision of an infantry officer: "Landscape was no longer scenery to me, it was *terrain,* and I judged it for tactical rather than aesthetic value." But now I can look upon the Vietnamese landscape as landscape. For the first time, I see Vietnam not as a battlefield, nor as a metaphor for disaster and folly and waste of lives, but as a country.

Which is why I cannot find Hill 22. The hill in my memory, stripped of vegetation, is a brown, muddy height ringed with barbed wire and scarred with foxholes, bunkers, trenches, and mortar pits, while all the hills before my eyes are covered with trees, mostly eucalyptus trees planted since the war.

Then a scrawny farmer in a checkered shirt sees us looking around in confusion and asks what we are looking for. When I tell him, he says, "Oh, sure, Hill 22. I'll take you there." His shirt is opened, and my glance falls on the tattoo on his chest. It says USA. The farmer, who gives his name as Pham Van Thang and his age as fifty-one, tells us that he is from these parts and had served with the South Vietnamese Army and been wounded by artillery fire.

Leading us to Hill 22, Pham says that there are quite a few former Vietcong in the neighboring hamlets and that he and they get along just fine. I am not entirely convinced that he is speaking the whole truth, and ask Thieu's opinion about Pham's veracity.

"He and the Vietcong were soldiers," says Thieu, short, stockily built, with a thick mustache that looks as if it's made from carbon fibers. "They talk and get along. They're not like the presidents of countries. Fuck all the presidents."

Thieu, I might point out, is from the North and a member of the Communist party, but is considered something of a rebel in this country; a poet willing to test the limits of the party's tolerance for dissent but savvy enough to know when to pull back. Martyrdom is not on his agenda. We climb a wide path through the eucalyptus, but the only thing familiar to me is the heat, and even that is not as severe as I remember it, probably because I'm not wearing a seventeen-pound flak jacket and carrying another forty pounds of weapons, ammo, and gear.

In a little while, something in the way the land unfolds stirs a memory, and I look off to the side of the path and see a round depression in the ground—the remnants of an old foxhole or mortar emplacement—and then a rectangular one—an old bunker. When we reach the crest of the hill, overlooking terraced rice paddies and tiered hills rising westward toward Nui Ba Na, falling southward toward the Song Tuy Loan River, I finally know where I am. Yet there is still a strangeness, brought on by the absence of the sounds that had become so grooved into my eardrums that I could not sleep without them for a long time after I came home from the war: the ominous rumble of distant artillery and bombing, the intermittent tickety-tack of automatic weapons fire, the eerie noise, similar to an owl's hoot, made by parachute flares drifting downward in the night.

A little way down the slope, at what's known in the soldier's trade as the "military crest," is a hole in the ground about eight feet square and six deep, half filled in with earth and partly overgrown with weeds, in which lies a rotted, stiffened, olive-drab poncho. I know, not with brain knowledge but with bone knowledge, that it's what's left of the bunker where I used to huddle with my radioman, Jones, under a roof composed of bamboo logs with three layers of sandbags on top. I climb in, and gazing through a kind of temporal telescope, see a blurred image of Jones and me, sitting with our backs to the muddy walls, listening to patrol leaders calling in situation reports in code-word jargon. *Charley two, this is charley two-one. Alpha sierra sierra romeo sierra.* The latter phrase was the Vietnam version of "all quiet on the western front." It stood for "all secure, situation remains the same," meaning that nothing had happened.

Climbing out, I observe a small, freshly painted pagoda a short distance away, and it flips another switch in my memory, which I share with my wife and companions.

"That was a ruin during the war, just a few jagged walls," I say. "It was a few yards outside our perimeter wire. One night, a couple of VC sneaked inside and lobbed grenades, or maybe they shot at us, I don't remember exactly. Didn't hit any of us. We dropped a sixty-millimeter mortar round on them. Didn't get them either. They were already long gone. All we did was blow a few more holes in the pagoda."

My audience looks at me expectantly. They are waiting for the punch line, for some point to the story. There isn't any, or, to put it in other words, the story's pointlessness is the point. It's a quark-size microcosm of the war.

I have another memory, but it is not one I share with my wife and the others. I have shared it with the approximately two million people who have read *A Rumor of War,* but I find myself unable to utter it face to face to anyone. It's certainly not a story to tell your wife, lest she begin to wonder just who and what it is she married.

Pretending that I have to take a leak, I walk a few yards toward the pagoda, then stop and in fact do take a leak. I'm not sure I'm peeing on the exact spot, but I know I'm close to it: the minuscule patch of alien earth where I stood, in the early morning blackness in late January of 1966, and said "How do you do!" to my own personal Mr. Hyde, the secret sharer of my soul.

Let me establish something: I don't really want to be here. I would rather be home in Connecticut, observing the quiet glories of a New England spring, than on this heat-stricken hill on the other side of the earth, resurrecting ugly memories better left interred. I'm sick to death of thinking about the Vietnam War, dreaming about it, and above all, writing about it.

But here I am, so I might as well, in what I hope is a last farewell and a final repudiation, piss into Mr. Hyde's face just to let him know what I think of him. Of course, it's my own face, so really I'm letting myself know what I think of me as the stream splashes on or near the ground where I stood laughing over the corpse of a nineteen-year-old Vietnamese boy killed by one of my patrols. He was one of two killed that night, in a hamlet called Giao Tri, about two kilometers from Hill 22. Earlier, an informer in the village had told us that both young men were members of a Vietcong sapper team—boobytrap and demolitions experts—and though I had ordered the patrol to capture them if possible, kill them if necessary, in truth I hoped my marines would find a reason to kill them. I wanted them dead, and to this day, I believe that the patrol knew I wanted it because they wanted it; wanted it because 34 men from our 140-man company had been killed and wounded in the previous month, 9 from our platoon, and almost all the casualties had been from mines and boobytraps.

And so we laughed over the corpse with the gaping hole in the side of its head, from which blood and brains leaked out. We roared hysterically when a marine kicked it in the ribs and said, "Oh, excuse me! Hope that didn't hurt." Yeah, we'd paid old Charlie back, and payback is a bitch. Ha, ha, ho, ho, for "Merry it was to laugh there," as the World War One poet Wilfred Owen wrote, "where death becomes absurd and life absurder. For power was on us as we slashed bones bare, not to feel sickness or remorse of murder."

And murder it was. The two Vietnamese turned out not to be Vietcong, but South Vietnamese draft dodgers, seeking refuge with relatives in the village. I said earlier that I did not know the names of the Vietnamese dead whose souls had become birds to cry their sorrow. Well, I do know the names of those two: Le Dung and Le Du, and we killed them because we thought they were the enemy, when in fact the enemy was us and what we had become.

We called it Purple Heart Trail, because so many marines had been killed and wounded on it. It wasn't a single trail, but a skein of paths and tracks that led through the jungle galleries bordering the Song Tuy Loan.

The next shrine on the pilgrimage is on the trail; it's the place where my platoon was ambushed on Christmas Eve, 1965. I can see it in my mind—a rice paddy with the river to its back, foothills to its front, a tree line on each of the other two sides, a dead tree standing where the rice paddy ended and the high ground began, a sagging barbed-wire fence running from the tree back toward the river. That description could fit any one of a thousand places around here, and I am once again disoriented by the changes in the landscape. Since the end of the war, the Vietnamese government has made great efforts to settle the rural areas, and what I remember as a hideous tangle of bamboo thickets interspersed with meadows of elephant grass is now under cultivation, mostly with sugarcane and tobacco. What had been a footpath is now a dirt road, big enough to handle motor vehicles, and new villages have sprung up along it. Some look prosperous by the standards of this desperately poor country, with many small, brick villas with stucco facing and tile floors instead of the usual thatch and bamboo and dirt floors. Electrical towers march across the countryside, bringing the blessings and curses of electricity to places that thirty years ago were lit only by oil lamps. Looking through one window, I see kids watching their new Sony TV.

We pass a shed, its roof supported by bamboo trunks with old GI helmet liners resting on their tops, cut across a sugarcane field, and come to the river, shallow in the dry season, and the river is the only thing I recognize. I sense that everyone is wondering what we're looking for, and why, so I describe the ambush: the dead tree exploding— there was an electrically detonated mine concealed at its base—the eruption of automatic rifle fire from the tree line, marines firing back, and the whole thing over in fifteen seconds. I was knocked down by the blast, but wasn't hit, the back of my flak jacket having absorbed the shrapnel. Five of my men were badly wounded, one with a sucking chest wound that brought a pink froth to his mouth, another with one arm hanging by a single strand of muscle, a third's face looked as if it had been clawed by a wildcat. Then carrying the casualties to a landing zone through the rain (the inspiration for my poem), calling in the medevac, the rhythmic chop of helicopter rotor blades.

As I tell this particular war story, a handful of Vietnamese gather around. This is still a remote part of the country, and foreigners are a very rare sight. One of the onlookers is a middle-age man on crutches, wearing a gray shirt and gray trousers, the left leg of which is folded and pinned back to the stump of his thigh. He asks Thieu who we are and what we're up to. Thieu tells him I'm an American veteran, visiting the scenes of battles long ago. The man, who says that his name is Doan Thu, nods and then tells us his war story.

"In 1973, when I was thirteen years old, I was bringing our cow home from the fields. The cow stepped on a landmine. The explosion killed it outright. My leg was badly mangled. I was taken to the hospital in Danang, where the doctors cut it off."

End of story, and I am sufficiently humbled to watch my words from now on.

A few kilometers upriver, closer to the somber loom of Nui Ba Na, lies the village of Hoi Vuc. People who have read the histories of the war are familiar with its big events, like the battles of the Ia Drang valley and Hamburger Hill, the Tet Offensive, and the fall of Saigon in 1975; but for the great majority of men who fought it, the war was mostly a matter of small-unit actions in obscure places that are not in the history books and never will be. Hoi Vuc, a village of perhaps one hundred families near the fork of the Song Tuy Loan and one of its tributaries, was one of those places; a hard-core, nasty place where an American patrol was all but certain to get into a firefight, or run into an ambush, or trip a boobytrap, or come under sniper fire. "Holy fuck! Hoi Vuc!" the marines in C company would groan whenever their mission took them within a kilometer of the village. There, early one evening in the monsoon, my own platoon had battled a platoon of main-force Vietcong, the rain-swollen Song Tuy Loan preventing them from closing with us and us with them, so we all we did was shoot at each for ten minutes or so. We killed three without suffering a casualty ourselves, but we came under heavy mortar fire that night, and called in artillery on the VC positions, our shells falling so close they were as much a danger to us as to the enemy, the air rent by screeches and blasts and shrapnel cracking overhead with a sound like cracking whips. I remember that, and the day a couple of weeks later, when my platoon was ambushed near Hoi Vuc, again by VC armed with an electrically detonated mine and AK-47s. Two of my men were lightly wounded, but a third had been hurt pretty bad, a PFC named Arnett, who muttered, as a corpsman shot him up with morphine, "This is my third Purple Heart, and they ain't gettin' no more chances. I'm goin' home." (In Vietnam, soldiers who'd been wounded three times were deemed to have done enough for their country and were automatically sent to the rear or rotated back to the U.S.)

Hoi Vuc was a very hard nut to crack, and one day, our regimental commanding officer took me aside, showed me his tactical operations map, and because I had fought in so many actions around the village, asked for my opinion of a plan he was devising to subdue the place once and for all.

"See these hills overlooking the ville, Lieutenant?" the colonel said. "I'm thinking I'll put marines and snipers on 'em, and then I'll call a B-52 strike in on the place. Carpet-bomb it, and if anybody lives through that, they'll come running out and the snipers will get them."

It was one of the moments when I did something I'm proud of. I talked the colonel out of his screwy scheme, pointing out that, one, he was unlikely to get authorization for a B-52 strike on one small village; two, even if he did, carpet-bombing would slaughter innocent women, children, and old men right along with the VC; and three, the hills were so close to Hoi Vuc that the huge bombs would likely kill the marines he planned to station on them.

We have difficulty finding the village, once again because the landscape has been altered, and also because its name has been changed. Thinh, the tourist company guide, discovers that it's now called Hoa Phu. He makes a few inquiries, and then leads us to it and to the village chairman, Truong Van Cuong, a small, forty-six-year-old father of four who cordially invites us to dinner and to spend the night in his house. This hospitable offer is so far from the greetings I was accustomed to receiving in Hoi Vuc that I don't know how to react to it.

Although Truong is village chairman, he is obviously not getting rich off his job. His house is like the ones I recall—a palm-thatch roof, bamboo and rattan walls, a dirt floor trod to the hardness of concrete, a household shrine with a bowl of joss sticks and a picture of Truong's deceased mother flanked by candles in blue and white ceramic holders, a couple of beds with reed mats laid over wooden slats, a small, fenced courtyard where roosters nibble on corncobs. There are three items that evidence a measure of prosperity: a small TV, a radio, and an electric desk fan to combat the stifling heat.

As Truong's wife pedals off on her bicycle to the local market to buy a chicken and vegetables, we drop our packs and sleeping bags in the courtyard and settle down to wait for the cool of evening to descend. While we wait, admiring the flowers the Truongs have planted around their fence, an emaciated, middle-age man wearing a green army shirt approaches us, and after learning from Thieu who we are, tells us that his house was burned down six times by U.S. troops, beginning in 1967, and that he was arrested three times, interrogated, and released.

He makes this declaration without rancor or bitterness, and then adds in the same matter-of-fact tone: "But I was never tortured. I don't blame the troops for what happened, I blame the U.S. government."

"I have to say, I'm just angry with my country," Leslie comments later. She is nearly thirteen years younger than I, and remembers accompanying her mother to a candlelit antiwar vigil when she was in high school. "What were we thinking of? This country was a threat? These people are lucky if they have a water buffalo!"

The questions are addressed to me, but I don't have an answer. Sometimes, events that are bewildering while we're living them acquire meaning in retrospect; but the more the Vietnam War recedes into the past, the more senseless it becomes to me; and it has never seemed so senseless as it does at this moment, waiting to be feted by the chief of a village our colonel once wanted to annihilate with B-52s.

Evening falls, the blessed hour in Vietnam, when the sun's curse is lifted. Peasants are coming in from the cane fields and rice paddies. A young woman leads a cow home from pasture. A young man with the torso of a bantamweight prizefighter drags a heavy boat up the Song Tuy Loan: he will pick up a load of sugarcane and float it down-river, and the next day, do it all over again. The scenes take me out of the past and into the present, which is none too bright in rural Vietnam, where, despite electrification and new roads, life remains a brute, stultifying struggle to survive from harvest to harvest. The legacy of half a century of warfare is partly to blame; so are customs and attitudes hardened in the cement of ancient traditions; and so are the repressive policies and economic mismanagement of the government, which, like the Chinese, is attempting to institute free-market reforms while maintaining a one-party dictatorship.

"You see Truong's floor, it's dirt," Thieu murmurs to me while Thinh and Truong's wife prepare dinner in the dark, smoky cooking shed. "Farmers and villagers like him, if they have a child in university, don't have the money to surface their floors. They don't know how to dream. They have no dreams beyond having enough clothes, enough rice to see them through to the next harvest. In many villages, the saying is, 'Pray for three bowls of rice a day and three shirts in the winter.' In my poetry, I try to show people how to dream. That should be the mission of all Vietnamese writers."

At forty-two, Thieu is one of Vietnam's "young writers," meaning that he was too young to have fought in the war. He's also young in the sense that he's daring enough to question the policies of the Communist party, whose often ruthless discipline helped Vietnam win the war. When I met him nine years ago, he frequently took me aside to deliver invectives like the one I've just heard. But, I ask him, hasn't the government liberalized considerably since 1990?

It has liberalized, but not considerably, Thieu says, then adds, "There is still no real freedom speech in Vietnam. I cry for my country in my poetry, but I have to cry quietly." Dinner is a feast—chicken, pork, rice, eggs, eggplant, cooked greens, and—this delicacy tests my and

Leslie's capacities to be good guests—the chicken's claws, boiled and sticking up out of a bowl. Truong fills our glasses with a Vietnamese rice vodka that tastes vaguely of almonds, and we drink toasts. He seems reluctant to discuss his memories of the war, saying only that his mother once invited some marines into her house to eat sweet potatoes, but they declined. He and two other villagers who join us after dinner are more eager to talk about the here and now. The word "NGO" comes up frequently. Nongovernmental organizations are seen here as a last hope for salvation from poverty. Perhaps an NGO will fund the building of a clinic for Hoa Phu, or a new school, the men say. There are so many kids in the village now that they have to go to class in shifts. As I listen, I think of an article I read recently in a newspaper: the *latest* thing in the America of the booming 1990s is to own a swimming pool with stereo speakers that play underwater and that are disguised as rocks to give that natural effect. We're not just rich, we're obscenely rich.

The Truongs' generosity doesn't end with the meal. They insist that Leslie and I sleep on their beds. We protest, and not just for the form of it, but the Truongs are adamant. Honored guests, even those with sleeping bags and air mattresses, do not sleep on the ground or the floor. Before bedtime, the Truongs turn on their TV, and several villagers come over to watch a drama with them. As the TV is only a few feet from my bed, I have to watch too. I don't understand a word, of course, but I wish I had a cell phone so I could call a few old war buddies and tell them that I'm in Hoi Vuc, the guest of the village chief, and watching television with him, his wife, and neighbors. I'm glad, when the program is over, that no one changes channels to CNN: the culture shock would kill me.

At two in the morning, answering nature's call, I pad outside through the courtyard gate and down a pitch-black path. If ever I'm going to suffer a flashback, it would be now, but I don't. Hearing crickets sing and frogs chirrup near the riverbank and in the paddies, I recall listening to those sounds on watch; listening for them to fall silent. That's what you listened for, the sounds of silence, and they weren't like the ones in the Simon and Garfunkel song. When the frogs and crickets stopped, it meant that someone—or a whole battalion for all you knew—was moving around out there in the black unknown beyond your foxhole, and you waited with every sense alert, every nerve tensed for a burst of gunfire, a grenade to come arching out of the underbrush. But now the chorus goes on without interruption, the ceaseless song of ordinary and peaceful night.

In the morning, shouldering our backpacks (I'm *backpacking in Vietnam,* for Christ's sake!), we slosh across the Song Tuy Loan and trek for two miles through wooded foothills, coffee and banana plantations, and isolated hamlets to the tiny village of An Loi, at the foot of Nui Ba Na. In the past, local villagers called it "Lord Mountain," for its height and the inaccessibility of its shadowed forests, spreading a canopy two hundred feet above the jungle floor. Ba Na belongs to the Truong Son mountains, the rugged range that forms the spine of central Vietnam and that's known to geographers as the Annamese Cordillera: a tropic wilderness that looks as you imagine the earth looked at the dawn of time. Whenever I think of Vietnam, that mountain is the first thing I remember. Soaring almost from sea level to an altitude of forty-eight hundred feet, with mists rising through the trees, it became the emblem of everything I found alluring, menacing, mysterious, and indomitable about Indochina. The mountain's crest, a long, serrated plateau, was the first to catch the light of sunrise; in the garish sunsets, it glowed like a volcano; at night its massive bulk occulted the stars in the lower heavens, and its blackness looked like a hole in the sky, a tunnel into the void beyond the cosmos. Tigers prowled the mountain's forests. Wild elephants had been seen there by reconnaissance patrols. Amethyst pythons thick as a man's leg coiled in the branches of the trees, and at the summit, we had heard, were the ruins of an old French resort, where colonial planters and merchants were said to have gone to escape the heat. The resort became legendary to us in 1965 and 1966, like the tale of some lost city. It was one of the riddles of Vietnam. How did the French build a vacation spa way up there? How did they get to it? There were no roads marked on our maps, only a few trails used by woodcutters and Catu tribesmen, the primitive, mysterious montagnards who hunted with crossbows.

Sometimes, looking up at it, we wanted to go to the top for the same reason the French did; according to what we'd heard, it was as cool as springtime up there, amid the mists and clouds. No chance of that. Ba Na was then deep inside "Indian country," which was what we called territory controlled by the enemy. We talked about returning to Vietnam in peacetime to climb the mountain and see if the ruins were really there or merely another myth of the war.

Climb it is now what I'll try to do, although I don't need to confirm the tales about a Lost Resort. Thinh has told us that it indeed exists. A twenty-two-room hotel and two hundred stone and brick villas had been built there by Vietnamese labor gangs between 1919 and 1930. Tourists were carried to the peak on sedan chairs borne by four to eight coolies, who trudged up a winding footpath dubbed the "Debay track," after one Captain Debay, a French marine who blazed the trail in 1902. Ba Na is once again a resort, Thinh informs us, operated by the Ministry of Tourism. A road has been built along Captain Debay's old route, and links up with a road that connects An Loi with Danang, some twenty-five kilometers away.

A van from the East Asia tourist company meets us at An Loi, where we are refreshing ourselves with warm Cokes at a roadside stand. When I tell Thinh that I want to walk up, he gives me the facts of life: the road up the mountain is fifteen kilometers long, that is, nine miles, a strenuous climb for a fifty-seven-year-old man in ninety-degree heat. But I insist on going on foot, making one concession to my age by tossing my backpack into the van. Thieu, who smokes two packs a day, also gets into the vehicle, telling us that and he driver will follow, in case we decide that riding is a better idea after all.

We set off, crossing a bridge over the Song Tuy Loan. We have to pay a fee at a toll gate, for Ba Na is now part of a national park (sparing it from the ruthless logging that has wreaked more devastation on Vietnam's forests since the end of the war than defoliation did during it). The road goes up in tortuous switchbacks. The slopes on both sides are extremely steep, climbing on the one side, falling on the other, the land below a quiltwork of greens—the dark green rows of coffee plantations, the paler green of eucalyptus and bamboo forests, the almost neon green of rice paddies, with brown rivers winding through it all and the coastal hills to the east shimmering in the heat. Rob, who is twenty-one years younger than I and in better shape, soon bounds ahead and disappears around a bend. Leslie, Thinh, and I trudge along, sweating in the ferocious sun, delighting in the moments when a cool breeze wafts down from higher elevations. We stop for a break in a little thatch shelter where a man and a woman sell soft drinks, tea, and, of all things, cigarettes; then we continue on, and coming around a sharp curve, gaze southward into a long, narrow valley that was called "Happy Valley" during the war because nothing happy ever happened there. It was where, on an April morning, our company received its baptism of fire, that martial sacrament. I picture the Vietcong, firing down on us from a ridgeline, Lemmon's platoon charging them in a frontal assault, while mine and Tester's platoon, advancing behind a mortar barrage, swept around the ridge to outflank the guerrillas. Looking at the valley now, more populated and civilized than it was then, serene in the sunlight, I sense something missing: the tension between beauty and danger. Without the danger, the landscape is merely beautiful; it is scenery.

After climbing another half an hour, Thinh and I calculate that we've covered only four kilometers, less than a third of the way. We're drenched in sweat, we've been guzzling freely from our water bottles. The twenty-three-year-old rifle platoon leader would have kept on, but not his middle-age descendant. Soon, the van picks us up. We pass Rob, cheerfully striding along. He says he'll finish the trek on foot. Switchback after switchback, the road takes us higher, past construction and maintenance gangs. Sometimes we look down on slopes where mahogany and tropical oak trees soar to heights of over 150 feet. The trees are more than three hundred years old, Thinh says. Reflecting on the fact that they were saplings when the pilgrims were looking out their cabin windows into the North American wilderness, I wonder if there was some connection between what we tried to do in Vietnam and our forebears' restless quest to conquer and subdue and remake the wild into their own image.

At Vong Nguyet, an old, stone-walled French hill station the Vietnamese have renovated into an inn and teahouse, it is raining lightly, and feels twenty degrees cooler than down below. We have lunch and wait for Rob, giving him a round of applause when he arrives. Leslie and I decide to walk the rest of the way with him. It's less than four kilometers. Half jokingly, which is to say half seriously, Thinh warns us that there are still tigers on the mountain. Figuring the chances of being pounced on are pretty remote, we climb through the drizzle. Cicadas sing in the trees, though "sing" may be the wrong verb for the noise they make—an unsettling screech that sounds like a Skill Saw cutting a two-by-four.

The first two kilometers are easy, but we choose to take a footpath for the last two and it isn't easy. But it is more rewarding than the road. We feel the power of the jungle as the yellow, muddy path twists and ascends into the clouds. Wild orchids bloom, vines and creepers festoon the trees, and then the first ruin appears, eerie-looking in the ribbons of vapor: a roofless villa, its stone walls crumbling and pocked with bullet and shrapnel holes—from which war, we don't know. There is another ruin farther on, and another, and the jungle is reclaiming them all; they look as if they could be a thousand years old instead of a mere seventy.

A final strenuous push, and we're at the summit, where we're met by an incongruous sight: a restaurant, a terrace with little tables and plastic chairs under umbrellas advertising Tiger beer, and four buildings with steeply pitched tile roofs that are supposed to resemble montagnard longhouses but look more like Swiss chalets made of Legos. A sign says, WELCOME TO BA NA RESORT. I feel a certain letdown. I wasn't expecting this. I'm not sure what I was expecting—maybe some mildewed bungalow with a chugging paddle fan, the ghosts of French colonials in tropical linens, sipping drinks brought by servants in silk brocade.

We sip cold Heineken brought by the restaurant staff, eat dinner while a hard rain hammers the roof, and afterward, listen to Thieu recite some of his poetry, which is very sad, and then a few lines from the eighteenth-century Vietnamese epic, *The Tale of Khieu*. It is also sad, a tragic love story. We ask, why is Vietnamese literature all so damned heartbreaking?

"War by war, death by death, storm by storm, this is a sad country, so its poetry must be sad," he says, chain-smoking. He pauses while a gigantic brown moth—it's as big as a bat—flits around a light. Then, looking at me, he says, "Tell me tomorrow what you dream about tonight."

He and I stand in the incandescent dawn, looking eastward toward the coastal plain, then westward toward the Truong Son mountains, rising and falling toward Laos. The dense mists in the ravines and gorges look like vaporous lakes.

"I dreamed that I was attacked by a python," I tell him. "It was coiled around me, crushing me to death, but I wrestled with it and broke its grip."

Thieu lights up and nods, but doesn't say anything.

Later, after we've explored more ruins and a waterfall, and encountered some jungle fauna—a poisonous centipede as long as a man's hand, with bright yellow pincers—we drive down the mountain. Just before we leave, a man named Nguyen Duy Tam asks for a lift. He's about five feet tall, weighs 120 pounds, and is carrying on a shoulder pole two bags of rice weighing 88 pounds. I do push-ups and sit-ups every morning, but I am barely able to lift the thing onto my shoulders, and then stagger like a drunk. Tam tells us that he carries a load like that up the mountain from his village, eleven miles away, almost every day, and then carries another load down. He's fifty-four years old.

"I bring rice and food to the road workers," he says. "I make thirty thousand dong [$2.25] a day. It takes me about four hours each way. I don't carry water with me because I never get thirsty."

I look at Leslie and Rob and remark, "This guy is the reason we lost the war."

After a night in the old port city of Hoi An, we drive down a rutted dirt road, through the Vu Gia River valley, some twenty miles southwest of Danang. We are headed for Hill 52 and Thuong Duc, the last two way stations on the pilgrimage. Whenever I feel a tendency to romanticize the war, whenever my memories become gauzy with time and I begin to see myself as a heroic character, leading marines into battle in my early twenties, I think of those two places to correct my vision.

The Vu Gia valley was an enemy stronghold, and our battalion were the first U.S. troops sent into it, in early January of 1966, on a search-and-destroy mission. It wasn't a big battle we fought here—our 850-man battalion suffered about ten per cent casualties, and I suppose we inflicted about the same number on the Vietcong and North Vietnamese army units we engaged. But, to my mind, all the pity and madness and ugliness of war are distilled into those two or three hours. Standing atop Hill 52, pitted with the remains of foxholes and bunkers, I look out across the valley, and hear the ghosts of the war more clearly than I have so far, feel them pressing closer, see them . . .

Helicopters swooping down into a landing zone under mortar and machine-gun fire. . . Two marines somersaulted through the air by a bursting shell . . . The battalion commander, the operations and artillery officers wounded, the operations chief with both legs blown off . . . My platoon, spread out on a low ridge, firing into a tree line. . . sixty-one-millimeter shells burst in front of us, behind us, fragments whine overhead, a swarm of lethal bees . . . I call in an air strike on the mortars . . . Napalm blooms . . . A lone VC, dashing across a paddy-dike to escape the flames, is cut down by a Skyhawk's cannon fire . . . D company pinned down by a nest of enemy machineguns dug into concrete bunkers. . . Our company sent through Ha Na village to take Hill 52 and deliver supporting fire for D company . . . Maddened by the fight in the LZ, we burn and blast our way through the village until there's nothing left but ashes . . . More airstrikes pound the machine gun nest for half an hour, bombs falling so near we sometimes feel the shock wave of the blasts . . . Night falls, the ashes below smolder . . . D company's wounded, somewhere off to our left flank, cry out in the darkness . . . An urgent request for morphine transmitted over the radio . . . D company's corpsmen have run out of it . . . Dawn . . . We form up and sweep eastward along the river, passing a field burned by napalm, where a pig gnaws the charred corpse of a human being . . .

I describe all this to Leslie, Rob, Thieu, and Thinh, and my wife's expression is more one of bafflement than horror. I might as well be telling her what life was like on some ghastly planet in another solar system. She returns to the van with Thieu and Thinh, but Rob and I stay to photograph the valley, which looks, and is, impossibly tranquil now. As we walk along, we surprise four kids who are playing on the hill. I guess they've never seen foreigners before, because three of them flee when they set eyes on our strange faces; the fourth, the smallest, looks straight at me and is literally frozen with terror. Then he screams as if he's having a nightmare. I murmur soothing words, but, inconsolable, he screams and screams.

I wonder if the boy's parents or grandparents have told him stories about the terrible men with red faces and long noses who came here with guns long before his birth; wonder if I am some sort of bogeyman come to life. I feel like running too. The memories here are too vivid.

Thuong Duc lies a few miles to the west, where the valley narrows, pinched between two high, gloomy ridges. The village nudges up against foothills on the south side of the valley, the hills climbing toward a mountain side that's almost sheer. A waterfall tumbles down it for several hundred feet, the water appearing motionless with distance, like a silvery ribbon draped over the dark jungle.

We trek up the nearest hill, where the U.S. Special Forces once had an "A" camp (later turned over to the South Vietnamese, who were overrun by Vietcong and North Vietnamese in the final offensive in 1975). At the old landing zone, a young farmer and his family have built a small thatch house and grow pineapples and bananas, which they offer us, with typical Vietnamese hospitality. As we sit eating with the farmer and his wife, I am afflicted with a weird double vision. *We are writers of blood and fire,* said our host at the writers conference nine years ago in Hanoi. *We saw war with the naked eye . . .* Yes, we did, and blood and fire are what I see now even as I look upon the faces of my wife and companions with the eyes in my head. Those in my mind behold, on this same hilltop, a battery of 105-millimeter howitzers shelling the ridge where the waterfall shimmers. In the distance, across the Song Vu Gia, a Skyhawk painted in green-and-brown camouflage screams in, drops napalm, and climbs, doing a barrel roll; all along the valley, smoke billows from air strikes and burning villages. At the LZ, radios crackle with desperate calls for medevacs or artillery fire; earlier, one of our companies ran into a battalion of North Vietnamese regulars. and in less than thirty minutes, 108 of the company's 172 officers and men were killed or wounded. The tall, patrician-looking colonel who stands beside me gazes out over the battlefield, and remarks, "My, it certainly is a lovely valley, isn't it?"

That was in April 1966, when I was serving as an assistant regimental operations officer and our regiment was sent into Thuong Duc on a search-and-destroy mission to clear the way for the special forces to build their camp. I helped plan the operation, though as a junior officer I did little more than dot the i's and cross the t's on the operation orders. But at one point in the planning, I played a more significant role, and it's another memory that haunts me to this day. Observing that the plan called for a battalion and an artillery battery to be dropped on the north side of the Vu Gia, I suggested that another battalion should land on the south side and establish a blocking position to cut off the enemy's avenue of retreat in that direction. My suggestion was taken up, but with one important difference: instead of a battalion—four rifle companies—a single company was to be committed to the blocking position. I protested vigorously, almost to the point of insubordination, telling the operations officer that to leave one company isolated, with a wide river between them and reinforcements, would be to invite disaster. *What are you talking about, Lieutenant? They're gonna have a forward air controller and forward artillery observers with them. Any trouble and they'll call the wrath of God down on Charlie. Firepower, lieutenant.* And so the company went and that was the one that ran into the NVA battalion, which taught a lesson in firepower by opening up all at once with machine guns, mortars, recoilless rifles, and rocket-propelled grenades.

Blood and fire.

We are put up in the headquarters of the Thuong Duc People's Committee—the town hall, a spacious, two-story villa. Taking a walk in the late afternoon, as thunder booms in the mountains westward, Leslie, Rob, and I discover that we are the main attraction in town. We can barely move, besieged by a horde of laughing, squealing school-children, all practicing their two words of English: Ha-lo, goo-bye. They grab our hands, jump on our backs. I stop and begin to teach them how to count in English, a favor they return by teaching me to count in Vietnamese. When they hear me say, "mot, hai, ba, bon," their delighted cries hit a level that pierces my eardrums. They are poorly dressed, a few need baths, they have no computers or visual aids in their one-room schoolhouse, only crude desks and copy books; but they are the sweetest, most innocent, and playful children you'll meet anywhere. And as they laugh and cavort, I think of a dreadful event perpetrated in Littleton, Colorado, by two American students who had more than these kids will ever be able to imagine, much less hope for, but who were nonetheless full of violence and sullen resentments and had tapped into the sucking moral black hole that lies at the core of modern American culture. We no longer have to go to the Asian jungles to find the heart of darkness, it's in our own backyard.

In the evening, we feast on rice, pork, and fish in the town hall, under a bust of Ho Chi Minh (never thought I'd do that, either), and in the morning, over breakfast tea, I have a conversation with the enemy. They are three former Vietcong: Trung Cong Phu, a seventy-year-old, gray-haired man with a direct gaze and the dignified bearing of an Asian venerable; Nguyen Trung Chinh, an intense, restless man who's sixty-six but looks twenty years younger; and Nguyen Thanh Duoc, who at fifty bears a striking resemblance to tough-guy actor Charles Bronson.

All three fought for years in and around Thuong Duc with the regional Vietcong army. Phu joined the Viet Minh resistance against the French in 1946, fought them for ten years, was arrested by the

Saigon regime afterward because he belonged to the Communist party, and spent another ten years in prison. Released in 1966, he immediately joined the VC and served as a medical corpsman with a local battalion until the war's end. Three decades of war and prison, but he feels no animosity toward Americans, only a kind of puzzlement.

"I never could understand why the U.S. was fighting in the war," he says. "I couldn't understand and asked myself. 'Why are these people here, killing us?' "

Chinh was with the VC from 1961 to 1975, sometimes as a political officer and organizer, sometimes as a guerrilla fighter. He took part in the Tet Offensive and lost a brother in the war. To him, there is no mystery about how Asian guerrillas were able to defeat the most powerful army on earth.

"The Americans were trained as conventional forces," he says, fidgeting with a pen. "They couldn't fight in the mountains and jungles, where we could appear and disappear. They couldn't win, because this land is our land."

Nor is there any mystery for the Charles Bronson look-alike, Duoc. Volunteering when he was only fifteen, he says he was ready "to suffer bombing, disease, and hunger." Duoc fought in the battle of Thuong Duc in 1975.

"There were moments of doubt that we could win, but they passed quickly. We fought the Chinese for a thousand years and won. We fought the French for a hundred years and won." Phu nods.

"The Americans were free in the sky in their helicopters, we were free in the ground in our tunnels and bunkers, and we knew the U.S. could not endure a long war. We have a tradition of long wars."

I ask each what is his most vivid memory of the war. They all three ponder for a while, and Chinh is the first to offer his:

"The day we liberated this area, we all cried . . . That's my clearest memory, my tears at liberation. I cried in defeat and I cried in victory."

But these three aging fighters are impatient with talk about the past. Their attention turns to the present and its intractable problems. Thuong Duc and its two neighboring villages have a population of thirty-six thousand, eight thousand of whom are school-age children, they tell me. Money is needed for a new high school, and also to repair the roads between the villages, and for medical equipment in the local clinic.

Phu takes the opportunity to give me a gentle lecture:

"This area was heavily damaged in the war. You as a journalist have a responsibility to write about it and to tell the world about the support we need to rebuild and heal the wounds of war."

And I promise I will.

Finally, it is time to leave. We pause for photographs, and then I shake hands with three men I would have done my level best to kill thirty years ago, as they would have done their best to kill me. As I walk to the van for the return trip to Hoi An, Thieu takes me aside for a moment.

"I've been thinking about the dream you had on Ba Na," he says. "The python was the past. By coming here, you've broken its grip."

OCEAN AND ISLANDS

voyager

1 9 9 7

I fell victim to the romance of the sea long before I ever saw an
ocean. Salt water was a good long way from the western suburbs of
Chicago, where I grew up and went to high school. That institution—Fenwick High School, a Catholic preparatory school for boys
in Oak Park, Illinois—was responsible for infecting me with sea fever. I
now treasure the education the Dominican priests gave me, but I was-
n't so appreciative then. Fenwick's medieval architecture, rigid dress
code, strict discipline, and regimen of Latin, college-prep math, and
Thomistic theology were stifling to a rebellious kid who wanted to be
a free-roving adventurer. Often—usually on winter afternoons, when
the drab Chicago light fell through the Gothic casement windows—I
would play a kind of virtual hooky by sailing away on imaginary voyages with writers I had met in my English and American literature
classes: Joseph Conrad, Herman Melville, Richard Henry Dana, Jack
London. Of them all, Conrad most abetted my mental truancies. I
shipped out with him more than with any other writer of the sea. What
a spell he cast on my impressionable mind, spiriting me away from
stuffy classrooms to dazzling tropic waters to Malay archipelagos and
the yardarms of brave ships, upon which brave sailors gave back "yell
for yell to a westerly gale."

In my junior year, our English teacher, a layman named Robert
Hlavin, assigned each of us to write a short story, just so we would
know firsthand what went into the making of one. My classmates
served up tales about their first dates or football games or drag races,
but none of that quotidian stuff for me. The hand of Joe Conrad's ghost

seemed to guide mine as I scribbled a sinister tale of a white man who sails up the Irrawaddy River in Burma, murders a native worker on a rubber plantation, and is then afflicted with guilt and with fear of the plantation owner's wife, the only witness to his crime. If my story was shamelessly imitative, it also was a flight of pure imagination. I'd never been farther from Chicago than Wisconsin; all I knew about Burma and the Irrawaddy were a few facts gleaned from my family's Funk & Wagnall encyclopedia. Nevertheless, Mr. Hlavin gave me an A, and suggested I submit the story for publication. I recall sending it to *Argosy,* and to a couple of other red-blooded, two-fisted men's adventure magazines sold on 1950s newsstands. Judging from the form rejection slips, the editors were not as impressed as my teacher.

This May (to make a temporal broad jump of thirty-eight years), I found myself thinking about that youthful literary effort as I stowed my seabag aboard the sailing vessel *Tudy,* moored at Anse Marcel harbor on the island of St. Martin, in the Lesser Antilles. I was amazed at my boldness in writing about a place and people I had known nothing about, and also a little envious of my sixteen-year-old imagination, liberated by my sixteen-year-old ignorance from the imprisoning need for verisimilitude. I had become a writer; behind me were nearly thirty years as a foreign correspondent, magazine journalist, and author of seven books: two memoirs, five works of fiction. But with that experience had come the recognition that imagination wasn't enough. I could no longer fly on the wings of fancy alone. I needed to get things right, and that tyrannical demand in my brain for factual accuracy, along with a story I had heard from my father-in-law, were what had brought me to St. Martin and on board the *Tudy,* a fifty-three-foot, sloop-rigged Swan. I was one of a crew that was to deliver her to Newport, Rhode Island, by way of Bermuda, a voyage of some fifteen hundred nautical miles.

This was the story my father-in-law, John Ware, told me one night at dinner three years earlier. He had heard it from an older first cousin he'd visited in Massachusetts. It seemed that in the early summer of 1899, their grandfather, William Mimms Ware, had put three of his four teenage sons on the family yacht, a forty-foot schooner called *Holly,* gave each ten dollars, and told them he did not want to see their faces until school started in September. The youngest of the trio, Winslow Ware, was my father-in-law's father, and only twelve years old at the time. He and his brothers sailed away from their home near Boston and somehow made it all the way to Cuba, where the *Holly* was wrecked in a storm. Rescued by Cuban fishermen, the three boys were brought to the U.S. Legation in Havana, where a consular officer cabled William Ware, informing him of his sons' whereabouts and asking that he send them money for ship's passage home. The money arrived, and the boys were back in Massachusetts in time for the new school term. That was all my father-in-law knew. The incredible thing, he said, was that his father had never spoken a word about this astonishing adventure, which led him to wonder if it had ever happened or was just some family myth.

Myth or not, the tale and the questions it begged teased me for the next couple of years. I wasn't interested in writing only about the voyage, but in the relationship between the old man and his sons, and in what could have moved him to expose them to such danger. By one of those happy coincidences that occur all too infrequently in a writer's life, I'd heard the yarn at the same time that I was pondering a novel about an old, aristocratic New England family with plenty of skeletons and the closets to hide them in. Over time, I managed to weave my father-in-law's true (or apparently true) tale into the history of my fictional family, and I had the plot of *The Voyage* (as the novel came to be called—another failure of imagination). But one essential element was missing; for all of my early attraction to the sea, I knew little about the sailing of boats. Having been to sea, briefly, in the U.S. Marine Corps, and having done some day-sailing in the Florida Keys and on Long Island Sound, as well as a lot of deep-sea fishing, I knew that a floor is a deck, a wall a bulkhead, and that to come about is to change a sailing vessel's course by turning the bow through the eye of the wind.

Such an elementary command of nautical facts, however, wouldn't be sufficient to carry me through the writing of a long novel about a long sea passage in a schooner. Nor, to repeat myself, could I trust my imagination to fill in the gaps in my knowledge. You see, I had married into a very salty family. On my mother-in-law's bookshelf is an ancient copy of the *American Coast Pilot*, its title page inscribed by one of her ancestors: CAPT. JOHN BLANCHARD, 1799. She is an avid sailor, the daughter of Fessenden Blanchard, author of many books on sailing. My father-in-law, before his death in March 1999, was a skilled yachtsman and coauthor of the *Cruising Guide to the New England Coast*, a yachting bible. My wife and sister-in-law had learned to handle a tiller right along with their ABCs. Those four had taught me a hard lesson: sailors aren't just finicky about using the correct terms and techniques, they're fanatics. Once, in one of my novellas, I had a character issue the command, "Jibe-O," a jibe being a maneuver by which a boat sailing before the wind is turned by swinging the main boom from one side of the boat to the other, so the mainsail takes the wind on its opposite side. Well, my wife and her family snickered for weeks at my error: the correct command, they kept reminding me, was "Jibe-*ho.*"

And so, as part of my research, I steeped myself in nautical lore and jargon. I still wouldn't trust myself to single-hand a dinghy more than a mile, but I sure as hell could talk the talk. Still, I sensed a lack. My literary hero, Conrad, had served nearly twenty years in the French and British merchant services before he started writing. Somewhere I had read that he didn't consider a ship to be truly at sea until it was a thousand miles from the nearest coast. I had hardly ever been out of sight of land—a shore-hugging, green-water dilettante who had only a fuzzy notion of what it was like to sail for long periods, out where the shore is barely a memory. I wanted to get that right, too, the sights, sounds, and smells of the experience, the feel and texture of it, assuming that any sailors who read my book would be as fanatical about that stuff as they were about technical details.

Eventually, a friend put me in touch with Captain Andrew Burton, who runs an outfit out of Newport called Adventure Sailing. Burton, a boyish-looking man in his midforties, is a delivery captain. Delivery captains, as the name implies, transport yachts from one port to another, often over great distances. That's a far cry from skippering cargo-carrying square-riggers; nevertheless, delivery captains are *working* sailors, among the very few seamen who still earn their bread under sail. Usually, they have to scrounge up their crews from among the wandering tribe known as "boat bums," but Burton has added a new wrinkle: for a fee, he will sign you up on one of his voyages. In exchange, you learn, among many other things, blue water helmsmanship, offshore navigation, and how to stand a watch in seamanlike fashion.

I sent Burton a check. Bought a one-way ticket for St. Martin, and joined him, first mate Herb Matthews (also the executive editor of *Cruising World* magazine), and my fellow paying crew members: Roger

Barnes, a retired book designer from Connecticut, Daphne Payne, a Canadian Great Lakes sailor eager for salt water, and George Lula, a Pittsburgh investment banker.

We set sail with the tide at midnight, under a double-reefed main—a smart breeze was kicking out of the east—Burton and I taking the first watch while Matthews and the rest of the crew went below to sleep. The silhouettes of St. Martin's hills gradually shrank and the lights of Anguilla, across the passage separating the French-owned islands from the British West Indies (an antiquarian name that seemed to come out of Conrad's time) gleamed through the darkness. The farther we pulled away from the lights ashore, the more the stars revealed themselves: the Big Dipper, low on the horizon, Leo directly overhead, the Pleiades, like a crystal spear point, the blue-white beacon of Sirius. We jibed (and you can bet I made sure to cry out, Jibe-*ho!*), taking a course due north to avoid two nameless islands. When we cleared them, we put the *Tudy* on a bearing of 015 degrees magnetic and cracked along at a bracing seven and a half knots.

Midway through the watch, a single-reefed jib was set. Andy, trimming this and that, increasing or decreasing the hydraulic pressure on the stays, moved across the deck with the grace and economy of motion of the veteran mariner he is—he reckons he's logged over two hundred thousand offshore hours since he began sailing at age five, off the coast of British Columbia, where he was raised. For all that, he doesn't look salty, but rather like an Ivy League graduate student. Nor does he roar and bellow like Hollywood sea captains. Noticing that I tended to oversteer, he corrected me in a quiet, almost professorial voice: "A Swan is a sweet, even-tempered, responsive boat," he said, as if the vessel had the virtues of perfect wife (or what unevolved, old-fashioned males like me think the virtues of a perfect wife should be). "You don't have to horse her, just give the helm a little touch, no more than a spoke in either direction. You *suggest* where you want her to go, don't *tell* her, and she'll follow."

I had some trouble getting the hang of it. The seas, running four to five feet, tended to lift the bow toward the wind, and I would overcompensate by turning the wheel too far to leeward. Also, looking down at the illuminated compass both dimmed my night vision and caused me to fail to anticipate the boat's motion in the waves. Thus began another lesson: if I kept Ursa Major a little to windward of the mainmast, Andy instructed, I would hold course without having to refer continually to the compass. This I did, and it occurred to me that when I was reciting my Latin conjugations at Fenwick, I would have killed to have the experience I was having now. It was thrilling to be steering by the stars, with the vessel's phosphorescent wake trailing like a ribbon of green fire over a black sea. Andy, meanwhile, was studying a pilot's chart of the North Atlantic with aid of a flashlight. The great, blue, watery unknown, after five hundred years of exploration, is now neatly divided into quadrants, in which the mariner can find the direction, average speed, and frequency of prevailing winds, the direction of currents, the average height of waves, the latitude of the iceberg line, the approximate track of the Gulf Stream, and so forth. How many sailors, I wondered, had died acquiring this information? Off watch, I went below, and had quite a rocky sleep in the cramped, stifling forward berth I shared with George Lula. I was rolled around on my bunk like a loose pin in a drawer. Awakening at 9:30, I managed the trick of making coffee, and an hour later, went above to relieve Roger Barnes at the helm.

"Course is zero-one-zero," Barnes said.

"Zero-one-zero," I repeated, and took the big wheel in hand.

Andy might not have looked or talked like a sea captain, but that didn't mean he was lazy about ship's discipline. He insisted that the new helmsman repeat the course to the off-going helmsman, because muffing a course exchange was all too easy. Insisted as well that the log be properly filled out, and that all lines be properly coiled and free to run, not for the aesthetics but to make sure they were ready for use in an emergency. While on watch, he expected us to develop the habits of attentiveness and anticipation, the two pillars upon which good seamanship is built. We were to keep a sharp eye on the rigging, on the sea and sky and weather, and try our best to foresee any problems that might arise. A mainsheet shackle backing out is very easy to fix, he'd told us; all you need to do is screw it back in. A mainsheet flogging wildly about the deck because the shackle has fallen out is a dangerous, difficult thing to fix. Good offshore sailors fixed the former problem and bad, the latter.

And I reflected, as the *Tudy* flew along in a steady seventeen-knot tradewind, that the values of the sailor ran almost directly counter to the values, or lack of them, in 1990s America, where sins were not only easily forgiven but not even recognized as sins. But when you are hundreds of miles from land in a fifty-three-foot sloop, sloppiness, shoddiness, and doing things halfway to right are sins, and certain to be punished by the unforgiving sea.

It has ever been thus, the conflict between the relaxed standards of the land and the exacting ones of the sea. I thought of the passage in Conrad's great novella, *The Nigger of the Narcissus,* when Captain Allistoun berates his crew for knowing half their work and doing half their duty. A crewman whines that they had done their best by the ship. Then, Conrad writes:

"'Your best,'" stormed the master. "You hear a lot on shore, don't you? They don't tell you there your best isn't much to boast of. I tell you—your best is no better than bad.'"

We put into St. George's harbor, in Bermuda, early in the morning of May 16, having covered over eight hundred nautical miles in five days. It had been glorious, tradewind sailing all the way. Some excerpts from my personal log:

> *May 12: 4:30 A.M.–7:30 A.M. watch: . . . Herb McCormick, relieving Andy, told me a yarn of a voyage he'd taken from Australia to Antarctica to pick up a couple who had wintered over in a prefab hut! Herb sailed across the famed Roaring Forties in a flat calm,* but ran into three gales on the way back. "Small, tightly wrapped, nasty little suckers," he said. "Winds to sixty, seas twenty to thirty feet . . ." *Sea stories are almost always about storms and disasters, but I imagine a lot of sailing has been and is like this, almost monotonous, staring at the empty, blue vastness . . .*
>
> *A thrilling sight—spotted three sperm whales, blowing on the surface. Each looked to be thirty-five to forty feet long, sticking their big, blunt, brown-gray heads out of the water. We cruised right past them, or they past us, the whales arching and blowing spray off our starboard bow . . .*
>
> *May 13: 1:30 P.M.–4:30 P.M. watch: Learning the fundamentals of celestial navigation from Andy.* (I needed to know this because my novel was to take place in 1901, when sailors could not have even imagined such wonders as loran and GPS.) *Andy took a noon sight, and fixed us within a mile of our position, as computed by the onboard GPS. Took a sight myself, using* the boat's cheap, plastic sextant. Andy didn't trust me with his, which cost $2,000 and is a beauty, a fusion of form and

function. It has the aesthetics of precision, it's an instrument that won't lie to you if you use it right, it's a moral object. Anyhow, I was sixty miles off, which Andy said wasn't bad for a first try. On his baptismal effort as a celestial navigator, he had marked his boat in the middle of Utah.

May 14: 10:30 A.M.–1:30 P.M. watch: Two nautical aphorisms from Andy and Herb: 1. "Sailors are the worst pessimists in the world. If things are good, they know they'll become foul later."
2. "Sailors don't have ETAs (estimated time of arrival), *they only have destinations." Even in this day of sophisticated electronics, satellite weather reports, etc., Herb elaborated, life for the sailor is so uncertain that he never fills in the destination blank in his logbook until he gets there. Last year, bound for Bermuda, Andy wound up in North Carolina because bad weather had forced him to change course.*

Saw a westing container ship toward end of watch, the first vessel we've seen in three days. What with the scarce bird life and the absence of any sea life, except for the three whales, the open ocean sometimes seems like an immense, watery desert.

May 15: 10:30 A.M.–1:30 P.M. watch: A sullen day that can't make up its mind how sullen it wants to be . . . Very light airs, so engine is on, assisted by the mainsail. Andy has us practice reefing because, he said, "We're likely to run into some dirty weather north of Bermuda . . ."

4 A.M. : Racked out of sound sleep by Roger. Call of all hands on deck. We're approaching St. George's harbor . . .

Bermuda was all pastel houses, golf courses, and gardens of hibiscus and bougainvillea—a pretty, decorous place except for the raucous White Horse tavern in St. George. There, Herb and I had a true sailor's night ashore, guzzling Dark 'n Stormys, a concoction of Gosling's rum and ginger beer that is the national drink of Bermuda. We were joined by a dark-haired character who greeted us as "fellow seaman," called himself "Bermuda Ray," and revealed that he was a convicted drug smuggler, recently released from serving a sentence in the Atlanta federal penitentiary. Celebrating his freedom, Ray bought us a few rounds, we bought him a few more, and the next morning, Herb rolled out of his bunk holding his head as if it were made of a fragile material, balique, say.

"You can get into so much trouble in Bermuda!" he groaned. "I want to get back out to sea! Out to the purity of the sea!"

An hour or so later, after topping off the fuel and water tanks, we motored away from the dock, but Andy did not want to leave St. George under power. He was inspired by a friend of his, who had once captained a 167-foot ketch. That skipper had seen his smaller sister ship depart the day before on its engine, and he did not like the look of her.

"So he got his crew together," said Andy, "and they raised the mizzen and jib and sailed off the dock at Falmouth. By the time they cleared the harbor, they were cracking on, with every stitch of sail set, bound for Panama. *That's* the way you do it!"

He turned us to, and we hoisted the main and jib. The *Tudy* ran across the harbor. We jibed, heading inshore, then came about smartly, and with the staysail raised, reached through Town Cut. Under Andy's and Herb's supervision, the four of us did a passably seamanlike job. We were functioning as a team now. Ashore, construction workers repairing a house stood on the roof and waved to us, because, I guess, the *Tudy* made a fine sight—a handsome vessel outward bound, her sails drawing nicely, with no more a wrinkle in them than if they were made of china.

What I found that I liked about sailing, as opposed to powerboating, was the craft of it. Its mastery requires that you master, not only the arts of reefing and steering but the effect of tides and currents on your course, the kind of weather portended by cloud formations, and a hundred other things big and small. Reading the wind correctly and trimming the canvas to it. Learning how to take advantage of every little puff. There is far too little craft in people's lives these days, too little in their working lives, too little in their leisure activities. Everything has become electrified, mechanized, digitized, and computerized; all the guesswork that makes any sort of travel interesting is being eradicated by gizmos—soon cars will be equipped with computers to tell you exactly where to turn and when—and so modern man suffers from a diminished sense of achievement because he isn't the one who achieves, the gizmo does. The importance of craft, that is, of meaningful work, is a theme that runs through much of Conrad's writing. "I don't like work—no man does," says Marlow, the narrator of *Heart of Darkness*. "But I like what is in the work—the chance to find yourself. Your own reality—for yourself, not for others, what no man can ever know."

Maybe that was why Andy insisted on clearing the harbor under sail—sailing was his art, and he both expressed himself and found himself in it.

Three days out of Bermuda, as we entered the Gulf Stream some four hundred miles off Cape Hatteras, we ran into the dirty weather he had warned us about. The red sun emerged over the horizon, like the head of some fiery infant from the gray sea's womb—it was as if the sea were giving birth to the day. A westerly wind piped up to thirty knots, Force 7 on the Beaufort Scale, a moderate gale. By eight in the morning, we had eight-foot seas whacking into us, just forward of the port beam. Andy ordered Herb, George, and me to triple-reef the main. Clipping my safety harness carabiner to a jackline, I hopped up on the cabintop and took hold of the main halyard, while George tended to the mainsheet and Herb stood braced against the mast, preparing the reefing sheets. I commenced to lower the sail toward the third reef point, but in a powerful gust the canvas (Dacron, really) toppled down on me, pummeling me like the wing of a maddened, giant bird. Somehow or other I got free of it, in time to hear Andy, at the helm, call out, "Hang on!" A big sea boarded the *Tudy,* the water sluicing over the decks, and I was damned glad to be harnessed in. Herb then had me uncoil the reefing lines while he attached the rings to the hooks. He tightened down on the sheets, and the sail was shortened, and all the while we were balancing ourselves atop the pitching cabin like ironworkers on wet girders. George, grinding a winch, trimmed the sail.

We had no sooner gotten the main reefed down than Andy said, "I don't like the looks of it! Burn it! Burn the main!"

Ashore, I was a writer of some modest reputation, George an investment banker; here we were just deckhands, and the skipper's word was law. Without a word of complaint and with drunken staggers, we worked our way over the cabin to the mast and lowered the main; then, clutching the boom, Herb and I flaked the sail, that is, furled it over the boom, securing it with sail ties and with a length of the preventer, which had parted earlier. This took a while, as every time the boat rolled in the mounting seas, the boom swung to one side or the other, threatening to knock us off our feet. Finally, it was done, and on a reefed jib alone, our ship was making eight knots through high, boiling waves, with spindrift twirling on their faces and in the troughs. Faces crusted with salt, sweating in our heavy foul-weather gear, we had the feeling that comes from getting a dangerous job done and done right, and it was a damned good feeling, the kind a man or woman will never get, feeding the pages of a sales presentation into a copy machine.

The wind backed from west to west-southwest, and keened up to thirty-seven knots, a Force 8 gale. A few gusts sent the anemometer past forty knots. From belowdecks came the sound of crockery and glasses shattering inside the galley lockers. Later, Andy turned on the radio to listen to the noon weather report from the NOAA station in Norfolk, Virginia. A cold front was coming down from Canada, and our skipper was more concerned about that than the gale. We did not want to beat against a thirty-knot nor'wester for our last 150 miles to Newport. It wouldn't be dangerous, just miserable, he said, adding that he wanted to make as much northing as possible to shorten the distance we would have to beat against the front. Beating, you ignorant, despicable land-lubbers, is sailing as closely as possible into a wind by alternating tacks, and is an exhausting business over long distances.

Quipping, "This is a race we're gonna lose, isn't it?" Herb agreed to press the boat a little. The reef in the jib was shaken out, and we tore along at over ten knots, eleven when we surfed down the waves. I was at the helm, and found it difficult to steer. With the extra canvas, she really dug in and went constantly to windward, so that I had to hold the wheel hard to leeward to keep her on course. But it was stirring to have her at my command. In sailor's parlance, she had a bone in her teeth, and when she plunged, the bow spray burst like exploding crystal.

Trying to sleep was not stirring. It was impossible, like trying to sleep in an earthquake. There was a cacophony of bangs, thuds, thumps, rattles, and pings as the ship rose and fell, and the seas rushing past the hull snarled like a pack of angry dogs. This uncomfortable experience caused me to reflect on my mission. Did I really have to do this for the sake of verisimilitude? Couldn't I have just read about heavy-weather sailing and made the rest up? Conrad had relied on direct experience in his first few novels, but the one literary scholars regard as his master-piece, *Nostromo*, was composed almost entirely out of his imagination. Published in 1904, the novel was set in a fictional Latin American coun-try, and was based on nothing more than a fragmentary tale Conrad had heard and on a fleeting glimpse he had caught of the Central American coast twenty-five years earlier. But in 1904, long before the present Information Age imposed its despotic reign of facts and data, it was eas-ier for readers to suspend disbelief and accept that a country called Costaguana existed and that Conrad had gotten it right.

At 1:30P.M., having slept not one second, I was back on watch, this time with Roger, looking like an old sea dog in his gray beard and knit watch cap. The wind was straight out of the southwest now, still at Force 8, with ten- to-twelve foot seas tumbling toward our port quarter. They were Gulf Stream seas, steep and crowded, and the wind, blowing across the course of the Stream, sometimes drew them into tossing cones. When a strong gust whistled through, tendrils of watery smoke swept across them, like dry-ice vapors across the slopes of dark blue hills. Swallow-size storm petrels plied this heaving wilderness, capturing tiny fish with their beaks (how they could see such microscopic prey in all that vastness was beyond me). Shearwaters glided and turned, white then brown then white again. I stood my half-hour trick at the wheel, handed it off to Roger, and sat down in the cockpit. The *Tudy* careened down a really big wave, maybe a fourteen-footer, and as she rose, another sea soared several feet above Roger's head, then curled and broke over the stern. It whacked us with the power of a baseball bat, almost toppling Roger while lifting me out of my seat and tossing me into the lifeline. I lay for a moment in the foot-deep water that swirled and foamed over the deck before, the bow rising again, it sloshed with a rush out the scuppers. If not for my harness, I would have been swept overboard.

Off watch again, back on at 10:30 that night, the wind down to Force 6—twenty-two to twenty-seven knots. I was just as glad to be above decks; below, the hollow boom of the hull crashing down into the troughs sounded like artillery fire. As the wind subsided to twenty knots, Andy called down to Herb to set a double-reefed main. The spreader lights were switched on, and in their glow, Herb and I scampered and skidded about to set the sail. Everything went wrong at once. First, the main halyard fouled in a shroud, and Herb had to shinny up the mainmast to free it, a hairy business on a rocking, rolling boat. Then a batten worked loose, its back end sticking out of the leach like an arrow. After we fixed that, a reefing line managed to kink itself around another. Once that was seen to, we settled down and soon, so did wind and seas. At one in the morning, the clouds parted and the moon came out, shining on the wind-pocked waves to make them look like ridges of hammered pewter in motion. It was an enchanting sight, but it didn't last long; half an hour later, a thick fog descended.

We sailed through it for the next twelve or fifteen hours, peering through the murk for ships, listening for the menacing thud of engines. On the twentieth, during the early evening watch, we acquired two hitchhikers—orange-crested warblers an awful long way from land. They were charming little birds, and very bold. One let me touch it. We gave them a ride home, amused by the way they hopped about the decks, miraculously snatching invisible insects out of thin air.

The fog lifted at last, blown out by the cold front. In the black early morning hours of the twenty-first, I was steering dead on Polaris, and all bundled up in sea boots, wool socks, and a foul-weather suit over a Polartec sweater and trousers. My body was warm, my face chilled by the twenty-five-knot norther, the icy spray flung back from the bow. Gayhead Light, on Martha's Vineyard, gleamed a welcome. At sunrise, with a literary Andy reciting lines from a Masefield poem, we raised Castle Rock Light at the approaches to Newport harbor. The enormous "cottages" of enormously rich summer dwellers passed by, then the stone walls of Fort Adams, where we bore off to starboard, toward Bannister's Wharf.

Soon, we were tied up and off-loading our gear. Because I was the least experienced of the crew, I felt a huge swell of pride when Herb clapped me on the shoulder and said, "You can come sailing with me anytime, you're a good shipmate, mate." I was also pleased to have done my little bit to finish a job—maybe not an important job in the grand scheme of things, for all we did was to deliver a yacht, a plaything—but a job nonetheless. Fifteen hundred miles of open sea in ten days, six hours. Not bad. Heading down the dock to call my wife to come pick me up, I found it pleasant to be walking on a stable surface; yet a certain letdown came with being ashore. Already, I missed the way the *Tudy*, under full sail, would gather herself as a racehorse gathers for a gallop. I was nostalgic for the sight of sperm whales and long-tailed tropic birds winging over the green swells off Bermuda. Most of all, I would miss the solidarity of a boat's crew, working together for a common purpose. I didn't know yet if I had learned anything that would be of use to me in writing my novel, and I didn't care. I was grateful to have been privileged to live out a fantasy born long ago, in a high-school classroom on bleak winter afternoons.

the ahab complex

1 9 8 3

L ike the Antarctic and the Amazon Basin, the Gulf Stream is one of the last places on earth where nature holds dominion and man is a mere intruder. Though remote stretches of it flow through the open seas or past uninhabited coasts, other parts can be reached without mounting a major expedition funded by the National Geographic Society. A short boat ride from the gimcrack high-rises of Miami will put you on it; it rushes just outside the trash-flecked green of Havana harbor, within sight of the Mafia-built hotels where Meyer Lansky used to count his chips, and where, now, Russians dance clumsily to conga drums and the bray of Latin brass. Across the Florida Straits from Havana, the Stream courses within twenty miles of Key West, the island city that's as much a refuge for smugglers, gunrunners, and redneck shrimpers as it is for young men who bump bottoms in discos where slide projectors flash pictures of unnatural acts on the walls.

Despite its proximity to these, and other, centers of civilization, the Stream is much safer from conquest and exploitation than either Antarctica or the Amazon. Man cannot build highways or time-share condominiums on it; he can't dam it, sink offshore rigs into it, mine it, fence it, subdivide it, my God, its flow is so powerful that he can't even properly pollute it. The only imprints he makes on it are evanescent: the wakes of his tankers, freighters, and warships, wakes that froth and roll, then vanish in the mighty ocean current Hemingway called "the great blue river."

I think of it as a place, and what a place, so long that its waters cool the Yucatan Peninsula and warm the harbors of Norway; so strong that its volume of flow in the Florida Straits alone equals a thousand Mississippi Rivers; so mysterious that oceanographers have yet to chart its maze of cross-currents and undercurrents, eddies and meanders.

It is as much a home to wild giants as the Serengeti: mako and great white sharks, broadbill swordfish, blue marlin and bluefin tuna weighing half a ton breed and hunt in the Stream. It is also a highway for these roving monsters, which follow it for enormous distances: tuna and swordfish travel it from New England to the Bahamas; marlin that mated in its Caribbean reaches have turned up off the coast of West Africa. None of these great fish, like, say, the great cats, can be ogled and photographed in parks and preserves. Anyone who wishes to see them must fish for them in the Stream, either commercially or for sport. The latter is by far preferable; although these species are caught on primitive handlines in some parts of the world—in Cuba, for instance, men still hook and fight giant marlin as Santiago did in *The Old Man and the Sea*—most modern commercial fishing is an industrial enterprise that gives the fish little chance to escape and no chance to demonstrate its power.

On the other hand, big-game fishing with sporting tackle not only gives a person an opportunity to see these huge brutes, it offers the sportsman or -woman the experience of feeling the awesome strength of a large predator without suffering serious injury or death in the process. He or she will suffer from sore muscles, exhaustion, dehydration, dizziness, blistered fingers, swollen hands, perhaps a few minor cuts and bruises, and possibly a torn ligament; but I've never heard of an angler being wounded or killed by a marlin or giant tuna. Big marlin and swordfish have rammed, and sometimes sunk, fishing boats with their bills; mako sharks have lunged over gunwales and nearly torn small craft to pieces; however, these have been freak incidents. Thus, danger junkies, like some of the weirdos I knew in Vietnam, would do better to find their amusement hunting polar bears with a .22. Of course, going far offshore in a small fishing vessel can be very charming for those who are charmed by risk. Sometimes, as when a nor'wester packing fifty-knot winds blows up out of nowhere, hurling mountainous seas at your boat, the experience can be so damned charming that you'd give anything not to be charmed anymore. Enough. Big-game fishing is not an inherently dangerous sport.

It is, like other forms of angling, fragmented into various cults, cliques, and castes. Within its circle is a smaller circle of billfishermen—those who pursue sailfish, swordfish, and the four species of marlins—and within that a still smaller circle of anglers who hunt giant marlin to the exclusion of all other fish. Given the abundance of gamefish—there are around fifty species—this sort of purism may seem foolish, perhaps a little crazy. Bill Robinson, formerly a first mate on a Key West charter boat, calls it "an expensive form of mental illness." To refine Robinson's analysis, marlin fishermen suffer from a rare psychological disorder that I call the Ahab Complex—an obsession to pursue and conquer a monster of the depths regardless of the consequences to one's bank account, career, and family life.

A number of fish in the Gulf Stream qualify as monsters. Each species possesses one or two qualities attractive to anglers, but in none is found the fusion of power, speed, endurance, size, agility, and an immeasurable virtue, character, that's found in the blue marlin. Of the four marlin species, the Atlantic-Pacific blue, the Pacific black, the striped, and the white, the first two are by far the largest. There is some debate as to which, the blue or the black, is bigger; a black weighing over twenty-two hundred pounds was harpooned off Australia, but commercial fishermen have reported catching Pacific blues of over twenty-five hundred pounds. The Atlantic blues of the Gulf Stream are smaller, though fish of half a ton are not unheard of. The current world's record on rod and reel is 1,282 pounds, and specimens of fifteen hundred pounds have been caught commercially. Their massiveness alone makes them awesome fish, but they are also among the fastest creatures in the sea, capable of sustained runs of over thirty-five miles an hour and bursts of sixty. This feat is nothing short of phenomenal: the resistance of water is seventy times that of air. The combination of size and speed makes the marlin one of the lords of the open ocean. With its swordlike bill, it can easily kill large prey (marlin have been found with 150-pound tuna in their stomachs),or defend itself against almost anything that swims. The swift mako shark is its only natural enemy, but even the mako generally cannot catch a healthy marlin. If it does, it's in for a fight: commercial fishermen in the Bahamas have reported witnessing combats between the two fish. The makos lost every time. That makes sense, because marlin bills strike with tremendous impact. They have pierced twenty-two inches of solid wood. A bill retrieved from a floating ball of raw rubber revealed a depth penetration of thirteen inches; no bullet on earth is capable of penetrating submerged rubber that far.

When it comes to endurance, swordfish and giant tuna may have the marlin beat, but not by much. That also makes sense, for the marlin is the embodiment of the principle that only the fit survive. First of all, no creature on earth that starts off so small—in the larval stage they are one inch long—grows so big. Second, out of every million eggs laid by a female, only ten reach maturity, so, when an angler hooks one that's lasted long enough to tip the scales at five hundred pounds, he has definitely not tied into a creature that's made of sugar candy. A short fight with one will last about an hour; two or three is more likely. The longest on record, with a huge black off Australia's Great Barrier Reef, went on for thirty hours. (The fish threw the hook and the angler was hospitalized.)

The marlin's agility is another of its prized attributes. Its spectacular aerial displays—you have to imagine an animal bigger than a grizzly and capable of more midair twists and turns than an acrobat—mesmerize anglers. Sportsmen value agility in a fight, and fish that jump, for some reason, are considered more "noble" than those that don't. Given their size and royal coloration—dark blue, purple, and silver—blue marlin are downright majestic when they lunge out of the water.

All four species are rare, which, of course, makes them much sought after. The blue is the rarest of all, not in terms of numbers (no one can make even a wild guess as to how many there are) but in terms of concentration. Blacks, stripers, and whites tend to travel in schools. The blue is a loner, wandering the oceans in male-female pairs, occasionally in "wolf packs" of four fish. In the Atlantic, they're scattered from the northernmost edges of the Stream to as far south as Cape Horn; and because little is known of their habits and migratory patterns, the angler who goes in quest of them must be willing to cover vast stretches of water and put in anywhere from twelve to seventy-two hours of fishing time just to hook one. If he manages to, he has, on an average, only two chances in five of catching it. Blues are as unpredictable as they're elusive. They have the strength and stamina of blacks, the speed and nimbleness of stripers and whites. In a fight they employ a wide repertoire of combative skills: they streak away from the boat with stunning acceleration, then turn on a dime and come at the boat, greyhounding as they come; they jump out of the water ten or twelve times in a row, corkscrewing in midair to wrap the leader around their bills or tails; they beat the waves to a froth with their heads, "walk" on their tails, sound a hundred fathoms, and, sounding, sulk in the depths, loggy as sharks, or they "bulldog"—shake their heads from side to side to throw the hook. Sometimes, in their frenzy, they ram their bills through the hull. And sometimes, rarely, but it has happened, they come to the boat, apparently beaten; then, as the mate takes hold of the wire leader, they sense their peril, and making a valedictory leap for freedom, impale the mate or cause the wire to snap like a steel whip that amputates his ear, fingers, or hand.

Even when gaffed, the fish can behave erratically. Last summer off Key West, an angler aboard Captain Steve Magee's charter boat hooked a blue so large that Magee is reluctant to estimate its size. The fish was alongside an hour and forty-five minutes later. As the mate, Robinson, held on to the leader, literally as a man holds a rope in a tug-of-war, Magee struck the huge marlin with a flying gaff. The fish roared under the boat, the great sickle-shaped tail raising a wall of water that washed over the deck, knocking off Magee's and Robinson's hats and sunglasses. The fish broke loose. Robinson hauled up the empty gaff-head. It was made of quarter-inch steel and it had been opened up like a coat hanger.

Having discussed the fish, I'll now turn to a somewhat less impressive creature, the fishermen. I use the masculine because big-game angling is a largely masculine sport. I don't mean masculine in the sense of machismo, although the sport is associated with he-man celebrities like Ernest Hemingway and Lee Marvin. Despite the size and ferocity of the quarry and the heftiness of the tackle (some big-game rigs weigh twenty-two pounds), you don't have to be a middle linebacker or drink kerosene as an aperitif to catch the monsters. Yes, Lee Marvin has caught plenty of big fish; so did Bing Crosby. So have a lot of women, for the sport requires skill, stamina and determination, not brute strength. Female anglers have boated marlin of over a thousand pounds. In the Florida Keys, the local record of 527 pounds was established by a five foot, two-inch, 100-pound woman who fought the fish for three hours. The reason why this sort of fishing is dominated by men lies not in the masculine body but within the masculine mind.

"Women can do as good a job catching marlin as men," said charter captain Frank Kerwin. "But women can take it or leave it. They'd rather catch something for dinner. Let a man just hook one and he goes crazy. He doesn't want to fish for anything else."

Norman Wood is a man who hooked one and went crazy. He does not fit the tough-guy stereotype of the big-game angler, and hasn't lost his mental faculties. An amiable, easy going Georgian who is now a real estate developer in the Florida Keys, Wood is quite sane except when he's twenty miles out in the Gulf Stream aboard his fishing boat, the *Petticoat III*. That is when the obsession takes over. On a recent voyage, the *Petticoat* ran into a school of dolphin, a prized gamefish that is also excellent table fare. Wood's wife, Shirley, began reeling them in for dinner. The skipper fumed impatiently on the flying bridge, then called to the cockpit below:

"That's enough. Let's get back to fishing."

Shirley replied that she was fishing.

"Dolphin aren't fish," Wood shot back. "Marlin are fish."

It began several years ago, when he caught his first blue.

"I'd been a light-tackle angler up till then. First I thought bone-fishing was the ultimate. Then tarpon fishing," he said. "But that marlin weighed three hundred sixty-five pounds, and when I saw it make twelve or fourteen leaps out of the water, I didn't want to fish for anything else."

And he hasn't. Since then, Wood has caught sixty-seven blue marlin (all but a few of which were released).

It would be an exaggeration to say that all men get excited about the sport. There are plenty of male sportsmen who find it intolerable, mostly because the fish are hunted by trolling. Artist Russell Chatham, an expert fly fisherman, once described trolling as the next most boring thing to an "unsuccessful bridge club luncheon." He went on to say that, when a fish is finally hooked, "and you are faced with the appalling prospect of an hour in the fighting chair, you simply would rather have a beer."

Trolling—trailing baits or lures behind a slow-moving boat—needn't be that dull; nonetheless, it is probably the least interesting method of angling next to still-fishing with a worm. "The peasant . . . with patient angle trolls the finny deep," said Oliver Goldsmith; and the monotony of it often pummels the sharpest mind into a peasant like stupor. Which is not to say that marlin fishermen are peasants. No peasant I know of could afford the outlay. The sport is no longer reserved for men who could comfortably play high-stakes poker with the emir of Kuwait, but it does require a considerable supply of ready cash as well as the time and freedom that money buys.

What kind of men are willing to pay large sums and endure hours of tedium simply to catch a big fish? Are they trying to compensate for some real or imagined inadequacy? You bet. But let's get one thing straight: I don't mean sexual inadequacy. No cocktail-party Freudianism, all right? No baloney about rods being phallic symbols and the overcoming of large fish a surrogate for sexual conquest. None of that nonsense, okay? For those of you who insist on believing that something dark and weird is going on here, I'll toss out a tidbit: all giant marlin, those over three hundred pounds, are females. Yes, they are ladies. Moreover, marine biologists believe marlin undergo a sex change at a certain stage in their development, so when a Lee Marvin wannabe hooks a big one, he's fighting a transsexual fish.

While you ponder the implications of those facts, I'll get on with my point. The inadequacy of which I speak is the inadequacy, the limitations imposed on men by their human natures. The human male is a predator, but he's a puny one compared to the competition. The blue marlin is the to Gulf Stream what the lion is to the Serengeti: the living symbol of its world, the beauty, might, and mystery of the Stream made flesh. Like the lion, it is a creature that seizes the masculine imagination and arouses in the masculine heart and urge to pursue and capture because it has been endowed, far more generously than men have been, with the virtues men prize. Catching one of these great fish is, furthermore, a team effort. It is common to say that the angler caught the fish, but in fact he caught it with the assistance of a skilled captain and mate. The camaraderie, the union of several men in a single quest, is probably some sort of throwback to those primitive hunting bands from which masculine society is thought to have evolved. In that sense, marlin fishermen are diametric opposites of fly fishermen. Fly fishing is a solitary sport that calls for a contemplative, cerebral nature; for its object is to outwit a fish. Marlin do not need to be outwitted because intelligence and wariness are not among their attributes. (When you weigh half a ton and are armed with a sword capable of piercing two feet of solid wood, you don't need to be smart or careful.) The satisfaction is in outlasting or outdoing the fish. The pleasures of the sport are athletic as opposed to intellectual. Marlin fishermen relish an engagement that calls forth all of their physical resources, and the elation, the somehow pleasant pain, the cleansing exhaustion that come after a hard-fought battle.

The Hemingway blue marlin tournament sponsored by the Cuban government in 1978 was my big-game initiation. I have mixed feelings about fishing tournaments, which turn a noncompetitive activity into competitive blood sport; but signing up for the tourney was the only way an American could fish the waters Hemingway had made legendary. Contestants were given dispensation from the travel restrictions between the U.S. and Cuba that had made Cuban waters, a mere ninety miles away, seem as remote as the South Pacific. Along with two fishing partners, Jack London and Dave Finkelstein, a six-foot, -seven-inch captain named Garrett Anger, and a five-foot,-six-inch mate, Dick Stammers, I boarded the *Candide II*, a much-abused thirty-one-foot Bertram that London, Finkelstein, and I had picked up for $19,900 several months earlier, and then spent a lot more money and hours and hours of labor fixing up.

We christened her "Candide" after the novel by Voltaire, because foolish optimism is the quality the sportfisherman must possess even above patience and perseverance. Sticklers for literary accuracy told us that we should have named the vessel after Dr. Pangloss, the character in the novel who proclaimed, in the face of overwhelming evidence to the contrary, that this was the best of all possible worlds. "Pangloss," however, sounded too much like an industrial wax. "Candide" had a better ring and made our point.

On a scorching day in early August, we fired up the twin Chrysler inboards, cast off from the docks at Key West's Garrison Bight, and set out across the Stream.

Upon pulling into Barlovento harbor five hours later, it became immediately apparent that we were the underdogs. The slips were filled with fifty- and sixty-foot Hatteras and Merritt and Rybovich fishing yachts, topped by gleaming tuna towers, with paid, professional crews. Alongside these vessels, the *Candide* looked like a dinghy. Compared to the state-of-the-art Fin-Nor and Penn reels clamped to the state-of-the-art rods, our old-fashioned reels, with their friction drags, looked pathetic, like something we'd picked up at a yard sale. Compared to the owners of the yachts and the expensive tackle, all of whom seemed to be Texas oilmen, London, Finkelstein, and Phil Caputo, all of whom were freelance writers, appeared to be peasants. And our chances of winning against such competition appeared to be nil. But there we were, in Castro's Cuba, and there was nothing for it but to try.

I had become reasonably competent at most forms of light-tackle angling, which I'd found to be what sportfishing is supposed to be: fun. Marlin fishing, on the other hand, was proving an awful disappointment. Trolling seemed an activity you could train for by sitting in front of a TV and watching test patterns all day. In three days of it, we'd hooked one fish, a docile, middling-sized male that came to the boat in five minutes, then sounded and cut the line on the running gear. No epic battle. No spectacular leaps. Nothing. The difference between expectation and performance was depressing.

We amused ourselves at night in Old Havana, which a quarter century of Socialist triumph had transformed into a slum. Vintage cars from my high-school days plied the narrow, colonial-era streets, and the Floridita bar and La Bodega del Medio, Papa's old haunts, sported photographs of celebrities long in their graves, movie posters featuring Rita Hayworth and Greta Garbo. I bought a *mojito* for a pretty Estonian secretary at the Soviet Embassy; she all but screamed in terror when she discovered that I was an American, and fled the bar. The Cuban government treated the *Yanqui* anglers to a show at the Tropicana, and the astonishingly beautiful, long-limbed chorus girls suggested that Communist rule wasn't all bad. Then it was back to fishing.

On the fourth day, London and Finkelstein were so fed up with catching nothing but severe sunburn that they decided to stay ashore and see a bit more Havana. Already showing symptoms of the Ahab Complex, I went out with Garrett and Stammers. We prowled the waters off Cojimar, a fishing village several miles east of Havana. There, in eight hundred fathoms, the Stream met an onshore current, creating an upwell that, a Cuban hardliner told us, brought plankton up from the bottom, squid that fed on the plankton, and marlin that fed on the squid. You know, the old food-chain trick. It worked for Hemingway. Fishing out of Cojimar in 1933, he caught the blue marlin that still stood as the Cuban national record on rod and reel: 468 pounds.

By noon, we were cooking in the microwave of a Cuban August. A breeze made the heat bearable. On the other side of the ledger, the breeze was blowing against the Stream, churning the water into a four-foot chop. Gazing astern, I saw, behind the *Candide's* wake a shadow like the shadow of a immense, torpedo-shaped bird, a shadow rising from the purple-blue of eight hundred fathoms. Stammers, sitting on the port side gunwale, jumped to his feet.

"Marlin!"

The port outrigger line snapped from the pin with a crack like that of a starter's pistol, the rod bending and the line ratcheting off the reel. Then the rod straightened. The mangled carcass of the bonito we'd been trolling flopped in the seas perhaps a hundred yards behind us.

"It's off," Stammers mourned, cranking in the line to put on a fresh bait.

"On the right!" Garrett bellowed from the bridge. He was a veteran Long Island charter captain, and I assumed his excitement wasn't theater. "It's a horse! On the right!"

The monstrous shadow reappeared behind the mackerel trolling on the starboard outrigger. The marlin, as marlin often do when enraged or in a feeding frenzy, "lit up." The fish turned a brilliant, electric blue from gill to tail; it looked as if a gigantic police mars light had flashed in the water. A split second later, the mackerel vanished in a furious boil, and the line was disappearing at an alarming rate. At full throttle, twenty-five knots, the *Candide* could not have pulled it off the reel any faster. Inexperienced, I tried to pull the rod from the holder without lightening the drag. It was like trying to yank a stop sign out of the ground; the forces of the drag, the boat moving in one direction, and the fish in the other had jammed it into the holder.

"Back off the drag!" Garrett yelled from the bridge. He gunned the boat forward to take slack out of the line. "Back it off!"

But when you see perhaps two hundred yards of eighty-pound-test line, pulled against a drag resistance of twenty-five pounds, evaporate in seconds, you're certain that the reel will be stripped if you lighten the drag an ounce.

Somehow I wrestled the rod free, and was shocked, even a little frightened, as the powerful fish jerked me across the deck to the transom, my arms and shoulders feeling as if I'd grabbed hold of a ski rope attached to a Chris Craft. Locking my knees under the gunwale, leaning far back, I saved the tackle, and maybe myself from going overboard.

"BACK THE GODDAMNED DRAG!"

I managed to, then maneuvered myself into the fighting chair, the rod butt into the gimbal. Raising the rod tip, I struck the fish hard three or four times, the speed of the boat helping me set the hook deep into the marlin's bony mouth. Still the line was peeling off with a sound like . . . well you can duplicate the sound by expelling a deep breath through clenched teeth as hard as you can, flicking your tongue behind your teeth at the same time. I did not see the fish, only the line going out at a shallow angle; 300 yards, 350, 400, 450. Stammers got me into the shoulder harness, which took the strain off my arms and allowed me to fight the fish with my back and legs, my feet braced against the chair's footrest. Keeping the rod tip high, I tried to slow the marlin, and might as well have tried, with rod and reel, to slow a 1,000-cc Harley.

"You settled down yet?" Garrett called from the bridge. "You gonna listen to your skipper? I should have been backing down on this fish yesterday. It's halfway back to Key West by now."

Backing down—pursuing a running fish stern-first—is a maneuver performed by a captain to prevent the reel from being stripped while at the same time avoiding the dangerous bellies that form in a line when chasing the fish head-on. This tactic also spares the angler the hideous job of retrieving several hundred yards of line on his own power. This marlin was running against the seas, which meant we had to back into them. What seemed like a ton of water crashed over the transom as soon as Garrett threw the clutches into reverse. Through the blur of salt spray, I saw the marlin's head come up, a gargantuan head, with a bill that resembled a cavalry lance, beating the waves into a froth.

Light-tackle fishing had been fun, but fighting the marlin was shocking, scary, surreal. Garrett and Stammers were talking to me like cornermen to a fighter. *Reel, reel, reel. Rod tip's too low. Raise it. That's it. Level wind, watch the line, damn it, it's piling up. That's it. You've got slack. Take up the slack when it's trying to throw the hook. Reel, reel, reel.* All the while, the fish's head was thrashing the water a long way off, the cockpit awash, the engines whining at full astern, and I, pouring sweat, guided the line onto the reel with my left hand, cranking with my right until I was winded as a sprinter at the end of a race.

I'd retrieved all but a hundred yards of line when the fish made its first sound, a shallow one. Rod tip low, I thumbed the reel spool, then raised the rod, the line within a few pounds of breaking strain. To catch a marlin or any big gamefish, you must break its will in much the same way a horseman breaks the will of a wild stallion. It's done by putting maximum pressure on the line, a procedure that eventually convinces the fish to come to the boat. The big blue was a long way from being convinced. It didn't budge. It held down, winglike pectoral fins outspread, creating incredible resistance. Reel, thumb the spool, raise the rod. Muscles strained, tendons pulled. Try again. Thumb the spool so you don't pull drag and lose line. Now lift. Pressure, pressure. Try to turn its head. Can't. Feels like I'm hooked to a submarine.

I was leaning well back in the chair, throwing my weight against the weight of the fish, the harness straps pulled taut, rod and line quivering from the tension, when the rod whipped to one side, cracking my wrist against the chair's armrest. Then to the other side. Then back again. Whap, whap, whap. The marlin was bulldogging, and the power in those swipes of its head was intimidating. Get control of this fish. It isn't just beating you, it's beating you up. The line hissed off the reel again, its angle decreasing sharply.

"Coming up!" Garrett shouted. "Take up the slack when it jumps."

The fish was not far astern when it broke water. It came out like a plane lifting off a runway, the blue-black javelin of its bill, the head with one big saucer-shaped eye that seemed to be examining us, the massive cobalt shoulders topped by a stubby, pointed dorsal fin, the pectoral fins swept back against a silver belly shining like a mirror in the sun, then the rest of its body, all twelve-odd feet of it, water streaming from flanks as royal blue as the Stream and barred by stripes glowing a neon lavender. It came out with its curved tail scything the air, its body shuddering not with the quick desperate spasms of a tarpon or sailfish but with a slow, stately grace, shuddering and arching into a crescent. The fish dived bill-first, sliding smoothly into the seas, its tail vanishing in a plume of spray. It was up again in an instant. This time it jumped straight out of the mystery of the Stream, a missile rather than a plane, a blue, purple-striped missile rocketing up until the tips of its tailfin were ten feet above the surface. It seemed to hang in midair for a moment, the powerful, sinuous twists of its body as lovely as anything I'd ever seen: then it flung itself over on its side, the splash of its impact like the burst of a six-inch shell.

"Jee-sus!" said Garrett. "It'll go six hundred."

The fish jumped three more times, and there was in each soaring leap a union of power and grace that arrested my heart and brought a tightness to my throat. For the next fifteen minutes the marlin leapt and made long runs that made the reel hot as an iron; it greyhounded across the ocean in one direction, turned and went off in the other; it pounded the seas with its head to dislodge the hook; it walked on its tail, whipping up a whirling mist like a waterspout before it flung itself on its side to run again. Such an explosion of energy would have exhausted any ordinary fish; and I understood why the ancient Greeks believed billfish were warrior-gods of the sea, the swordsmen of Achilles who had been transformed into fish after they'd drowned themselves in grief over their hero's death.

At the end of an hour, I felt as if I had played four quarters of football, but the marlin showed no signs of tiring. Garrett was backing down hard when the impeller on the starboard engine's raw water pump froze, causing the engine to overheat. He had to shut it down, and, on one engine, pursue the fish head-on. The line bellied dangerously. I reeled until it came tight again. The fish, which seemed to sense we were crippled, sounded. I tightened the drag as much as I dared, and rising off the seat, threw all my 165 pounds against the marlin. It did not slow for a second, running line down as fast as it had run it out, the reel so hot that Stammers had to pour fresh water on it to keep the drag washer from scorching. A third of the line was gone by the time the fish stopped, about a hundred fathoms below. That is when the most honest phase of the fight began; honest because, when a marlin sounds, the angler cannot rely on a boat to help him retrieve the line he's lost. On his own power, he must fight the fish for it, sometimes an inch or two at a time.

The marlin and I fell into a grueling contest. I would pump it toward the surface until the hundred-foot marker (a strand of dental floss wrapped around the line) appeared. Sensing its peril, the fish would bulldog, extend its pectorals, and hold so fast I felt I was snagged on a coral head. Then, with contemptuous ease, the marlin would sound once more. All I could do was watch the line slant ever downward into the fiery blue, down through the leaning pillars of sunlight and sparkling blooms of plankton.

I think it was on the fish's third sounding that I felt a sense of utter defeat. I was fairly strong and well conditioned, but it was demoralizing to see the fish stripping line from me as though I were a child. Also, it was appalling to think that I would have to fight for every inch once again. The marlin began to assume mythic proportions in my mind; maybe the ancients were right. The bloody fish was a god. Deity or no, I was convinced it could not be beaten, at least not by me. I guess the only thing that stopped me from handing the rod to Stammers was the fear of disgrace.

I was sitting in my customary position, bent into a question mark, the sun working me over with the zeal of a Chicago cop clubbing a radical, when Stammers said:

"Two hours."

I was aware only of the rod, the taut line, the solid, immovable weight below, and a numbness in my back. Closing my eyes, which burned from sweat and crusted salt, I imagined how the great fish looked, long and streamlined as it held in the current. I think I loved it then, loved it for its might and stubborn valor, and regretted my own lack of nobility, my vanity. That fish was a record-breaker, and after all I'd been through, I wanted it. Wanted it more than anything. Silently I asked forgiveness for what I was going to do. I'm sorry, I can't help it. If I catch another, I'll release it. And the one after that. And the next, but not this one. I *want* this one.

Thumbing the spool and lifting again, I felt an odd lightness, which for a very long, sickening second, I mistook for a pulled hook. When the line came tight, I realized I'd turned the marlin's head. Lifting, I turned it again and the piety I'd felt a moment before was overcome by a triumphant, savage glee. (And I wonder if that excitement of dominating the indomitable is one of the darker attractions of the sport.) Instead of inches, I gained yards at a time. I wound the marker onto the reel. Stammers put on the gloves with which he would wire the fish. The double line popped to the surface and went onto the reel, and then the fish was on the surface, lying exhausted on its side, and it looked as though it went on forever.

Garrett, bounding down from the bridge, unlimbered one of our two flying gaffs. Stammers got a wrap on the wire. In advance I decided to be calm and sportsmanlike when they screwed up and lost the fish. Garrett hit the fish hard and high up. Though it had seemed spent, the marlin smacked the hull with its tail and dived under the boat, thrashing with its last strength. Garrett hauled it up by the gaff rope, and

Stammers struck with the second gaff. The great fish, bleeding, rolled once and again, the blood green in the water, rolled a third time and died. We tail-roped it and struggled for fifteen minutes to winch it aboard. I slumped in the chair, staring dumbly at its length, two feet longer than the cockpit deck, the massiveness of its blue shoulders, fading to slate, the stripes whose glow was dimming. I was sore from my neck to my ankles, my wrists bruised, hands swollen and blistered, but I could have flown.

On one engine, it took us over two hours to limp back to Barlovento harbor, where the fish was weighed: 569 pounds. We'd beaten Hemingway's record and whipped the Texas oilmen, winning the tournament by a margin of fifteen pounds. I was thrown in the water by Garrett and Stammers—a ritual always performed when an angler catches his first marlin.

Being a person with some unfortunate insecurities, one who seems to require visible proof of his achievements in the way of framed awards, plaques, and trophies, I had the fish mounted back in Key West and found a wall at the Full Moon Saloon to hang it on. It hangs there now, its grand colors restored by the taxidermist's art, twelve feet, three inches of fish suspended above a document certifying that it established a new blue marlin record for Cuba. Yes, folks, irrefutable proof that I am no gee-hawing bass fisherman, but a twenty-four-karat big-game conquistador.

Today, five years and some two dozen marlin battles later, I'm a bit conscience stricken. It was all for pride and vanity. At least loony Captain Ahab had the decency to die with Moby-Dick. I now prefer to tag and release marlin, boating them only when they're exhausted and the choice is between killing them quickly with a gaff or leaving them to the sharks, an act as unconscionable as leaving a wounded animal in the brush. After all, if the essence of big-game fishing is the contest, then the angler has proved his point when the marlin comes to the boat, beaten. There is no real justification for killing it. It's only fair to point out that these fine ethics of mine haven't been tested. None of the marlin I've caught since that first one has exceeded 250 pounds, so it was easy to let them go. I seriously doubt I would have the saintliness required to release a "grander"—a thousand-pound fish. Of course, the surest way to avoid any moral dilemmas is to stop fishing for them, spend my weekends playing golf or watching twenty-two men bash each other for possession of an oval-shaped ball.

That isn't likely. I haven't become a marlin purist—there are simply too many other types of fishing I love—but I go for the big blues when they make their runs through the Florida Straits in the spring and fall. Yes, it can be extremely monotonous, but one of the pleasures of marlin fishing is not knowing exactly where the fish are or when they'll strike, or the sudden, unexpected appearance of that shadow in the blue water, then the huge shoulders and the dorsal fin cutting a wake, the bill slashing and the captain hollering from the bridge, "Marlin!"

Another pleasure is simply going far out on the Stream, where the land and the lighthouses drop beneath a horizon as straight as a ruler. The great blue river can be tranquil as a trout pond one day; the next it's wild with mounded seas, spray blowing off the crests of the waves like snow off mountaintops. Sometimes the Stream is riotous with life; at other times you swear it's part of the Dead Sea. Always it makes you aware of what is genuine and what is false, what is important and what is trifling. For when you are on it, you know that everything happening in it, from the silent blooms of plankton to the vast migrations of fish to the lethal ballets of hunter and prey, was happening long before all your ancestors were born and will be happening long after all your descendants are dead.

blue water blues

1 9 9 3

Angling is an act of faith, whether it is done by dipping a worm at the end of a cane pole or by casting a gorgeously tied fly with a graphite rod that inflicts sticker shock on all but those with incomes like Michael Milken's before he went to jail. Professional guides will tell you that success in fishing is three-quarters knowledge and skill and one-quarter luck, and that's true if you're a guide. For the average hacker, the role blind fortune plays is much greater. Anglers are gamblers by nature, the types who'll hang in a poker hand to draw to an inside straight or fill a four flush.

But sometimes a sure thing comes along, or seems to. Sometimes the fisherman is certain that all he needs do to catch more fish than he's dreamed of is to show up, and showing up, said Woody Allen, is ninety percent of life.

Which was why I showed up in San Diego in November as one of eighteen anglers who were not going on a fishing trip so much as participating in an event: The World Angler Bluewater Fly Rod Classic. It was to have the flavor of a pioneering expedition—a search for new angling frontiers like the quests I had read about as a boy in the books of Zane Grey. Aboard a ninety-foot mother ship, the *Shogun,* we would sail southward from San Diego to the rich fishing grounds off Mexico's Baja Peninsula, and using only fly tackle, attempt to capture pelagic beasts that are usually the quarry of big-game fishermen armed with giant reels and trolling rods. Striped marlin, yellowfin tuna, and most elusive of all, wahoo.

The adventure and the unusualness of the experience drew me

more than the chance of making the record books. Long-range fly fishing on the open seas had been tried only twice before, in 1991 and 1992, and most of the anglers had been professionals who are to fly fishing what Nick Faldo is to golf and Boris Becker to tennis. The names included Steve Abel, chairman of the Abel Reel company, Ed Rice, producer of the International Sportsmen's Exposition, Stu Apte, and others. These world-class anglers had set out to prove that long-range blue water fishing was possible for fly-rod enthusiasts, and they had succeeded beyond even their not inconsiderable expectations.

The fly-rod enthusiast who heard or read the tales of their exploits and didn't feel his or her pulse rate shoot into triple digits had to be suffering from clinical depression. Tales of twelve anglers at once hooked into huge wahoo, of yellowfin tuna in such numbers they raised standing waves when they boiled. Records were broken faster than china in a nasty domestic dispute. Abel caught a 64.1-pound wahoo on twenty-pound tippet and a 54.7-pounder on sixteen. Trey Combs, a noted outdoor writer and an accomplished fresh and saltwater fly fisherman, boated a 12.4-pound black skipjack on eight pound, while a California angler, David Inks, captured a thirty-eigh-pound-nine-ounce yellowfin on twenty.

Our trip would include some of the pros from the two previous voyages, but as the first commercial venture of its kind, the anglers in the "Bluewater Classic" would be paying customers and club players like me.

I was relieved. Oh, I'm all right as a saltwater fly fisherman. Through many years of hard work and practice I have managed to achieve an acceptable level of mediocrity; that is, I'm good enough not to make a complete fool of myself. Anyway, I hadn't signed on to impress anybody. There was the adventure I mentioned before; also, Connecticut, where I live, is a good place to be away from in the late autumn, when New England's iron skies and early dusks remind me of the line in the opening paragraph of *Moby-Dick:* "Whenever I find myself growing grim about the mouth; whenever it is a damp, drizzly November in my soul . . . I account it high time to get to sea as soon as I can."

But my main purpose was to change an uncanny streak of bad luck that was testing the outer limits of my Dr. Pangloss optimism.

Over a span of three years, I had gone south to Belize in pursuit of tarpon and bonefish, north to Martha's Vineyard for striped bass, west to Montana for trout. I'd come back from those and other forays not exactly skunked, but the next thing to it. An all-day float down the Yellowstone netted me two small rainbows. "What was I doing wrong?" I desperately asked by guide as we hauled the McKenzie boat ashore. "Not a damned thing," he drawled from beneath his Marlboro man Stetson. "Yellowstone's a funny river sometimes." Nights of casting for stripers in the Vineyard with zero results. The worst day occurred in Baja in the summer of 1990. Surf casting one morning in a beautiful, lonely bay in the Sea of Cortez, my wife and I caught one small grouper and eleven plastic bags.

So now it was back to Baja, or, rather to its offshore waters, where the wahoo schooled like sardines and the boiling yellowfin raised standing waves. Surely now my albatross would fly away, surely now I would once again believe with conviction that this is indeed the best of all possible worlds.

Well, fishing is a metaphor for life; things never turn out quite as good you hope or as bad as you fear.

From San Diego, the *Shogun* steamed southward for two days and a night. We were bound for the San Pablo Ten, part of an underwater ridge that runs for some fifty-five miles off Baha, its distance from shore ranging from twenty-five to almost a hundred miles, its depths from forty to ten fathoms, with its western slopes sheering down into the abyssal darkness of the biggest ocean on earth.

The *Shogun's* galley was transformed into a temporary tackle shop as eighteen anglers rigged and rerigged and rigged again. Flies and streamers were tied by Alan Richey, a supervisor on the Trans-Alaskan pipeline, and by Teddy Lund, at twenty-three the youngest member of an otherwise middle-aged to elderly crowd. The rest of us tied tippets of various classifications, from gossamer four-pound test up to twenty-pound. Dan Byford, a technical advisor for Umpqua Feather Merchants in Oregon, gave lessons on saltwater leaders to the several freshwater enthusiasts aboard and sharpened our hooks on a small, electrically powered grinding wheel.

Byford is something of a philosopher, and I liked his metaphysics. Technically minded though he was, he paid homage to the big role chance plays in fishing.

"You can't control the weather and can't control the fish or the seas," he told me after gazing with disapproval at one of the class tippets. "Sharp hooks and good knots, those are the two things you can control, so you might as well do it right."

And so, dawn till dusk on our second day out, I tied monofilament until my fingers were swollen. A low-pressure trough had moved in, the wind had risen, and the swells grew to eight to ten feet, which made rigging a queasy business.

Was it mal de mer that caused a sudden, inexplicable gloom to wash over me late in the day? I was on the stern deck, taking a break and chatting with Whitey Bozeman, a sixty-eight-year-old oil consultant with a mustache the color of a first communion shirt, when an evil voice whispered in my head, "This trip isn't going to be like the other two. It's going to be a bust because you're a Jonah." Readers with training in psychology will recognize this sort of thinking as characteristic of an adolescent who thinks he's the center of the universe. Okay if you're an adolescent. I was fifty-two.

To shuck off the premonition's spell, I climbed to the pilothouse for a talk with the *Shoguns*'s skipper, Captain Frank LoPreste. The adjective "legendary" is too frequently applied to fishing captains, but it fit LoPreste, a fifty-year-old with forearms that belong in an arboretum and a chest to match. Descended from Sicilian fishermen from the island of Lipari, LoPreste is considered the pioneer of long-range fishing off Baja. As the owner or part owner of a fleet of blue water boats, he has led sportfishing expeditions to the Revillagigdos Islands, a remote archipelago lying some 370 miles south of Baja, and to the even more remote Clipperton atoll, the easternmost islands of French Polynesia. He has guided so many anglers to record-breaking catches it would take the length of this article to list them all. In short, he is the sort of skipper to give a fisherman confidence.

His face half lit by the glow of side-scan sonar, radar, and depth-recorder screens, LoPreste was studying a chart while mate Kevin Shelly steered and Norman Khagawa, the Shogun's young co-owner and co-captain, scanned the horizon with binoculars. LoPreste outlined his game plan. We would drop anchor at the San Pablo Ten early in the morning and fish there for skipjack and small yellowfin tuna to loosen everyone up and accustom them to the *Shogun*'s fishing methods. Afterward, we would make our way southward, seeking wahoo and mahimahi, then prowl the waters off Bahia Ascension for striped marlin and sailfish, large schools of which had been spotted by other long-range vessels. Our last stop would be a series of banks, bearing names like "Thetis," "Uncle Sam," and "Potato," where we could expect yellowfin in the hundred-pound class and giant wahoo.

A word about the wahoo. Bearing the unwieldy scientific name of *Acanthocybium solanderi*, it is the largest of the mackerel family, growing to over one hundred pounds. With a long, sleek, silver-blue body barred with dark blue tiger stripes, muscles that can propel it to speeds of sixty miles an hour, and teeth like a bandsaw's, it also is a perfectly designed predator. The wahoo is generally a nonschooling fish, a lone, roving killer of the deep sea; but in places like Baja's offshore waters, it occasionally assembles in large numbers. When hooked on light tackle, its speed and power are almost frightening. Only a handful of anglers in the world have caught one on a fly.

Much encouraged by my chat with LoPreste, I went back below. We ate a splendid dinner of shrimp sautéed in garlic butter (the ship's two cooks, Monte and Mike, regularly turned out meals that would make most restaurateurs ashamed of themselves), then rigged some more. By ten-thirty, my bunkmate, Tony Oswald, and I were in our small but comfortable stateroom, rocked to sleep by Mother Ocean.

What is the allure of fishing? What draws the angler to stream, river, or lake; to deep sea, estuary, or tidal flat? I think it is the charm of not knowing what will happen, the sense of mystery. There is too much that is known about the modern world, and too great a desire in the hearts of modern man to know even more. We want to forecast, predict, chart, graph, plumb, sound, or otherwise take the measure of almost every aspect of life. Satellites tell us what the weather will be like five days from now, CNN keeps us up to the second on developments in Bosnia, amniocentesis shows us the sex of a child months before it's born, and now, the media breathlessly announce, we can link our home computers to information highways and access the world at the touch of a button. We are overfed on information and undernourished in wisdom and a sense of wonder.

Wisdom is a matter for philosophers, but fishing can restore the lost wonder of childhood. There is a mystery in all forms of angling—why did the trout strike this fly now when they wouldn't give it a second glance half an hour ago?—but the mystery is deepest on the big blue water, a realm less known than outer space. You can see an evening rise on a trout stream, see bonefish tailing or tarpon rolling on

the flats, but when a school of wahoo streak in like a salvo of silver tor-
pedoes, or marlin shoot to the surface out of waters that could drown
the Smoky Mountains, they usually do so without much warning,
often with none at all. Their appearances occur so unexpectedly it's as
if they have sprung full blown into life at the moment the angler sees
them. They seem like apparitions, summoned up from a dark and
secret world.

The rattle of the anchor chain woke me at four A.M. Tony, who is
head of World Angler and a veteran of the previous two trips, wisely
stayed in bed. I was full of the neophyte's excitement and got dressed
and climbed up to the galley for a cup of coffee. Thinking I would be
the only one awake at such an hour, I was surprised to hear voices out
on the stern deck and the sweet hiss of airborne fly lines. Out there in
the predawn blackness, Bob "R. T." Trosset and Carlos Solis were casting into what looked like a void while mate Kevin Shelly stood atop the
huge bait-well, tossing live sardines to chum up whatever swam below.

R. T. is a top Key West guide I have fished with for the past twelve
years. He was responsible for my making the Baja trip, having told me
about it when we were tarpon and bonefishing in the Keys the previous June. Solis, a Havana-born Miami native, is an international investment adviser for Merrill Lynch and an amateur angler who is better
than most pros. He can cast a fly one hundred feet with either hand.

Well, if anybody was going to catch the first fish of the voyage it
would be one of those two. And, I reasoned, if I wedged my unworthy
self between them, I might get sloppy seconds. I went around to the
side of the galley house and took my Sage twelve-weight from the rack.

I might point out here one of my misgivings about blue water fly
fishing. It seemed to contradict what I had been taught to believe was
the essence of fly fishing: solitude, elegance, and delicacy. First, I was to
share deck space with seventeen other anglers. Second, everything
about this endeavor seemed gargantuan and brutal. The Shogun was
more ship than boat. The bait-well Kevin stood on was almost as big as
a backyard swimming pool and contained no less than two and a half
tons of live sardines. Then there was the tackle. Of the seventy-five
rigged rods in the racks, my tarpon-size Sage with its Fin-Nor reel was
among the smallest. Most of the others appeared to have been made by
a hockey stick manufacturer, and the flies attached to them were literally as big as hummingbirds. What would Izaak Walton have to say

about this? I wondered. *I dide observe that the tackle of these anglers was veree bige and sauvage-lookinge It was notte me idea of whate flyfishinge shoulde bee.*

Puny Sage in hand, I joined R. T. and Carlos. Kevin said the depth-recorder had marked tuna about eighty feet down. I made a medium cast upcurrent. Let the fast-sink line drop and drift back, then stripped in slowly. A pastel dawn broke, revealing the barren brown mountains of Baja's western coast.

"Boil!" Kevin hollered. "Tuna!"

Thirty to thirty-five yards astern, the fish were devouring the live baits. Carlos cast into them with his left hand. I attempted the same with my right, making a nice pitch of eighty-odd feet, but still ten feet short. I began to strip my green-and-white streamer, felt a take, set the hook, and the rod bowed into a U. the line hissing off the reel as the fish sounded with electrifying speed. In a moment, R. T. was hooked up. We two danced an odd ballet for several minutes as we followed our fish back and forth across the beamy stern. I passed my rod under his to avoid crossing our lines: he passed his under mine. The tuna fought with the tenacity for which the species is famous, plunging straight down, shaking their heads. I had caught blackfin before on fly tackle in the Atlantic, boating one that came in at twenty-seven pounds. Judging from the tussle the yellowfin was giving me on a rod that could break a big tarpon's will, I estimated that it would weigh in at thirty pounds.

When Kevin gaffed the fish and tossed it flopping onto the deck, I figured a trick had been played on me by the Lord of the Sea. This could not be the tuna I had hooked. In the midst of the fight, the Lord of the Sea had exchanged it for one much smaller, a ten- to twelve-pound rat. Yet there was my streamer hanging from the rat's lips, so the only trick was the one I'd played on myself by assuming that a yellowfin fights like a blackfin.

R. T.'s was soon brought to gaff. It was about the same size as mine. We were the heroes of the morning, we had caught the first fish of the voyage. But thinking about the struggle I'd had with such a small prize made me wonder what a thirty-, forty-, or fifty-pounder would do to my tarpon-killer rod, and I began to look upon the hockey sticks with a kinder eye.

Our catch that morning proved a false good omen. For the next two days, we worked vast stretches of water and caught a few middling-size mahimahi and skipjacks; but the big tuna, wahoo, and billfish eluded us. The expedition was not coming close to fulfilling our high expectations. A mild gloom fell over anglers and crew. We fought against it by maintaining an air of sportsmanlike cheer. If it was a bit forced, it was better than saying the hell with it and sulking in one's bunk.

Much has been written and said about the benefits the lessons of competitive sports bring to life's more serious endeavors. I'd like to put in a word for sportfishing. It does teach patience and perseverance—rare virtues in an age of instant gratification—but it also can teach you how to hope when there isn't much reason to. That's a good skill to have when coping with the bad hands life deals us all at one point or another.

The phony angler—usually some Ralph Lauren yuppie outfitted with the most expensive equipment money can buy—will give up after a few bad days, telling himself, "This is a waste of time, it's unproductive, it doesn't pay." The true angler, in his patched waders and threadbare vest, will fish a river all day without a strike and still feel his heart beat with anticipation when he comes to the next bend; he knows a legendary brown or rainbow awaits him in those pools and riffles below.

So it was with us. The spirit of Dr. Pangloss infected us all each dawn. Surely this will be the day when magic happens.

And it almost did for Carlos Solis late in the morning on our fifth day out. We were cruising the Thetis Banks, off a bleak headland called Punta Lazaro, when LoPreste and his crew spotted pods of frigate birds circling and diving in the distance. That's a sign that baitfish are being driven to the surface by predators, and a welcome sight to eyes that have scanned the horizon for hours and seen nothing but, well, the horizon.

LoPreste steered the Shogun toward the frigates. Far off, the pod resembled a puff of smoke against the wispy mare's tails that brushed the sky. Carlos and R. T. were in the casting positions at each corner of the stern deck, waiting to see what came up. Only three anglers could fish at a time, two in the stern, one from the bow. To give everyone a fair shot, a rotation system had been set up, with each fisherman assigned a number. When one angler hooked up, the next took his or her place. (Two of our eighteen were women.)

"Those are marlin under those birds. Marlin!" LoPreste announced over the P.A. system.

Those of us not fishing scrambled to the bridge to watch or take photographs. From that vantage point, I was able to see birds working in every direction—frigates, boobies, and gulls, some circling, others diving into the boils and splashes made by billfish in a feeding frenzy. I had never seen so many marlin and sailfish in one place in my life; hundreds, thousands for all I knew, were spread over several square miles of ocean.

"Marlin!" howled Mason, one of the mates, from atop the bait-well. Or was it Mason's identical twin, Jason? I don't recall, only that wild, electrifying cry, "Marlin! Marlin up!"

A sight to cause cardiac arrest in the healthiest heart: the big dark dorsal and tailfins, the blunt bills slashing the sardines Mason pitched overboard to draw the fish into casting range. There were two striped marlin, each between a 120 and 150 pounds, and they lit up in their excitement as if they were made of blue and purple neon. I don't know why billfish give off this brilliance when they are feeding or angry, nor what chemical reactions cause it. It is one of the most beautiful and awesome displays in nature.

One marlin, throwing off pulsing, brilliant colors like a strobe light, streaked toward R. T.'s streamer, took a pass at it, then circled and seized Carlos's fly.

Carlos's demonstration of coolness under pressure should have been videotaped and sent to fishing clinics everywhere. He moved backward with small, nimble steps, clearing his running line from the deck; then, as the fish came taut, he dropped his rod toward the horizontal and set the hook hard four or five times, driving the barb into the marlin's bony mouth.

Twenty yards from the boat, the fish cleared the water, blue-green flanks barred with lavender, and the whole lovely eight or nine feet of him haloed by a rainbow mist as he shook and writhed in midair and water drops flew from his body into the sunlight. Carlos "bowed" to him, as you do to a jumping tarpon to prevent its throwing the hook, reeled down, and hung on as the fish planed up out of the water at an angle, slammed down belly-first, lunged again, and then, like a figure skater finishing a routine with a spectacular flourish, went straight up, twisting as he did, arched over, and slipped bill-first into the water with such perfect form he hardly made a splash.

Someone said, "He'll go one-thirty easy."

The marlin sounded. Carlos fought him deep for perhaps fifteen minutes, and fought him as proficiently as I have seen anyone fight a big fish on light tackle.

The marlin made a run, burning off three hundred of the nine hundred yards of backing on Carlos's Abel reel. Away off, we saw the fish greyhound left to right, turn abruptly, and greyhound in the opposite direction. The arc went out of Carlos's rod and a heartbroken look came over his face as he reeled in his thrown fly and the striper leapt away and vanished.

An hour later, Trey Combs and I were in the stern positions, casting to a dozen striped marlin and sailfish. The sight of that many big billfish swirling only thirty feet away, the marlin with their brilliant stripes, the sails with their ribbed dorsal fins unfurled, almost gave me a case of angler's buck fever. The trick in this sort of fishing is to time your cast so your fly lands simultaneously with the teaser baits. I got two follows, and a third marlin swiped at my fly but did not hook up. Trey made a textbook-perfect cast, his fly dropping into a boil, and hooked into a sailfish. I reeled up, watched the fish make an acrobatic jump, and suppressed an unsportsmanlike thought: "I hope he loses it so I get another shot." He didn't, bringing the sail in after a halfhour fight.

My shining moment of glory, which Sir Walter Scott said 'tis worth an age without name, came that night. I caught a fourteen-pound black skipjack on sixteen-pound class tippet, which made it nearly twice the size of the current world record. I would like to say that this catch was the result of skill, of making a perfect presentation with the right fly; but all I'd done was blindly cast into a boiling mass of fish so frenzied from teasing they would have eaten goose feathers. The fish that struck my anchovy imitation happened to weigh fourteen pounds. It was raw luck; any one of his much smaller mates could have hit the fly.

The next day was our most unproductive, a day of stunning monotony as we trolled for wahoo with artificial lures. If one struck, LoPreste would stop the boat, a mate would start chumming to keep the other fish around, and the anglers would cast to them. That was the theory. The trouble was, we did not get a chance to put it into practice. Not a fish, nor a sign of one. The blue water blues fell over the boat once again.

"What we have done," Teddy Lund wryly observed, "is bring the total boredom of trolling to fly fishing."

LoPreste theorized that the dearth of fish was due to the lack of a strong ocean current, and there was nothing we could do about that.

The next morning, after a windy night on a pelagic roller coaster, our luck changed—a little. A big wahoo struck one of the trolling lures. Others were soon splashing behind the boat. R. T. was up. He made a short cast, let his fly sink well down, and began to strip in line very slowly. Wahoo are not genteel creatures. When feeding, they rocket through a school of baitfish, killing and crippling as many as possible, then swoop back to devour the casualties—"An ugly little tale of predation in a primeval, violent world," as Tony Oswald put it.

R. T.'s excruciatingly slow retrieve was supposed to make his fly imitate wounded prey. His rod tip bent suddenly, his running line leapt from the deck, and in less time than it takes you to read this, the fish had run out two hundred yards of backing.

"Fastest run I've ever experienced," R. T. said later. "It was like I'd grabbed a live two-hundred-twenty-volt line."

The fish turned on a dime and streaked toward the boat—a favorite tactic of wahoo when hooked. With a look of total concentration on his face and with LoPreste shouting in his ear, "C'mon, R. T.! We need this fish!," Bob desperately reeled up the slack. The wahoo came tight and made another astonishing run, but that was all that was in him. What wahoo have in speed, they lack in endurance. A quarter of an hour later, he was on deck, bleeding from the gaff wound below his dorsal, his dark stripes fading, his long jaws with their razor-wire teeth opening and closing harmlessly. Co-captain Khagawa cracked him twice in the head with a club, he shuddered and lay still, his blood washing out the scuppers with seawater.

"Ah, the delicate, elegant sport of fly fishing," I quipped to Lund, who was to catch the only other wahoo of the trip.

That afternoon, we came upon another mass marlin convention, and the *Shogun*'s two skiffs were lowered to pursue them. I was assigned to one, along with Oswald. Mate Kevin Shelly would be our skipper. "Skiff" was hyperbole; the craft was a fifteen-foot Zodiac with a folding wooden deck and a thirty-horse outboard, that is, a rubber life raft.

But as soon as we set off, I knew that this was the adventure I had come for. To be equipped only with a fly rod, chasing marlin many miles offshore in an inflatable skiff, made me feel small and vulnerable, but also exhilarated, more a part of the dreadful, exciting drama of predation than I could be aboard the big boat.

We headed toward a large flock of frigates. There was something elemental about the sight of them, soaring darkly against the pale sky, then diving, then rising to soar and circle again.

"Frigates are low on the water," said Kevin, a salty old hand who's done every kind of fishing there is. "They're not just looking, they're doing business."

My teeth rattled as the skiff banged over the six-foot swells. Soon we were under the birds. Marlin were zigzagging all around us. The fish lighting up now and then, iridescent blue in the dark blue of the sea, and the sunlight streaming into the depths and appearing to converge at some point far, far below, and us in the raft, practically at eye level with the monsters swimming only two rod lengths away. Any closer and we'd be in the water with them.

"Jesus Christ, look at 'em, look at 'em!" Oswald was shooting pictures with his motor drive whining. "My God, look at 'em all."

There had to be forty fish in that one school. About a dozen cruised the surface; the rest were undersea at varying depths: long, dark shapes restlessly moving through greenish clouds of baitfish.

I stood to cast, and it wasn't only the skiff's rocking that made me unsteady. I had borrowed R. T.'s fifteen-weight billfish rod. It had the casting ability of rebar and the eight-inch billfish streamer at the end of it would have been shot if it were duck season. Still, I managed to lay out a forty-footer. The fly dropped a foot or so from a striped marlin that wasn't feeding but basking. While I let the fly sink, Kevin tossed out a couple of dead sardines to get the marlin in an eating mood. The line angled down into the sunlit water. I began a slow retrieve, stripping in two inches at a time, and something big rose out of the blue darkness and flashed beneath the fly. I kept retrieving at the same speed. The fish turned and followed the streamer toward the skiff. It was a Pacific sailfish, a very big sailfish, the biggest sail I'd ever seen, and it was leisurely tracking my fly, its dorsal looking as wide as the jib on my wife's sailing dinghy back in Connecticut.

"Hit it, you huge gorgeous S.O.B.," I said silently because I truly was unable to speak. "Hit it! Hit! Hit!"

The sail followed the streamer right on in, until I had no line left to retrieve, only leader. A mere arm's length away, he turned, his big round blue-back eye fixed on us, and then he planed away, sounding and sounding until he disappeared.

The school went down and we went bouncing and slamming toward another pod of diving frigates half a mile off. The fish beneath them were all marlin and all big. As we slipped into a trough, I saw one batting bait on the crest of the swell, and he was ten feet and two hundred pounds, and I was looking up at him, then straight at him as the next swell lifted us. These fish were hotter than the others. They were feeding, though not with any great zest. Sort of snacking. Like guests at a cocktail party.

I stood, noticing out of the corner of my eye a nearby panga with three Mexican snapper fishermen in it. We must have been a sight. I could almost hear them remarking, "More crazy gringos!"

Fly casting from a rubber raft in six-foot swells was like fly casting from a surfboard. I blew my first pitch, stripped in, and cast again, aiming for one of the smaller fish in the school. The big one was too much marlin for fly tackle. If I stuck him, the result would be tragic at best, disastrous at worst. Hooked marlin have been known to charge boats, and if that beast punctured the skiff with his bill, we would join the food chain—and not at the top.

The small marlin wasn't interested in my offering, but the big fellow glowed like a sign and turned on it. His bill, slender and sharp as a lance, his dorsal fin black, his shoulders humped out of the water, his caudal fin moving back and forth with slow, powerful sweeps—it was a sight I knew would stay with me for a long time. He followed the fly to within petting distance, then dived, and the last we saw of him was his tail sliding beneath the swells.

Though we fished all afternoon, I never hooked, much less caught, a marlin. My bad-luck streak was holding; yet I felt no disappointment. Perhaps I was putting a Dr. Pangloss gloss on things, but I felt privileged merely to have been so close to so many of those magnificent fish, and to have seen them in all their beauty and power. Such experiences, stored up in the memory, are to the spirit as an extra layer of fat is to the body—something to live on in times of want.

yorke island

1 9 9 9

I am fascinated by islands for a lot of reasons, but mostly because they are microcosms of human society. The powers and emotions that move people in the greater world are often too vast and complex to grasp at once; but on an island, the conflicts of the heart and mind are reduced to a comprehensible scale, as in a stage play. That sort of thing interests me because, as an *American* writer, I find that the vastness, diversity, and incoherence of my country is too much for my limited brain to make sense of. I've often envied British writers, particularly those of the nineteenth and early twentieth century. Those tidy social novels of Jane Austen and George Eliot, Henry James and Thomas Hardy. Their island-nation seemed to grant them a clarity of vision; social mores, values, and outlooks were (and still are) pretty much the same in Stoke-on-Trent, London, or Devon. But the United States? Think of it—Point Barrow Eskimos and Miami Cubans, Hawaiian pineapple growers and Maine lobstermen, Montana ranchers, Harlem shopkeepers, and Silicon Valley dot-comers are all citizens of the same country. The sharp differences in their environments make their experiences and views divergent. It's difficult for a writer to sort through all that clutter, find the emotions and longings they share in common, and then write about them in such a way as to make the Montana rancher understand the Harlem shopkeeper, or vice versa.

It's no accident that when I quit my career as a foreign correspondent in 1977 and returned to the U.S. to write hardcover novels, I didn't move to the heart of the heart of the country, but to an island: Key West. I found Key Westers a diverse lot. Descendants of white

Bahamians (known as "conchs"), Cubans, blacks, gays from New York and Chicago, macho shrimpers and fishermen from the South, made up the population, but their confinement to ten square miles of land surrounded by water created a certain homogeneity and formed a society in miniature. I could get my mind around the place; and yet, for reasons I can't explain, I've never written about Key West, nor about other islands I've been to: Martha's Vineyard, Nantucket, Block Island. The one island that did capture my literary imagination was Yorke, a speck of coral rock, palm, and mangrove in Australia's Torres Strait.

I visited Yorke in 1985. For ten weeks on assignment for *Esquire* magazine, I'd been roaming the Outback with two friends, also fishermen and sailors. Accustomed to the sea, we had begun to feel oppressed by the dusty, scrubby, endless expanses. That arid immensity seemed to deny the *possibility* of ocean, seemed to suggest that every drop of salt water had evaporated and left the planet a desiccated wasteland.

We decided to fly to the Torres Strait islands to give ourselves a dose of sea air before facing the Outback once again. Aboard a small plane, we left Cairns on a sparkling, chilly day in July (July is winter inthe Southern Hemisphere), bound for Yorke, which lay somewhere between the tip of Cape York Peninsula and the south coast of New Guinea. With us were Joseph Mosby, the island chairman, his wife and children. They were returning from a visit to Brisbane. Stockily built, with a broad face and burned-cork complexion, Joseph was a classic-looking Torres Strait islander. He laughed and smiled a lot, but seemed somewhat insecure about his position because he took every opportunity to remind us that he was "the boss on Yorke, I crack de whip."

Captivated by what I saw below—a brilliant world where light, sea, and air appeared to fuse into a unity—I wasn't paying much attention to Joseph's place in the local pecking order. The Strait, named for an early Spanish explorer, appeared as an immense sheet of turquoise, inscribed with green punctuation marks. Here and there, surf ringed barely submerged reefs that showed darkly through water so clear you would not have known it was water if it wasn't for the ripple of sunlit waves. Toward the east, where the Coral Sea welded its dark blue to the paler blue of the sky, a squall hung like a vast, gray curtain.

The squall swept down on us, the plane yawed and pitched, and our young pilot was squinting through the rain-spattered windshield for a break in the clouds. When one appeared, we saw a spear-shaped island, with an islet a few hundred yards off its pointed end. Soon, a gravel and crushed-seashell street, lined with brightly painted bunga-lows on stilts, showed through the palms and mango trees below. At the far end of the village rose the coral-block steeple of an Anglican church.

The pilot, a cocky kid with a baseball cap emblazoned with a pair of surfer's feet and the slogan, HANG TEN, set us down on the grass airstrip. We were pleased by what we saw as we rode into the village on a cart pulled by a tractor. With its tidy cottages, its gardens of bougainvillea and hibiscus, its fishing dinghies pulled up on deserted beaches striped by sea wrack, Yorke, thank God, had been bypassed by mass tourism and commercialization. It could have been a setting for a Conrad or Somerset Maugham novel—and not just for its tropical envi-ronment. All the stuff of human drama was there as well, as we learned during our two and a half days there. The drama was generated by the old conflict between traditional customs and modern demands. At that time, the Queensland government, which administered the islands, was seeking to make them more economically autonomous through one of its agencies, the Island Industries Board. The board's purpose was to encourage development of local enterprises, most involving commercial fishing. The emissaries of the new economic order on Yorke were Ross and Dale Gardner, the island's only two permanent white residents. In the best traditions of the religious missionaries of old, the thirty-some-thing couple were struggling to convert the natives, not in this instance to Christianity, but to the values of market capitalism.

It wasn't easy. The fishermen often would not put to sea because the moon was in the wrong phase, or because the wind was blowing from the wrong direction, or simply because they didn't feel like fish-ing. Nor did they have any taste for the hard, messy work of cleaning, filleting, freezing, and packaging their catches for shipment to the mainland. Ross and Dale did that themselves, sometimes working late into the night.

"The islanders are different, they have no regular working pat-tern," Ross observed diplomatically as I spoke to him near the small fac-tory where he processed the catches.

As government employees, he and Dale were also reluctant to blame government policies. Not so reluctant was Yorke island's grand old man, Eldridge Mosby, then sixty-seven years old and known in his community as "Uncle Elda." In his view, the government was undermining its own plans to improve the islanders' self-sufficiency by keeping them on the dole and paying them unemployment benefits.

"Dey got no incentive to work. Dese pellas t'day, ta them, it's near enough, that'll do, bye 'n bye;" Uncle Elda told us one breezy afternoon in his bungalow. Except for the pidgin dialect, his words could have been spoken by one of today's Republican congressmen.

A pearl diver in his early youth and later captain of his own pearling lugger, Uncle Elda still had a powerful chest and arms, and when he strode down the village street in his swirling lavalava, his carriage was almost royal. He was a fascinating character, who regaled us with tales about his pearling adventures and about his unusual ancestry.

"I got little bit white-man touched," he said, meaning that he was a grandson of an American, Ned Mosby. A nineteenth-century whaler from Baltimore, "Yankee Ned," as he came to be known in the Torres Strait, married a native woman called Queenie and sired a number of children, one of whom was Uncle Elda's father.

He was proud of his background, and when he let slip that he considered his nephew, Joseph, a "disgrace ta de Mosby name," we began to learn that there was a struggle on Yorke for its identity. As the designated chairman, Joseph was Queensland's man on the island; he signed the welfare and unemployment checks, channeled government benefits to his supporters and withheld them from his adversaries, much like a ward boss in Chicago or Boston. Joseph upheld the status quo. So claimed Uncle Elda, who said that he'd often told his nephew to "stop sayin' 'Yes, boss'" every time a government official came for a visit.

Uncle Elda hoped to see the day when all the Torres Strait islands would be culturally as well as economically free of the Australian mainland. Sometimes he wished he'd been alive in his grandfather's day because then he could have influenced the change to European ways.

"We'd be making' laws of our own by now. But now, we half an' half, not one ting or the other," he said wistfully. "We sorta been canceled out, like in a box with a foot on top of it. We ain't been released."

Discovering these conflicts, aspirations, and frustrations did not sour our visit to Yorke island; they enriched it. Sure, the scenery was enchanting, but the island wasn't some designer paradise, manufactured for the amusement of tourists; it was a real place, burdened and yet enlivened by the desires and fears of real people.

I fell in love with it, and knew I would write about it someday. I'm not sure why. Possibly because the clash between the traditional and the new was writ large on that small place. The story simmered in my mind for more than a decade, and then, last year, in a creative burst of only two weeks, I wrote a short novel out of the raw material Ross, Dale, Joseph, and Uncle Elda had unwittingly provided to my novelist's brain ten years before. One caveat, though: my story is a dark one involving alcoholism, jealousy, and murder. The fictional characters are not intended to resemble their real-life models!

I've never returned to Yorke. Maybe some love affairs are meant to be short and to be savored in the remembering rather than in the living of them. And two images I do remember, apropos of the island's central conflict, are of Uncle Elda. In the one, he is standing in the shallows, his lavalava drawn up to his knees as he puts new line on his traditional handline rig; in the other, he is sitting in his bungalow, watching an American video on his VCR, powered by a diesel generator. I don't know if he's still alive, but I hope that he somehow found a way to open the box and release his fellow islanders.

lost keys

1 9 9 1

N ot long ago, the Florida Keys had the power to quicken the blood and stir the soul. It was a place like no other on this continent, a tropical wilderness where mangrove islands shimmered in silver seas so clear you could drop a dime ten feet down and tell if it landed heads or tails.

It was magic, and what made it so was its wilderness—the dangers lurking in its beauty. It might have been advertised as "paradise" in the tourist brochures, but it could bite, sting, scratch, and sometimes kill you. Sharks as long as spongers' skiffs cruised the placid, sunlit waters. A careless boatman could get lost in the mangrove mazes and be driven mad by the skeeters or die of thirst and exposure, if a croc, gator, rattler, or coral snake didn't get him first.

The weather, touted by the Chamber of Commerce, was unpredictable, subject to sudden storms, the worst being the one the ancient Taino Indians called *hurukan*. When one of those roared ashore, the low, flat islands offered no refuge from the smashing winds, from frothing tidal surges twenty feet high. The Russells could have told you about that: the pioneer Keys clan numbered seventy-seven souls at dawn on September 2, 1935; at sundown, after the great Labor Day hurricane blasted through the Upper Keys, eleven were left.

The Keys could do that to you, but they could also enchant you with the emerald silences of their hardwood hammocks or the sight of roseate spoonbills lofting out of an island rookery. They could dazzle you with their crown jewel—a barrier reef running along the Atlantic side for two hundred miles, ablaze with coral colonies that were home to nations of fish, from palm-size damselfish to giant hammerheads.

Above all, the islands offered solitude and sanctuary from the jangling, overcrowded twentieth century. As recently as the late 1940s, the Keys outside Key West were still so wild and sparsely inhabited that the federal government considered incorporating them into Everglades National Park. A mere fifteen years ago, a fisherman could pole the backcountry flats all day and seldom see another boat, or hear anything except the squawk of herons or the splash of pelicans diving on a school of pilchards. I know, because I used to do it.

The Keys were my home for twelve years before I left them in 1988, in sadness and disgust. It was there I raised my two children and made some of the closest friends of my life. I wasn't a seasonal "snowbird" who stayed only for the balmy winters, but a year-round resident, enduring the long, broiling summers when, during hurricane season, each dawn brought with its glory the chance of catastrophe. I fished the islands' waters, dived for lobster and brought my catches to the table. I explored the out-islands' meandering channels and hidden lagoons and the drowned canyons of the reef. I learned to read the subtle signs that herald changes of season in the tropics, which have more wonder in them than the explicitness of turning leaves and falling snows. I studied the circuits of the winds, so I didn't need the Coast Guard weather channel to tell me when a norther was getting set to blow. I have been all over this country and in most parts of the world, and have never loved any place more than those islands that hang like a broken jade necklace from the marshy tip of Florida.

I loved them not just for their beauty but for their uniqueness. The are the only tropical environment in the continental United States, home to some of the rarest plants and animals in the world. And the coral reef is one of the few between the Tropic of Cancer and the Arctic Circle. If it is ever lost—and it *is* being lost—it will be lost forever.

Which is why I hate what is happening to the Keys. Greed and stupidity are killing them.

Watching a beloved place die evokes the same emotions as watching a loved one die: grief as well as rage. Driving down U.S. 1 from Miami one warm afternoon earlier this year, I would feel like tossing firebombs one moment and weeping the next. When I first drove it in 1976, the fabled Overseas Highway possessed a certain ramshackle charm: two narrow lanes passing over forty-two aging but picturesque bridges. A weather-beaten marina here, a funky clapboard café there; salty bars frequented by fishermen and lobstermen and warm-water riffraff; ma-and-pa motels; palm and mangrove wilds in between; uncluttered views of a sea that glinted like pewter in its reach for the lighthouses marking the reef. Beyond the reef, where the sea turned to cobalt, a northing freighter might be seen, catching the Gulf Stream to save fuel. All that began to vanish in 1983, when the Florida Department of Transportation finished a multimillion-dollar reconstruction of the highway. It was widened for most of its 150-mile length—linking the mainland to Key West—to four lanes in some places. New bridges, soaring concrete arches that resemble freeway overpasses, replaced the ones completed in 1912 for Henry Flagler's Overseas Railroad, the highway's forerunner.

To paraphrase something the naturalist Joseph Wood Krutch once said: If you want to preserve a place, don't build a road into it, and if you do, make sure it's a bad one. The old highway used to daunt most modern travelers, who can't seem to go anywhere without an interstate and conveniently spaced exits for food, fuel, and lodging. U.S. 1's new, improved version, I saw last winter, drew traffic as dense as rush hour on the Connecticut Turnpike—a sluggish, fuming river of rental cars, vans, tour buses, pickup trucks towing sailboats and motorboats, gas-greedy Winnebagos driven by self-indulgent senior citizens whose bumper stickers boasted that they were, har-har-har, spending their grandchildren's inheritance.

The cavalcade passed through a wasteland that looked like Coney Island or the Jersey Shore, with Sunbelt glitz thrown in. Acres of mahogany and Jamaican dogwood and gumbo limbo trees had been cleared for blocks of time-share condos, complete with phony British or French spellings (Harbour View, Ocean Pointe) to give them an air of class their architecture belied. Fast-food franchises and chain motels, like some aggressive new species, killed off most of the funky cafés and ma-and-pa motels. Sea views were rare except from the bridges; otherwise, my eye was blocked or distracted by such gimmicks as a mechanical gorilla waving its arms to beckon motorists into a T-shirt shop, huge fiberglass models of marlin tempting would-be Hemingways to sign up for a charter, and plywood great whites that invited me to "pet a shark!"

Such grotesques, I thought, were more than eyesores. They were acts of vandalism against the beauty of sea, sky, and island. The Keys, once a place like no other, had become like any other place in America: noisy, congested, ugly.

So much frenzied development struck me as more than the result of shoddy zoning laws. It seemed an attempt by people utterly lacking in humility before nature to assure themselves that they were the masters of their environment, to control it with a grip as firm and lasting as the concrete they spread so lavishly. If that was true, then all those highway signs flashing familiar logos—Exxon, Burger King, Holiday Inn—were false beacons of safety, rather like the deceitful lights the old-time wreckers planted on the reef to lure ships to their destruction and the wreckers' profit. Only now the lights were lights of self-deception, for to live in the Keys is to live at sea, and the sea always has dominion. To prove that, all it had to do was shrug its broad, blue shoulders, as it had in 1935.

Fifteen years ago, Big Pine Key was a rural crossroads of perhaps fifteen hundred people. Now its population is more than three times that; the eleven-square-mile island some thirty miles north of Key West is the fastest-growing community in the Keys, with a proud new shopping mall and subdivisions where, only a decade ago, there had been forests of slash pine and silver palm.

I turned off U.S. 1, driving toward a friend's house down Key Deer Boulevard. Along the road, yellow signs warned: SLOW, ENDANGERED KEY DEER. They reminded me that Big Pine is something more than a fast-growing community: it's a battlefield for one of the bitterest ecological fights in the country.

Roughly one-third of the island is taken up by a United States Fish and Wildlife refuge for the Key deer, a miniature offshoot of the eastern whitetail that adapted ages ago to the island's limited space and food supply. The species, which grows no larger than the average dog, is among the most imperiled in the country. It has become to the Big Pine citizens what the spotted owl is to the loggers of the Pacific Northwest.

Once hunted nearly to extinction, then brought back by careful management from a population of a few dozen animals in the 1950s to about four hundred in the 1970s, the Key deer's new predator is the automobile. An average of thirty thousand vehicles travel the Overseas

Highway each day during tourist season. and roadkills have reduced the herd to between 250 and 300. Overdevelopment has also destroyed their natural habitats, including acres of wetlands, and dried up or depleted some of the freshwater supplies the deer need to drink.

To save them from potential extinction again, the Fish and Wildlife Service, joined by conservation-minded citizens, proposed expanding the refuge to include privately held lands, some of which already had homes on them. To battle the measure, contractors, real estate brokers ,and homeowners have banded together. The fight, which is still going on, is vicious because it isn't the usual nature lovers versus big-money developers. The struggle pits a government agency and powerful environmental lobbies against ordinary homeowners, mostly blue-collar workers, some of whom came to the Keys in the booming 1980s and can't afford to live among the croissant-and-cappuccino set in gentrified Key West. There are things the residents would like to have but right now don't: a town hall, recreation facilities, an elementary school for their children. These are more than conveniences; they transform a collection of houses and stores into a community, with an identity of its own. But if plans for expanding the Key Deer Refuge go through, Big Pine won't be able to make the leap. Worse yet, middle-class people whose homes or vacant lots are targeted for acquisition may be forced to sell at prices well below market value.

What had drawn me to Big Pine Key was the destiny of the reef.

The one who had called my attention to it was Jack London, an old friend with whom I'd spent many delightful days fishing for tarpon and bonefish in the Keys backcountry, and for sailfish, marlin, and tuna in the Gulf Stream. Boston-born, London moved to the Keys in the late 1960s and was almost immediately hooked by their strange allure.

"It was like no other place I'd been," he says now. "There was a sense of wonder, of wildness, a unique spirit that's now been commercialized."

London is no sentimentalist. but a hardheaded businessman who made enough money restoring and selling old houses to retire at age fifty. He's been so distressed by the concrete tide washing over the Keys that he often considers moving to his mother's native Ireland, where he owns a house. Then, last year, he decided to take a stand. He ran on an environmental platform for commissioner of Monroe County, an area that covers the Keys as well as half the Everglades National Park. His opponent, Gene Lytton, a leading member of a pro-development group of politicians known as the "concrete coalition," was considered hard to beat, but the political neophyte, London, defeated him by the widest margin in Monroe County's 124 year history. Conservationists, perhaps mistakenly, interpreted London's lopsided victory as a sign of changing attitudes in the Keys.

After taking office, London discovered even more about the alarming facts of ecological damage in the Keys. Their Spanish discoverers called the Keys *Los Martires* (The Martyrs) because their twisted shapes suggested suffering. To London, the name started to take on new meaning. When he moved to Monroe County more than twenty years ago, its permanent population, including Key West's twenty-five thousand people, was only about fifty thousand; today it is close to eighty thousand. During the peak winter months, seasonal residents and tourists bloat that number to about 140,000. Nature did not design the fragile islands to support so many people, and the Keys are showing the effects. Most severely damaged is the reef, an aquatic marvel visited by hundreds of snorklers and divers each year. Its corals are bleached and diseased, and a 1986 study by Dr. James Porter of the University of Georgia showed that it is dying at a rate of four percent a year.

London set out to do what he could to save the reef both for its own sake and because tourism is the mainstay of the Keys' economy; about 1.5 million people from all over the United States, Europe, and Japan visit the islands each year. "The thing that attracts people to the Keys are its waters and reef," London told me one afternoon at his house on Summerland Key. "Why should someone come here all the way from Canada, or Miami for that matter, to dive on an algal reef or ride a glass-bottom boat to look at dead coral?"

But, he adds, far more than tourist dollars are at risk. Pointing southward, to where Niles Channel opens out to the bright Atlantic, he describes what he believes would be the greater loss.

"All the kinds of wonderful creatures that live out there would be lost, too," London says. "Three hundred species of fish! It's not just pretty rocks out there. That reef is a whole ecosystem, the mother of all things in these waters, and to fail to *attempt* to save that magnificent spectacle due to avarice and stupidity and shortsightedness would be more than infuriating. To my mind it would be criminal."

Those sentiments eventually led him into an association with Brian LaPointe, a marine biologist from Big Pine Key, whose theories about the causes of the reef's decline have made him a controversial figure, in scientific as well as political circles. No one denies the reef is in grave trouble. Too many people scientists and laymen alike, have seen the damage. But according to the conventional wisdom, the deterioration has been caused by boat groundings, anchors, and too many careless divers standing on the corals or bumping against them. A number of experts blame overheated waters resulting from global warming or natural causes such as nutrient-rich waters from deep ocean upwellings.

LaPointe did not disagree with those diagnoses, but argued they were only partial explanations. The reef's public enemy No. 1, he had come to believe, was man and his waste. Some seven hundred tons of nutrients—nitrates, phosphates, and ammonium—are dumped into Keys waters each year. Three hundred fifty tons come from a large secondary sewage treatment plant in Key West. (Secondary treatment strips pathogens but not nutrients from wastewater.) The remaining 350 tons come from the thousands of septic tanks and illegal cesspits throughout Monroe County, which ranks sixty-sixth out of Florida's sixty-seven counties in soil suitability for septic tanks but *first* in septic-tank density per square mile. Storm-water runoff, leaching through the porous limestone, has been washing the contaminants into canals and near-shore waters. Tides and currents then carry them to the reef, promoting the spread of oxygen-devouring algae, which probably makes the reef more vulnerable to lethal blights like black-band disease.

When London read LaPointe's findings, he concluded that the answer to saving the reef lay ashore. Improved sewage treatment plants would have to be installed; the blitzkrieg of backhoes, bulldozers, and cement trucks would have to be slowed down, and perhaps stopped altogether. Otherwise, within twenty years, the entire reef probably would be an algae-covered sepulcher. Indeed, much of it already is. I should see for myself, London suggested, inviting me to join him and LaPointe on a diving trip to Looe Key Marine Sanctuary, which lies off Big Pine Key.

The term "marine biologist" conjures up in my mind an image of a bespectacled academic. LaPointe, a tall, beefy sun-bronzed man of forty, looks instead like a slightly out-of-shape tailback. Trained at

Woods Hole Oceanographic Institution, he is known in marine-science circles as an expert in coastal eutrophication—the overloading of near-shore waters with nutrients.

LaPointe is not a shy or retiring man. In the mid to late 1980s, after his research convinced him that human waste was the reef's killer, he did not confine publication of his findings to obscure professional journals. He aired them in the *Miami Herald* and *Florida Keys Magazine,* a glossy periodical for tourists. Aware of the negative effects LaPointe's conclusion might have on growth, developers and real estate interests marshaled other studies to disprove them. Pro-development newspapers branded LaPointe "Dr. Guano" and "Professor Sewage."

"They couldn't believe that we were killing the reef with our high standard of living," he told me one afternoon during a visit to his home, which sits on a canal at the far end of Big Pine Key. "It's like the stages of someone goes through when he learns that a loved one is dying. First there's denial, then anger, then bargaining, and, finally, acceptance."

The end result of unchecked eutrophication is a marine desert. To see this, LaPointe and I merely had to walk out the back door of his house to the canal. It was so devoid of fish and plant life it might have been lined with concrete. When LaPointe moved to the Keys in 1982, the canal bottom was carpeted with healthy turtle grasses, the water teeming with mangrove snapper. Three years later, the grasses were smothered under mats of algae. "This is the final stage," LaPointe says, *"complete death."*

We then climbed into a twenty-foot Mako and headed out to Looe Key. The "sanctuary" was a parking lot of boats, flying red-and-white diver's flags and tied off to mooring buoys to spare the reef from anchor damage. But as I was about to see, the *QE2* could have dropped her anchors on that reef and it wouldn't have made any difference.

Having dived on Looe Key in the mid-1970s, I could remember the billows of tropical fish, the vibrant formations of elkhorn, brain, and boulder corals shimmering in clear waters. What I saw now was like revisiting the house I grew up in and finding it had been sacked by vandals. Vast stretches of dead coral, resembling rubble from demolished buildings; elkhorns bleached to a dirty white; boulder corals afflicted with black-band disease, which leaves ugly scars that look like huge skin ulcers.

LaPointe said the water was clearer than it had been in months, yet visibility was reduced by clouds of phytoplankton, which trap sunlight and heat up the water, further stressing the corals. I guessed I saw about half as many fish swimming through those ruins as I'd seen fifteen years ago.

An hour later, at the end of our dive, we stood on a shallow part of the reef that was as lifeless as a sidewalk before dawn. A charter captain nearby called out to us, urging that we not stand on the corals. LaPointe, cleaning his mask with a glob of algae, laughed derisively. "That's like telling someone not to stand on a drowned man's chest," he said, "because you might stop him from breathing."

If I thought Looe Key was in bad shape, LaPointe had warned, wait till I saw Sand Key. I wasn't sure I wanted to, for Sand Key was another reef I remembered fondly. I used to snorkel there with my two boys in the mid-1970s, and still recall their delight as they explored a real-life wonderland instead of some plastic Disneyworld replica.

Sand Key lies seven and a half miles from densely populated Key West, and is straight in the path of the outfall from the city's sewage treatment plant. As LaPointe and I took a boat out to Sand Key with Craig Quirolo, who, with his wife, DeeVon, heads a conservation group called Reef Relief, we could see the sewage boiling out of a pipe some four thousand yards from shore. It left a huge smear of pea-green water, sweeping seaward on an outgoing tide.

I mentioned to LaPointe that some scientists disagreed with his theories, arguing that the pollutants affected only near-shore waters— those within two miles of land—but weren't reaching the reef itself, which is three and a half miles from shore at its closest point.

"Look where it's headed!" he shouted. "What do they think, that there's a fence out there at two miles with a sign: 'No pollution allowed beyond this point'?"

Once Quirolo moored near the rusting tower of Sand Key lighthouse, LaPointe and I dived in. Whatever the cause, *something* had devastated Sand Key beyond my worst imaginings. If Looe Key was a disaster, Sand Key was a submarine holocaust. We cruised the reef for an hour without seeing a single piece of coral that wasn't dead or dying. The great rack of elkhorn now looked like fossilized antlers; the once purple sea fans had turned into pale skeletons. A blue-green scum coated the brain and boulder formations, and everywhere were meadows of algae, waving their slimy tentacles in the ocean currents. The only fish I saw in any numbers were chubs, pecking at the flesh of dead sea urchins.

After we surfaced, I noticed that some people, at least, didn't seem greatly disappointed by the reef. A short distance away, dozens of snorklers were paddling around a charter boat. I wondered aloud why they'd spent their money to look at what amounted to an underwater gravel pit.

"They're probably used to places like the Jersey Shore or Lake Erie," Quirolo replied. "So, to them, this looks just fine. But pretty soon this is going to look no different."

The Barrier Reef is just one of many marine resources in the Keys that have been ravaged and plundered in recent years. Fish trapping, which is expected to be outlawed early next year, has almost wiped out whole populations of some species, including herbivorous fish that once could be counted on to crop foreign algae from the corals—all of which only accelerated the reef's decline.

Ten years ago, schools of king mackerel migrated past the islands in seemingly inexhaustible numbers. But by the middle of the decade, unrestrained commercial netting had decimated them. Shrimp boats used to converge on Key West from all over the Gulf Coast, harvesting up to ten million pounds in a season. Then, to feed the needs of a boom-ing Florida— one thousand new residents *a day*—drainage of the Everglades was intensified. This, combined with recent droughts, has made part of the once brackish Florida Bay as salty as the open sea, destroying, in the process, nurseries for juvenile shrimp and the entire Keys shrimp industry. As for those backcountry flats where I poled my skiff, well, they have become a playground for Jet Skiers who tear up the bottom, scatter the bonefish schools, and terrify the birds from their roosts and rookeries.

Today, preservationists are resting their hopes for the Keys' eco-logical recovery on two government measures. One is a growth-man-agement plan required by the state of Florida that will reduce new con-struction in Monroe County by as much as sixty-five percent. The other is an act of Congress that late last year designated the entire Florida Keys as a national marine sanctuary. But how those efforts will save the reef isn't clear, not to me anyway.

If LaPointe's theory is right, new and centralized sewage treatment facilities will have to be installed throughout Monroe County. That will cost, according to London, as much as three hundred million dollars. Where's the money going to come from? In the meantime, it's going to take the federal government at least two years to formulate regulations for the new national marine sanctuary. And as Looe Key proved to me, calling a place a sanctuary doesn't necessarily make it one.

What about the growth-management plan? It is already raising thorny legal issues. The United States Constitution guarantees citizens the right to just compensation for their property if it is taken by the government under right of eminent domain. But there are no constitutional provisions about the rights of landholders whose property is not confiscated but rendered valueless by ordinances that prohibit building. And with some twenty-six thousand vacant lots remaining in Monroe County, how will their owners be compensated?

"We're at the cutting edge down here of critical issues with national ramifications," London says.

The main reason for this is geography, which has imposed limits on growth in Monroe County as obvious as the line between sand and sea. The county's inhabitable parts comprise only 110 of its nearly 1,800 square miles. Thus, Monroe County finds itself in the vanguard, facing a problem right now that will eventually confront other parts of the country as population increases, open spaces shrink, and the rights of home- and property owners collide with the need to preserve precious natural resources. Regardless of what the states, or the federal government, mandate, Monroe's citizens are going to be the ones to decide when their community should stop growing, and to determine how many people is too many people.

These questions were all raised in July at a hearing on an interim development ordinance that would have halted all new construction permits until the state-required plan went into effect. The ordinance was vigorously opposed by homeowners and developers, even though its purpose was not to save the Key deer or coral reefs, but to save lives in the event of a hurricane.

The National Weather Service recommends a twelve-hour evacuation time for hurricane-prone regions. But in the Keys, the most hurricane-prone area in the United States, evacuation time is an estimated twenty-seven hours—because of too many people and only one route out. If a storm like the one in 1935 struck again, the consequences would be appalling.

It almost happened in 1988, when the worst storm ever recorded in the Western Hemisphere, Hurricane Gilbert, roared through the Caribbean with two-hundred-mile-an-hour winds. "If that storm had hit," recalls Bob Herman, who as Monroe County's director of growth management is a leading member of the area's evacuation team, "we would have had an eighteen-foot storm surge in the Upper Keys, twelve to fourteen feet in the Lower Keys, and twelve-foot waves on top of that." The average elevation in the Keys is about six feet above sea level. Even the highest point, eighteen-foot Solares Hill in Key West, would have been awash.

With that in mind, the county commission directed the drafting of the interim development ordinance. But when the hearing to debate the measure was called, it became clear that not even the prospect of being buried under a three-story wall of water was enough to convince some people that development had to stop.

A large, angry crowd of property owners, construction workers, and builders—wearing bright yellow shirts emblazoned with the slogan ENDANGERED SPECIES: FLORIDA KEYS CONTRACTOR—packed the room at the Key Colony Beach auditorium in Marathon. The day of the hearing, Thea Ramsay, a pro-development activist from Marathon, took out radio ads urging people to attend with ropes in their hands. Taking her at her word, one man showed up with a hangman's noose, which he and others at the back of the room brandished throughout the tumultuous ten-hour meting. The lynch—mob atmosphere kept many supporters of the ordinance from attending; when those who did tried to express their views, they were booed and shouted down. The measure went down in defeat: three to two.

But in November, after months of bitter debate, Jack London came up with a compromise proposal that the commission eventually adopted. London's plan limits the county to issuing only 270 new building permits a year—a sixty-five percent reduction from the previous rate of growth.

Still, I am skeptical about the prospects for eco-salvation in the Keys. Two weeks from now, Dr. James Porter is expected to announce that the reef's decline has accelerated to an alarming rate— its life expectancy has now dropped to only ten years. It is getting harder and harder to remember what the Keys have been for most of their history, a tropical frontier, as described so memorably by Peter Matthiessen in his recent novel, *Killing Mister Watson.*

Yet there are still people alive who recall the hardships of home-steading in what is now a sun-drenched playground. In a recent maga-zine interview, eighty-seven-year-old Lillian Spencer Roberts depicts her life on a pioneer plantation on Key Largo seventy-five years ago: mosquitoes so thick they covered the side of her family's house; croco-diles in the mangroves; marauding panthers clawing at the doors at night; clearing the land, planting and picking tomatoes; cutting wood under a scorching sun. And every summer, the Taino Indians' big wind—*hurukan*—lurked just beyond the horizon, waiting to rage ashore and wipe out in a twinkling all she and her family had built through years of heartbreaking labor.

I was thinking of Lillian Roberts's story the day I went diving on Looe Key with London and LaPointe. As we sat in the Mako, resting between dives, a seventy-five-foot cabin cruiser rumbled up to a nearby mooring. Two dozen teenagers crowded the vessel. They hauled a set of enormous speakers onto the deck and began blaring heavy metal, drowning out the sound of wind and gulls and the sea's gentle breath as it washed over the dying reef.

Watching the partiers dance and toss beer cans into the water, I thought that if it ever came down to a choice between them and the skeeters and crocs Lillian Roberts had to endure, I knew for certain which way I would go.

dry tortugas

1 9 9 6

There are posters and T-shirts sold in Key West inscribed with a quote by Hemingway: "I am going to get to Key West and away from it all." I was thinking about that as two friends and I approached the island after a day of flats fishing in the Marquesas Keys, a beautiful, lonely atoll some twenty-one miles due west of Key West. There, in solitude and silence, we'd poled the shallows for tarpon and permit, and watched breaching eagle rays and man-o'-war birds riding aerial currents on wings like black boomerangs. Hemingway would have felt at home with us in the Marquesas, but the scene that greeted us on our return would have caused him to make a beeline back to his grave in Idaho. The sky was speckled with the brilliant parachutes of parasailers, as if the island were being invaded by an 82d Airborne grown suddenly fond of garish colors. The sea was an aquatic madhouse of Jet Skis buzzing in pointless circles with a sound as soothing as chain saws. All along the shore, where there'd been little more than mangroves twenty years ago, rose the pastel battlements of new condos and hotels. It was pretty clear that Key West had become a place to get away from, especially if you were a serious angler, or even a not-so-serious one who merely wanted some good fishing and escape from the banality and racket of our congested and malled civilization.

Which was why we—Alan Richey, Stu Dunn, and I—had decided on a four-day light-tackle expedition far from the madding crowds. Dunn is a Chicago-area dentist who is nicknamed "Little Doc" for his five-foot-five-inch frame and his medical degree. Richey's job on the Trans-Alaskan pipeline had made him beyond eager for a few days' fishing in the subtropics. "I need this, I really need this," he kept saying in the rounded drawl of his native Alabama. "This" was the Dry Tortugas.

Dry Tortugas. It has a ring of adventure, no? The Spanish "tortugas" suggests the foreign and the remote—anyway, it sounds better than its English translation: turtle—while the adjective "dry" creates a barely audible undertone of dread, a suggestion that this place may not be altogether pleasant. The Tortugas are not foreign, but are very much a part of the United States—a U.S. national park. Yet they seem to be in another country. The last islands in the chain of the Florida Keys, they rise out of the Gulf of Mexico some seventy miles from Key West. Out there in the middle of a vast blue-green wilderness, they look like some geological afterthought, and their improbability is heightened by their most improbable feature—Fort Jefferson. This huge structure was built on the Tortugas' largest island, sixteen-acre Garden Key, between 1846 and the beginning of the Civil War to guard the sea-lanes into the Gulf. The invention of rifled cannons made its thick, brick walls obsolete before it was finished. During after the Civil War, it became a kind of American Devil's Island—a prison for Union deserters and for Dr. Samuel Mudd, the luckless physician who set John Wilkes Booth's broken leg after the assassination of President Lincoln. Thus, in the last century, the Dry Tortugas were synonymous with exile and desolation—a tenuous outpost of the American empire plagued by hurricanes and yellow fever.

Even today, accessible only by seaplane or boat, they strike the visitor as isolated and vulnerable—a few spits of sand, coral, and mangrove exposed to whatever blows Mother Ocean decides to throw at them. It looks as if she could wipe them off her face with a casual brush of her hand. And in bad weather, the passage to the Tortugas, across a treacherous body of water called Rebecca Shoals, can be nerve-racking, even deadly. Its bottom is littered with the wrecks of nineteenth-century schooners and twentieth-century yachts, of shrimp boats and barges and the oceangoing tugs that towed them. Then why go to the Tortugas? Two reasons. One is the fishing. They are the last angling frontier in Florida, providing, in quantity and quality, the kind of fishing that was commonplace in the Keys. The second reason is related to the first. I don't fish merely to catch fish, but to be in the good places where good fish are. This means places where the water's clean and the people are few. This means the solitude of wild or semiwild places. Not that the Dry Tortugas are at the edge of the known world—they just look as if they are. Anyway, the idea was to recapture the way it used to be in the Keys without going to Belize, Honduras, the Bahamas, or anywhere that required a visa.

We left Key West on a breezy April morning aboard Captain Robert Trosset's *Spindrift,* a twenty-five-foot open fisherman that was going to be our fishing boat, but we would live aboard a mother ship, a forty-eight-foot Viking christened the *Thunnus* and crewed by Captain Brian Bennett and cook and first mate Laurie Steele. The *Thunnus* also carried our food, ice, and 250 gallons of gasoline for the *Spindrift's* outboard. R. T. is a pioneer of light-tackle fishing in the Tortugas. A brawny, black-bearded, roaring boy, with a passion for salt water by day and rum-and-Coke by night, he is a rare creature: a native Floridian. After graduating from the University of Florida, he took a job as a life-insurance salesman. Less than two years later, when it became apparent to him and his employers that he lacked the temperament for reading actuarial tables and persuading people that they really needed more coverage, he began guiding professionally in the Keys. Since then, he's guided his clients to one hundred world records, and before our Tortugas trip ended, he would have his one hundred and first.

We passed over Half Moon Shoal, taking a few minutes to futilely cast flies to schools of permit, then entered the darker waters of Rebecca Channel. By this time, the Marquesas had fallen below the eastern horizon and the Tortugas lay beyond the western. We were in an open boat on the open, rolling sea. I know people who become phobic when they are out of sight of land. I'm not one of them. Big water excites and invigorates me, and I give no thought to what a petty creature I am, to the utter ease with which Mother Ocean could snuff me out. This isn't bravery, but a failure of imagination, perhaps of intelligence.

At midday, we raised Pulaski Light, marking the westernmost edge of Rebecca. Less than half an hour later, Trosset declared, "Land ho! Ha! Old R. T. got you there, right on the money!" Fort Jefferson appeared. At first, it seemed like a hallucination, some fantastic construct of a sea-dazed brain, but as we drew closer, its redbrick walls gained substance and reality, which shouldn't have been surprising: They're two stories high and eight feet thick. The sight of twenty masts and flying bridges crowded in the harbor disappointed me. I was greedy for isolation, wanted us to have the whole place to ourselves. But I was cheered by the a smoky cloud dancing over Bush Key, a cloud composed of a hundred thousand sooty and noddy terns. These remarkable seabirds fly across the Atlantic from Africa in March and April, without touching land. They mate and sleep in midair and build their nests in the Tortugas.

We crossed the aquamarine channel between Garden and Loggerhead Keys; then Trosset turned the helm over to me and broke out his cast-net. Hard up against Loggerhead's sand-fringed shore were schools and schools of pilchards, a whole bloody university of pilchards, darkening the waters. Guides use these small, herringlike fish to entice gamefish within casting range of a jig, plug, or fly. I brought the *Spindrift* almost to within the shadow of Loggerhead Light, Trosset directing me to go right, go hard left, his eyes tracking the ever-moving billows of fish. Throwing a cast-net is an art unto itself, and he gave an admirable demonstration, corkscrewing his shoulders, then tossing the net so that it opened like the white, gossamer wings of a gigantic butterfly; then he struck, and hauled up nearly one hundred pounds of the baitfish, the big, fat kind that are called "razorbellies" for their sharp-edged stomachs.

With the live-well filled, Trosset opened his sacred text— a thick log of loran numbers that mark reefs, wrecks, shoals, ledges, sometimes a single coral head—and we headed out to one of his secret spots.

By the time we reached it, Loggerhead light had vanished, as if swallowed by the sea. There wasn't land or another vessel in sight, and Trosset's depth-recorder marked a mound of fish hovering over the wreck. It looked on the screen like a miniature mountain. We dropped a bottom rig to catch grouper or snapper for dinner—this would be the angling equivalent of what safari hunters call "shooting for camp meat." Our real quarry were king mackerel, blackfin tuna, bonito, and horse-eye jacks, which we hoped to catch on fly or light spinning tackle. Two weeks earlier, one of Trosset's clients had caught a sixty-pound king at this very spot.

He started chumming with live pilchards. The way this is done isn't pretty; it won't please people who have seen *A River Runs Through It* and who go in pursuit of steelhead with their rods in expensive leather cases and barbless hooks on their flies. But let us remember that fishing is not lyric poetry; it's blood sport. You chum with pilchards by poking out one of their eyes; this causes them to swim in erratic circles near the surface, which in turn draws gamefish up from the depths. Another technique is to bounce the pilchard off the transom as you toss it into the water; stunned; it will flutter as it swims, sending signals of distress.

That afternoon, the pilchards gave their lives almost in vain. Richey caught and released a handsome fifteen-pound bonito on fly, I hooked a horse-eye on fly (the horse-eye is a very sporty fish on light tackle), but lost him to a 250-pound hammerhead that obviously had not seen *A River Runs Through It,* because it ripped the jack into bloody tatters, leaving me with only a head to reel in. The giant kings and tuna did not show up, and we had to content ourselves with grouper and mangrove and yellowtail snapper. But what grouper, what mangroves and yellowtails! We caught ten- and twelve-pound red grouper on almost every drop, mangroves of six to seven pounds, and yellowtail of five. My largest yellowtail, caught on a jig, went just under six pounds. Bottom fish in those numbers and sizes can hardly be found in the Lower Keys any longer, but they're routine in the Tortugas; anyone who thinks that overfishing and overdevelopment of coastal areas don't affect fish stocks would change his mind if he compared our catch rate with that of someone fishing off Key West. Had we kept all we caught, we could have provided dinner for every vessel in Fort Jefferson harbor for the duration of their stays.

That night, aboard the *Thumnus,* Laurie Steele cooked us a grouper dinner that would have cost twenty-one dollars a plate in Miami. We crawled into our bunks early and were rocked to sleep by the gentle swells in the harbor. At some ghastly hour of the morning, I was awakened by a high-pitched thrumming, a sound such as a strong wind makes in a boat's rigging. Stepping out on deck, I saw that the wind had kicked up, but the sound was coming from the terns on Bush Key. A three-quarter-moon shone on the island, the birds clearly visible in its light: thousands of them were swooping and darting, all crying at once to make a single cry. And to their lullaby, the wild song of a wild place, I fell asleep again.

The next day was one of those trials that all saltwater anglers endure. It seems to be the penance we must suffer to merit the sea's grace. As old salts would say, it had breezed up a bit. Twenty knots out of the southeast, a sky smoky and menacing. We donned foul-weather gear and, for an hour, rode over frothing blue ridges, bearing southwestward to where the Gulf Stream purples the water and the wahoo swims. That's what we were after. The wahoo is a silvery, blue-barred mackerel whose strikes and runs on light tackle are almost frightening. But the sea did not shed her grace on us. She beat us up as her waves rose from three to four feet, then four to six. We were drenched with spray, despite our slickers, and bashed into the gunwales until we felt as bruised as running backs. We returned to the *Thunnus* at sundown, again with a hold full of bottom fish but no wahoo, tuna, or kings. Shivering and tired, my face as encrusted with salt as the rim of a margarita glass, I went straight for the galley and my bottle of scotch.

Day three brought a magnificent golden dawn and more wind— twenty-five knots now. Trosset, who is six feet and weighs 220, was much amused by the picture that Dunn, Richey, and I presented as, holding the grab rails in a collective death grip, we stood side by side in our yellow slickers. Richey at five-eight and I at five-seven were not much taller than Dunn. "You look like three little canaries lined up there," Trosset roared.

We motored eastward for ten miles, until we spotted a shrimp boat whose crew were cleaning the nets of "trash" after a hard night's dragging. The shrimper, the *Captain Travis* out of Tarpon Springs, sometimes vanished almost to her gunwales as she dipped into the troughs, her outriggers with nets hanging resembling the wings of some Jurassic bird. Trash to a shrimper is anything other than a shrimp. It's all relative. One man's trash is another man's chum. Pulling up alongside the *Captain Travis* in such heaving seas was tricky, but Trosset managed it. The exchange was made: two cases of Bud for two ten-gallon buckets of trash, consisting of crabs, shellfish, various species of baitfish, starfish, and creatures I couldn't identify, mystery-men from the dark, protean world beneath us. The trash was to supplement our live pilchards, to be sent forth over the tossing waters in a greasy, irresistible slick. No, not pretty, not elegant. But it worked.

Anchored astern of the shrimper, we soon had big kings crashing and skyrocketing all around the *Spindrift*. Mixed in were the boils of bonito and a few blackfins. There was something thrilling in the fury and speed of their strikes. Alan made a long cast with his fly rod and was immediately hit by a big king. I then took his spot, cast, let the fly sink, gave it a couple of twitches with the rod tip, then began a slow retrieve. I was trying to make the streamer appear like a crippled pilchard, for kings, like their wahoo cousins, like to slash into a school of prey, wounding as many as possible, and then return to snap up the casualties.

The strike was sudden and shocking. The twelve-weight rod bowed and I was almost instantly into my backing, the taut line quivering like a high-tension wire, throwing off droplets of water as it sliced through the swells. On a fly rod, a king mackerel's first run gives you a feeling of barely contained panic, a sense that things are out of control. Several minutes later, I settled into the fight. One of the pleasures of light-tackle fishing is the muscular connection to nature, feeling a wild creature's power and vitality transmitted into your arms and back through the medium of line and rod.

In a quarter of an hour, the king came up, long and bright gray, his back and flanks sparkling with a pale, iridescent green. He appeared to go close to thirty pounds, a nasty piece of business, jaws studded with teeth like chunks of broken glass.

Richey's king was about the same size. We released both, then Trosset and Dunn each hooked up on spinning tackle. Terns wheeled overhead, frigates soared above, and there we were, alone and a long way from land, catching big fish. As the morning wore on, we began to catch bonito on fly, and kept catching them until our arms were sore. More exhausting was trying to keep our balance in the heaving boat; the sea turned us into spastic clowns stumbling and tripping from bow to stern and back again. In the early afternoon, as the wind blessedly began to die down, I saw a pod of exceptionally large bonito boiling off our bow. I cast into the middle of the boil and didn't need to make a retrieve. A fish snatched my streamer as soon as it touched water. The line ran out for a hundred yards, and I thought for a while that I'd hooked a blackfin. Then the fish sounded, and I had to work him back foot by foot. When, at last, I had him near, I reached over to grab the leader to release him, but had second thoughts. The type of bonito often called "little tunny" or "false albacore" average twelve to thirteen pounds, and this one looked considerably bigger. Actually, it was the biggest I'd ever seen. I called to Trosset for a judgment.

"That's a fly rod record," he said flatly and gaffed the fish. On his hand scale, it weighed in at nineteen pounds, two and a half ounces over the existing record on twenty-pound tippet. Trosset shook my hand and said, "Nice job." I considered saying something gracefully humble, like, "Oh, I was just lucky," but decided that honest pride was preferable to false humility, and so thanked him.

We went to Fort Jefferson harbor to weigh the fish at the official weigh station—nineteen pounds it was. While I filled out the paper-work, two seaplanes carrying bird-watchers put onto the beach. Moored there on the white sand, with wind-bent palms for a backdrop, they gave the place the look of a tropical outpost.

We set off again. Toward dusk, we made a drift, and were casting to crashing kings when a sailfish came up. Its arrival put us all, even the veteran Trosset, into an indecorous flap. "Cast, cast, cast to him!" he shouted to Richey and me while Dunn watched the boat rod on which we were drifting a live pilchard. I tossed a blue-and-white streamer; the sail, with his big dorsal spread, swam toward it, eyed it, and turned away with disdain. Richey presented a more realistic creation that he'd tied himself but hadn't given a name to. The sail turned on it. "He's got it! Hit him, hit him!" Trosset yelled, but Richey was a split second late on the strike and the fish swam off. Trosset instructed Dunn to reel in the live bait—he would use it as a teaser. "There's . . . something . . . on it," Dunn said as he cranked in line. The rod bent, line peeled off with a hiss, and the sail leapt in the distance. So we fly fishermen had to sit back and reflect on the efficacy of live bait over feathers as we enviously watched the sail perform his acrobatics, his blue-and-pewter sides glint-ing in the falling sun. Dunn has him boatside in twenty minutes. We posed him for photographs, then revived and released him. Oh, it would have been grand to have caught him on fly, but it had been a joy just to watch him greyhounding in the late, jeweled light, a perfect climax to what had been, after all, one fine day of fishing.

That evening, relaxing with a cigar on the *Thunnus*'s bridge after another of Steele's feasts, I felt every whack the sea had given me, felt in my sore arms and shoulders every run of every fish; yet I felt better, younger somehow, than I would have lounging by the fireside at home. I guess that was so because our vitality is restored not by ease but by effort. Modern life offers us few chances to test our mettle, so we have to seek them out. Looking up at the stars arcing horizon to horizon, I recalled something Joseph Conrad had written: "By all that's wonderful it is the sea, I believe, the sea itself . . . the sea that gives nothing but hard knocks and sometimes a chance to feel your strength— that only. . . "

After a final day of good fishing, we were motoring past Key West harbor and a pall settled over us. Again, a sky dotted with parasailers, again a sea desecrated by Jet Skis, again a huge cruise ship disgorging passengers eager to buy T-shirts and trinkets.

"Look at that!" Trosset said with a mixture of scorn, anger, and regret. "I remember when the waters around Key West were like the waters around the Tortugas. Now it looks like a fucking carnival."

And so we made plans to go back to the Dry Tortugas, where we could fish alone under the soaring frigates and, rocked by the sea, fall asleep to the song of birds that mate in the sky.